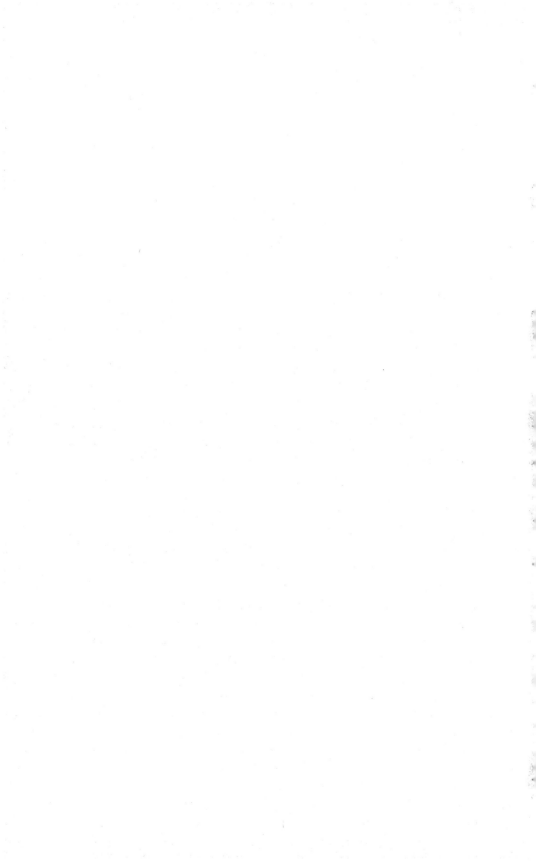

PREVIOUS BOOKS BY PAUL FISCHER

A Kim Jong-Il Production

A True Tale

of

OBSESSION,

MURDER,

and

THE MOVIES

THE MAN WHO INVENTED MOTION PICTURES

PAUL FISCHER

SIMON & SCHUSTER

New York   London   Toronto   Sydney   New Delhi

For Crosby
And for all those who continue to believe in the
power of a bright screen in a dark room

&

In memory of Jacques Pfend,
without whom this story could not have been told

CONTENTS

PART FIVE **MOTION PICTURES** (1889–1901)

AUTHOR'S NOTE

There are two typical histories of the birth of the cinema. To the French, the brothers Auguste and Louis Lumière invented the movies one legendary night in December 1895, when they held the first-ever commercial showing of a motion picture in the basement of the Grand Café, on Paris's Boulevard des Capucines. This was the evening, as the story goes, on which Parisians—still lethargic from their Christmas feasts—were sent shrieking out of the screening room by the Lumières' *Arrivée d'un Train en Gare de la Ciotat*, in which a locomotive charges straight at the audience, and the evening on which men whose last names would become famous—Gaumont, Pathé, Méliès—realized that this would be the medium to make their fortunes. The aptly named Lumière brothers are emblems of French national pride, lionized in history books and the collective consciousness. After all, it is their invention, the Cinématographe, that gives the entire medium its name.

In the United States, it is another mythical figure of the nineteenth century who is credited with originating the next century's defining medium. Thomas Edison—celebrated by his countrymen in his own day as the Wizard of Menlo Park—first sold tickets to view moving pictures in a peep-show device, the Kinetoscope, in 1894. Edison, the self-made working-class genius from the Midwest, is as foundational to the modern American self-identity as the Lumières are to the French. Edison, he of the telegraph, the phonograph, and the light bulb. Edison, whose thousand patents and partial deafness and pithy quotes ("I have not failed—I've just found ten thousand ways that won't work"; "Genius is one percent inspiration and ninety-nine percent perspiration"; "Opportunity is missed by most people because it is dressed in overalls and looks like work") have become the stuff of legend. This is the person, American schoolchildren learn, who came up with the movies. His Kinetoscope was the first machine on which motion pictures—a series of still photographs captured by a single lens, then shown at sufficient speed to create the illusion of motion—could be experienced by the public. So what if the Lumière brothers were the first to throw those moving pictures onto a screen? That, Edison contended, was not a matter of innovation but *presentation*.

Neither of these versions of history is the truth.

The following pages tell the true story of what happened before. Before Edison's Kinetoscope, and before the Cinématographe. It is the story of Louis Le Prince, who, in 1888, made the world's first motion picture—and then vanished.

It's a ghost story, a family saga, and an unsolved mystery. It's the story of an invention that, in the words of one of the first people to witness it in action, made death seem not so final, at the end of a century when humankind had already domesticated space, light, and time. Most of all, it is the story of one family, of a man who foresaw the world to come but did not live to see it materialize, and of the power of obsession and vision; of the previously impossible achievements they can make possible—and of the wreckage they leave behind when they betray you.

Key primary sources used in the writing of this book include the correspondence, manuscripts, and other documents in the Louis Le Prince Collection, held in the Leeds Philosophical and Literary Society Collection at the University of Leeds Library; firsthand recollections in the possession of the descendants of Louis Le Prince, including unpublished memoirs by Lizzie and Adolphe Le Prince as well as sworn affidavits given by third-party witnesses and collaborators; objects, documentations, and artifacts, including Le Prince's cameras and surviving pieces of film, held at the UK National Science and Media Museum in Bradford; historical records held at the West Yorkshire Archives; and materials in the Merritt Crawford Papers, collected between 1888 and 1942 and preserved at the Museum of Modern Art in New York. Writing on Thomas Edison was supported by primary documents in the Thomas A. Edison Papers, curated and collected by Rutgers University; and original case files for the lawsuit in which the Le Princes participated were found at the National Archives at New York City. I am further indebted to over twenty-five years of research into Louis Le Prince's life conducted in France by the historian Jacques Pfend, who generously opened his work to me. The usual sources—including but not limited to census reports, immigration records, passenger and crew lists, city directories, patent records, newspapers of the period, and other official documentation—were used to corroborate timelines and events. Notes and a bibliography can be found at the back of this book. Any passage in quotation marks is a direct quote from a written account, diary, letter, memoir, court transcript, or contemporary document.

All remaining errors are mine alone.

THE MAN
WHO
INVENTED
MOTION
PICTURES

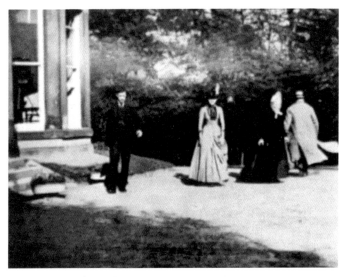

Still from *Roundhay Garden Scene*. (Courtesy of Laurie Snyder / UK National Science and Media Museum, Bradford)

The image is a scratchy, faded monochrome, thick with thousands of microscopic silver crystals. As it moves—because it is, in fact, a succession of images, transmuting stillness into movement—the picture skips and stutters. The edges of the image tear and fray, parallel ribbons of black rolling upward on either side, made uneven by wear and time.

Here is what the moving images show: On a flat, cold lawn, four human beings stroll in a loose circle. The young man in the foreground, dressed all in black, swings his arms wide in gleeful exaggeration, and the old man in the far corner imitates him, his coattails flapping behind him as he turns. There are two women between them, one young and one old, too, the first in a formal, tall hat and hooped dress, the second in a white bonnet and sober black frock.[1]

All four of these people, as we watch them now, are long dead. They are ghosts. We are watching them because a man preserved them, by the alchemy of forces even he could not yet name—atoms, electromagnetic waves, and quantum energy—in silver and light.

PROLOGUE

O n October 14, 1888—in the fifty-first year of Queen Victoria's reign—a Frenchman by the name of Louis Le Prince, resident in Leeds, England, gathered his family on the front lawn of his in-laws' country mansion for an experiment. The day was Sunday. The weather was bright and cold.

Le Prince was a tall, soft-spoken gentleman, six foot three in his stockings, at a time when the average man was nine inches shorter. The most striking aspect of Le Prince's appearance at this time—he was by then forty-seven years old—was his beard, white as snow and cut in the flamboyant style known as the Hulihee: long, fat muttonchops on the cheeks, combed outward and wavy, connected by a thick moustache, the chin shaved smooth. Though his appearance alone made him hard to forget, it was his character people found most memorable. He was a calm man, according to those who knew him. Frederic Mason, a mechanic who worked by Le Prince's side for nearly three years, thought him "in many ways a very extraordinary man, [even] apart from his inventive genius, which was undoubtedly great."[2] He was, Mason said, "well built in proportion, slow moving, most gentle and considerate; and although an inventor, of an extremely placid disposition, which nothing could ruffle . . . also extremely just."[3] Le Prince's treatment of his men seemed a reflection of his feelings on the entire species: he was trusting, but exacting; passionate, but guided by reason; patient, though he held fast. He believed in progress. He had fought in uniform as a young man—had seen, up close, his own share of suffering and death—but he hadn't lost his faith in the goodness of people. And he believed, firmly, that the new machine he had invented, which he would now demonstrate for his family—a heavy box of Honduras mahogany balanced on a sturdy, four-legged stand—would do more for human advancement and fellowship than any other invention before it.

The device, which Le Prince called a "taker" or "receiver"[4] of animated photographs, weighed nearly forty pounds. The wood was fresh, red, and raw. The brass accents still shone. On the front face of the box were two lenses, one below the other, the first a viewfinder and under it a "taking lens," through which light would enter the dark interior of the box. Inside, stretched around two metal drums, was a long roll of paper manufactured by the Eastman Dry Plate and Film Company of Rochester, New York, coated in a gelatin emulsion, silver salts suspended in animal collagen. The paper base was flexible, but the chemical compound was dry and brittle. When the time was right, Le Prince would turn the hand crank on the side of the mahogany box, and the paper roll would begin advancing upward: out of the first drum; briefly between the lens and a shutter, light passing through the glass and exposing each paper frame; then into the second drum, coiling itself back into a spool. Photons would activate the silver halides in the emulsion. The gelatin would hold them fixed in place. If all went as expected—if Le Prince spun the crank at the right speed, and with regularity; if the paper didn't rip; if the emulsion absorbed enough light—the blank paper would come out of the process covered in translucent miniature reproductions of reality as the lens had seen it: ten to twelve images per second, clear and defined enough to be run back, light now shining *through* the film rather than *on* it, to reproduce that reality at will. Already Le Prince planned to project the motion pictures—to splash them, life size, on a blank screen. He would give them color and one day synchronize them with sound. Events that could previously only be witnessed once would be available to be replayed as many times as desired. Something that had happened on one side of the planet would be viewable, with just a few days' delay, by an audience at the opposite end of the world. The past would become available to the future. The dead would move, and walk, and dance, and laugh, anytime you wished to see them do all these things again, even decades after their bodies were buried and dissolved in the ground. No human experience, from the most benign to the most momentous, would again need to be lost to history. All of it could be "taken"—could be "received"—and kept, then reproduced and shared, exactly as it had once been.

Le Prince had yet to succeed in making this possible. Every previous attempt had ended in disappointment. But he must have known that today, Sunday, October 14, 1888, would be the day he would succeed, like a conjurer, in willing light, time, and silver to combine into a force that could capture life itself.

His confidence was reflected in his choice of performers. Until now he had never taken his camera away from the workshop and had never pointed its lens at anyone other than members of his work crew. Today, for the very first time, Le Prince had enlisted the help of outsiders.

Le Prince assembled his four actors—his son Adolphe; his father-in-law, Joseph; his mother-in-law, Sarah; and Sarah's close friend and former employee Annie Hartley—near the house's bay windows. He asked them to stand on the grass and reminded them of the task they had agreed to complete. Annie Hartley would remember being confused about what, exactly, Le Prince hoped to achieve with that gigantic camera he said could somehow make photographs that *moved*.

Louis laid his hand on his camera's crank and called out to his actors to perform. Adolphe and Joseph walked in wide, expansive circles. Sarah wobbled in a straight line. Annie tapped her feet. Louis's hand turned and the mahogany box rattled like a machine gun. Inside the paper frayed as if it might rip.

It didn't. The microscopic silver grains, flooded with light, began to transform.

The images captured by Louis Le Prince that day form the first motion picture ever shot in human history. They were the culmination of four years of furious, costly work. Other men—in America, France, Germany, eastern Europe, and elsewhere—had taken part in a long race to become the world's first filmmaker, their passion and determination equal to Le Prince's. He was aware of some of them and suspected the existence of the others. Several of them had the backing of wealthy bankers and capitalists. Louis Le Prince—a studious polymath, trained as a chemist, whose peripatetic lifestyle had seen him live in four countries and work as a teacher, a painter, an industrial draftsman, and a potter—had beaten them all, and done it almost single-handed. He'd had no outside funding, no laboratory, no employees. He had spent every penny of his own money, defying the counsel of friends and colleagues. He had worked day and night in cheap rented premises, assisted only in the end by a ragtag few tradesmen. Patent officers had rejected his first designs as witchcraft, not science. Bailiffs had knocked at his door and threatened legal action.

He had pressed on through it all, and was about to be vindicated. After years of toil and uncertainty, the future, finally, was bright.

Later that afternoon, Le Prince and his son emptied the camera of its contents, a job that required covering the machine in a large black cloth to protect the film as it was removed and sealed away from the light. The dark sheet was new, sewn and cut just for the occasion by the wife of his mechanic, Jim Longley, and handled with the reverence one used with a shroud. They carried the camera and the case containing the fragile ribbon of undeveloped images back to their workshop on Woodhouse Lane, in the center of industrial Leeds. The next day, Monday, October 15, Longley began the work of developing the film. Longley, forty-three, was careful and precise about his work. He was an inventor himself—he held a patent for an automated ticket-issuing machine, one of the first of its kind in the world, which was eventually used on city omnibuses and in the turnstiles of Leeds's professional sports grounds. He understood the caution required. In the dark of the shop, drapes drawn over the few windows, Longley dunked the paper film in a succession of chemical baths, each mixture drawing further detail out of the emulsion. Finally, he removed the film from the last tank and moved it to a "developing reel," around which, loosely coiled, it was left to dry. The negatives were then transferred as positive images to a new base—paper, probably, but perhaps glass plates. This was the work "print" that was later fed into Le Prince's projector prototype, which he called a "deliverer" of images. When Le Prince returned to the workshop, pointed the projector at a blank wall, and turned it on, the shadows of his loved ones splashed out of the machine's lens against the white stone like specters. The live dance performed the previous day under the autumnal sun replayed itself, indoors, in grays and blacks. Adolphe, standing near his father, watched *himself* stride forward across the lawn, like a man haunted by his own double. The silver had held its place, the paper had not torn, the mercury and iodine had sharpened the vision: the experiment had worked.

Ten years after that motion picture was shot, a sensational lawsuit was raging, its outcome hinging on Le Prince's "garden scene," as he had come to call it. Its developments were regularly covered on the front pages of international newspapers, and its outcome would determine who, in the eyes of the law, was the inventor of motion pictures. It was a court case that would shape the movie industry for the rest of the twentieth century, and one in which Thomas Edison, the world's most famous inventor and the self-proclaimed creator of motion pictures, stood accused of theft, fraud, and perjury. The trial's catalyst was the disappearance of Louis Le Prince, who, two years after shooting the garden scene, had boarded a train in the South of France—and was never seen or heard of again. His body was not recovered. It would be seven years—the period required by law for a missing person to be declared dead—before his family could take control of his patents and other intellectual property; by then, Edison had already made a fortune showing moving pictures, and the Le Prince family went to court to prove the new medium was not his to exploit.

Le Prince's disappearance had not been solved; his final fate remained unknown. His wife, however, had a theory. Louis, she said, had been kidnapped and killed—and the man who ordered the murder was Thomas Edison.

PART ONE

THE CRIME

1890–1891

THE TRAIN

September 16, 1890

The train to Paris, which had been expected at 2:37 p.m., pulled in five minutes behind schedule.

Albert Le Prince didn't see his younger brother, Louis, very often anymore. Louis had moved away from France over twenty years ago—and if that wasn't enough, lately he had been consumed by his work on a mysterious moving picture machine. Now Louis had come to visit, delighting Albert's four children. The children were still grieving their mother, who had died just three and a half years earlier, a week before her thirty-eighth birthday. Louis had a way with young people. He took them—three girls and one, the youngest, a boy—on long walks through the parks of Dijon, enchanting them with descriptions of New York City, where his wife and children lived—the restless metropolis that was growing bigger day by day, overtaking London as the largest city in the world; a city of mansions built by bankers hoarding their fortunes and of tenements bursting with immigrants seeking their own; a city Thomas Edison had spent the last decade filling with electrical light. Dijon, by comparison, seemed tame, so provincial it may as well have existed in a different reality. He told them stories of his own five children, all about the same ages as their cousins, who were waiting for him in that city. On evenings when Albert was detained at work, Louis sat with them at home, entertaining them and giving them English lessons, correcting their pronunciation and suggesting books for them to read. His lists of recommendations were endless, from fiction to textbooks. Uncle Louis had a curiosity about the world, about the way things worked, about chemistry and engineering and art. He shared that curiosity with them as if it grew more bountiful for being spread around, and it did. Marie, writing later of spending time with her uncle, described it as a delight.[1]

The visit, however, was brief: three days. It would be Louis's last for the foreseeable future. His moving picture device, Louis confided to Albert, was all but finished. As soon as he was back in Leeds, in the north of England, where he had been working on the invention, he would return to the United States with it, this time for good. His assistants in Leeds had packed up the machines in special padded traveling cases; his wife had rented a historic mansion in uptown Manhattan, as a venue from which to unveil to the world this most modern of inventions. Nearly all the arrangements had already been made.

Louis and Albert were less comfortable together than Louis was with his nieces and nephew. When the middle-aged brothers spoke—"not," Marie wrote of her father, "as much as he wished to do"[2]—the conversation was often about money, of which neither brother had much at hand, Louis having spent the best part of a decade experimenting in animated photography, Albert adapting to life as a widower and single father. Louis was sure the motion picture device would change all of this. It was the kind of creation, according to him, that could alter the course of humankind. Imagine being able to experience the life of a person from the opposite side of the planet: to see how he existed, and to understand the rhythms of his world. Imagine doing so not through the pages of a book, but as if you had been transported instantly into that faraway place, and it existed vividly in front of your eyes, with all its sights and sounds. Imagine such a tool being used in education, entertainment, science, and diplomacy. Was that not certain to revolutionize the human experience, as drastically as the railroad and telephone had?

Louis spoke of these possibilities often. He believed in them with a fire he had never felt for anything else.

Albert—older, more levelheaded; a man who made money constructing necessary buildings—may have had his doubts.

The weekend passed; Monday arrived. On Tuesday the sixteenth, a sweltering day, Louis awaited the afternoon express back to Paris, from where he would make his way—via Brittany, London, Leeds, and Liverpool—back to America.

Later, after it had become clear that September 16, 1890, was one of the defining days of his life, Albert traced the steps he had taken that Tuesday. He replayed every word said and every gesture made. He told his sister-in-law—Louis's wife—about walking him to the platform, and, he said, told the police every detail as well.

The train station at Dijon was less than a kilometer away from Albert's home on rue Berbisey in the city center, a strip of elegant white stone town houses belonging to the city's merchants and politicians. Albert's was one of the smaller, more modest buildings, its ground-floor windows opening right out to the sidewalk.

Under a kilometer, from there to the station: fifteen minutes by foot, substantially less by horse-drawn carriage, past the twin towers and central spire of the gothic Cathédrale Sainte-Bénigne rising over the town. It was just after midday and the streets were busy. Until the railway had come to the city in the 1850s, Dijon had been on the decline: long home to royalty and nobility, seat of the influential fourteenth- and fifteenth-century Duchy of Burgundy, much of it was destroyed in 1789 by revolutionaries and rioters. For sixty years its infrastructure sat unrenewed, its streets grew filthy, swaths of its surrounding countryside wasted away unused. Dijon was, Victor Hugo wrote in 1839, "melancholy and sweet,"³ proud but lethargic, gallant but impoverished.

Then the steam train came, connecting Dijon to Paris to the north and Marseille to the south and to dozens of towns and hamlets in between. Now, from the beating heart of the terminal in the center of town, tracks branched out in all directions like arteries, pumping life into the municipality. The streets around the depot filled with shops and restaurants, and suburbs spread outside the city's ancient walls to accommodate a growing population. This was Dijon as Louis and Albert saw it that day: vibrant and entrepreneurial, fast urbanizing and industrializing.

Louis, Albert, and Albert's children arrived at the paved forecourt outside the train station. Le Prince originally intended to travel on the morning train, but after Albert was detained by a professional appointment, Louis had chosen to wait so he could properly say his goodbyes. As Albert later related it, they had reconvened at midday, settling the matters they had not managed to discuss in the previous three days, mostly about a family inheritance to be divided between the two of them; and then "all the family went to the station with [Louis]; he was in good spirits, and while waiting for the train laughingly showed his nieces the little trinkets he had purchased for his daughters as souvenirs."[4] Louis was meeting friends in Paris, with whom he would sail back to England, by night ferry to Britain's southern coast, then by rail to Leeds. It was Tuesday; by Friday Louis Le Prince planned to be aboard a steamer pulling out of Liverpool with its bow aimed at New York.

As the locomotive pulled in, they made their goodbyes. If Louis's embrace with his brother was particularly effusive—or, on the contrary, unusually restrained—Albert did not record it in any retellings of the day. Louis collected his luggage and boarded the train. Albert later said he had seen him do so. His daughter, twenty-one-year-old Marie, confirmed it.

In Paris, Mr. Richard Wilson, banker of Leeds, Yorkshire, and his wife waited for Louis Le Prince.

Wilson and Le Prince had been friends for nearly twenty years. They were members of the same institutions, Richard was Louis's banker, and he owned several pieces of Louis's art. They had traveled to France together and then gone their separate ways: Richard and his wife to sightsee, Louis to meet his brother in Dijon. They had agreed to meet again in Paris for the journey back to England.

But Louis did not appear.

At some point that night or the next day, unable or unwilling to delay their return home any longer, the Wilsons made their own way back to Calais. Wilson did not appear to feel undue concern. Perhaps he assumed Louis had decided to stay in Dijon a little longer, whether by choice or by obligation. Le Prince was usually a courteous man, and while he could have used either the telegraph or one of the new telephones, by now installed in every French rail station, to give Wilson advance warning of this change of plans, it wasn't uncommon, in those early days of long-distance communication, for this sort of thing to happen. Someone was delayed, something unforeseen had come up, you would simply see them a few days later than expected.

So the Wilsons boarded the ferry alone, presuming Louis was still with Albert in Burgundy. It would be weeks before anyone realized Louis Le Prince was, in fact, gone. Somehow, somewhere between Dijon and Paris, he had vanished.

MARKING TIME

October 20–November 11, 1890

Seven weeks later, Le Prince's wife Lizzie, forty-four years old, stood waiting on the Battery Park waterfront, the cold November wind coming in off the New York Bay with a force strong enough to loosen her hair out from under her hat. Her daughter Mariella, twenty—the same age Lizzie had been when she'd met Louis—stood by her side. Louis Le Prince had boarded the train to Dijon nearly two months earlier, and his wife had only just learned he had never arrived in Paris with it.

For the last three years—up until that visit with Albert—Louis had lived and worked in Leeds, Lizzie's hometown. He had returned there from New York, where the family had moved in the early 1880s, to take advantage of the wealth of his father-in-law, Joseph Whitley, in his mission to perfect his motion picture camera and projector. Whitley, ironmonger of Leeds, had access to workshops, tools, and staff Louis could not afford himself. He sailed back to England alone, leaving his family behind in America, expecting the work to take a matter of months. It stretched out to three interminable years. Lizzie and the five children visited in the summers—when they could afford it. Cash was scarce. To make ends meet, Lizzie worked as an art teacher and wrote articles for women's journals. She and the children moved from home to home, eventually renting an old house on a hill, uptown in Washington Heights, where woods still stood and Manhattan still felt like the countryside. The mansion reminded Lizzie of her home outside Leeds, where the middle class also lived in big houses on quiet hills, comfortably removed from the crowded, noisy city below. The house had been neglected for years: passed down from hand to hand, haggled over in inheritance disputes, its lawns overrun with weeds and its orchards cracked and rotting. Restoring the place would fill the quiet hours as Lizzie waited for her husband to come home, and preparing it as the venue in which he would eventually premiere his invention made her feel a part of his work, even while he was an ocean away. The entire family longed for Louis to return—and, with him, normalcy.

Louis's homecoming had inched closer and closer all year, with agonizing slowness. "It will take me another ten or fourteen days to complete the new machine," Louis had written his wife in late March 1890. "This is absolutely my last trial and I trust it will answer perfectly."[1] Two weeks later he remained on that schedule: just "a few days more and I will be through with the machine,"[2] he confirmed.

"What a relief it will be," he added in his next letter. "I shall scarcely believe it is over after all this anxious tugging, waiting, and trying again."[3] By summer he declared the work finished and started planning the journey back to New York. He arranged to bring along his father-in-law, Joseph Whitley, by now widowed and ill, to see out his old age with his daughter and grandchildren in the New World. By September, Louis was in Dijon, saying his goodbyes to his brother and his family.

And then the letters stopped coming.

Louis and Lizzie wrote each other every week, almost without fail. This time, however, Lizzie knew her husband was busy with all that had to be done before his departure. A month without letters might not have mattered as long as Louis was back home, for good, at the end of it.

September turned to October without a word. Then came October 20, a gray, cloudy day. Winds and thunderstorms had battered the city the day before; a policeman had been struck by lightning and thrown fifteen feet across Westchester Avenue in the Bronx. New York woke up on the twentieth to pavements glistening and gummed with fallen leaves. Engineers from the Edison General Electric Company spread out across the city to repair fallen electrical and telegraph wires. Steamships that had remained docked in New York harbor overnight, hatches battened down against the deluge, began unloading their passengers, a great mass of travelers—wealthy businessmen and desperate immigrants alike—heaving into Battery Park.

Among those ships was the RMS *Umbria*, the largest, fastest, and most luxurious vessel in the Cunard Line fleet, a seven-ton, single-propeller behemoth that plied the regular service between Liverpool and New York. Among the *Umbria's* thirteen hundred passengers was Joseph Whitley, who had celebrated his seventy-fourth birthday at sea. He was accompanied not by Louis but by a distant relative, thirty-three-year-old Arthur Oates.[4] Oates knew only that Le Prince had failed to return to Leeds from France and that it had been decided—by Whitley's doctors, his family, or both—the old man had best leave for America before his health made it impossible. Lizzie had a brother, Jack, but he was then in Germany on business and unable to come home to England. Joseph needed accompaniment, so Arthur had brought him. When she saw her father, Lizzie thought he looked "dangerously ill."[5]

She brought him to the old house uptown, where he could spend time with her and his grandchildren, and where Phoebe, the Le Prince family's longtime nanny and housekeeper, could help look after him. (It is unclear how long Arthur Oates stayed in New York before returning to England.) But Joseph's condition continued to deteriorate. "My father's case grew hopeless," Lizzie wrote later, "and in grief I wrote to my brother and my husband, urging the latter's immediate return, and expressing wonder that I had no letters."[6]

Her dispatch to Louis went unanswered. From Germany, Jack wrote his brother-in-law letters and wires of his own. They received no reply either. Jack messaged Richard Wilson, the banker, who let him know he and his wife had traveled back from Paris without Louis. This prompted Jack to contact Albert Le Prince in Dijon, who told him Louis had left over a month earlier, and conveyed his own astonishment at the situation.

No one knew where Louis Le Prince was. Albert and his children were the last people to have seen him alive—a whole five weeks earlier.

And so, as Lizzie put it, "the search began."[7]

The world was vast then. The Atlantic—before storms could be reliably predicted and avoided, before transcontinental phone calls and wireless, before airplanes—was a gantlet to be overcome. Letters from one side of the sea took days to reach their recipients on the other. News in England—a death in the family, a disappearance—would have to wait several days to be read in America, and vice versa. Lizzie could not make the journey to Europe herself. She could not afford it; she could not leave her children; she could not abandon her dying father. Dijon was thirty-seven hundred miles away, Louis had been there six weeks earlier, and both expanses, of distance and of time, seemed formidable and insurmountable. Together they raised questions as dark and unanswerable as the ocean.

What had happened on that train? Had Louis suffered an accident or fallen victim to violence of a more nefarious kind? Not only had there been no communication from him, but there had been no notice of his having been found or assisted; Albert had let Lizzie know the rail company had not recorded any incidents of any kind on that particular service. Was Louis alive? Where was his luggage—it was not found on the train—and if he was dead, where was his body? Had he been robbed while the train sped through the French countryside and thrown out the carriage door and into the darkness? Was he lying injured in a hospital, or lifeless in a ditch? Had he in fact made it to Paris but been attacked as he walked out of the Gare de Lyon minutes before nine p.m.—grabbed by the collar, stripped of his belongings, and hurled into the Seine? It was known to happen: the Paris Morgue was, newspapers said, filled with waterlogged corpses. Or could Louis have made it as far as the Channel Ferry, hurrying to catch up to Richard and Mrs. Wilson, and somehow fallen over the railing of the night boat and drowned, in a different dark body of water? Was he hiding? Running from something, or someone—or had he been caught by it, or by them? The Dijon–Paris line also led, in the opposite direction, to Marseille, a doorway to North Africa, its sun-drenched harbor home to countless merchant shipping vessels and international criminal enterprises; a "mouth ready to swallow the entire world,"[8] in the words of one novelist, to which countless people went to disappear or be disappeared. Had Louis reversed course, abandoning one train and boarding another, headed south rather than north? From Marseille one could end up anywhere.

At night Lizzie lay alone in her bedroom. Elsewhere in the house slept the children: Mariella, twenty; Adolphe, eighteen; Aimée, sixteen; Joseph, fifteen; and Fernand Léon, thirteen.

Lizzie had rented the Jumel Mansion, as the house was known, in the spring. In the autumn, as darkness encroached earlier each night, the house could feel sprawling and even cavernous. Eighty-five hundred square feet over three aboveground floors and a basement, in a grand colonial style that already felt ancient, it was filled with long, dark hallways that neighbors whispered were haunted. Eliza Jumel, the socialite after whom the house was named, was rumored to have killed her first husband; her specter, bonneted and somber, had been seen by previous residents at the first-floor landing or at the balcony, occasionally silent, sometimes wailing. In the dark it was a restless house, its living inhabitants as tormented as its dead.

Lizzie felt helpless. From Europe, Jack and Albert "assured" her, she later wrote, "that I could help them better by staying in New York, in case [Louis] should arrive there, than by leaving my family and coming to help them."[9]

"Watch incoming steamers and passenger lists," Jack advised.[10] It was still possible that Louis was on his way to America. He had been delayed, some unforeseen circumstance had forced him to remain silent, but he might yet be on any one of the ships crisscrossing the Atlantic every day.

Starting in late October, in the mornings after breakfast, Lizzie and Mariella dressed for cold weather and made their way downtown.

They walked or took a carriage to 155th Street and then paid five cents each to board the Ninth Avenue elevated train. Its wooden carriages rocked past apartment windows, its engine belching coal gas over the West Side. They left Washington Heights, which was still almost the countryside, traveling along Central Park, where sheep still grazed on the meadow, and then over the open-air markets and tenements of Lower Manhattan. Alighting at Battery Place, on Manhattan's southern tip, the two women had only a five-minute walk to Castle Garden, the sandstone fort that had been New York's port of entry for immigrants and visitors. Mother and daughter spent the next hours visiting shipping line offices on Steamship Row and checking their passenger lists, scanning for Louis's name. They had yet to find it. Having exhausted the available ledgers, the two women then proceeded along the waterfront to the end of South Street, where they lingered outside the Barge Office and Emigrant Landing Depot, studying the faces in the arriving crowds.

Until April 1890, newcomers to the United States had been processed within the circular fort of Castle Garden itself, on a man-made island two hundred feet off Manhattan's tip. Once an incoming steamer had cleared quarantine, its passengers disembarked, with their luggage, onto a small fleet of barges and steamer tugs that took them to "America's Open Gate,"[11] as some called the Castle. Here, under the watchful eyes of New York City policemen, whose main duty was to ensure the foreigners were not fleeced, robbed, or assaulted by loitering criminals and swindlers, immigrants were examined by a doctor and registered their names and personal details with state clerks. Those who were found to be ill or destitute were sent by steam ferry to hospitals or detention centers on nearby Wards Island. Everyone else filed into the Castle's huge atrium, where, under its domed roof, they could exchange their gold and foreign currency for US dollars, peruse available employment opportunities on the labor exchange's notice board, or purchase train tickets to destinations elsewhere in North America. Their business done, they crossed a walkway over the water and entered the United

States proper through a gate into Battery Park, the country—and their futures—before them.

Castle Garden was legendary. Immigrants wrote home to Europe about entering New York Harbor and being overwhelmed not just by the brand-new, copper-colored Statue of Liberty standing proud and welcoming over the bay, but also by the cacophony of the Castle, every inch of its hard floor occupied by men, women, families—German, Irish, Russian, Norwegian, Italian, Greek, Turkish, British—sleeping, eating, shouting, conversing, the fashions worn and the tongues spoken sundry and alien. There were no visas, and few travelers carried passports. The Castle had opened in 1855; in the thirty-five years since, the building had welcomed nearly ten million immigrants to the New World. Among those to have been processed through the fort between 1875 and 1890 were four-year-old Erik Weisz, who in 1890 would begin work as a professional magician under the name of Harry Houdini; a twenty-eight-year-old Croatian engineer obsessed with electricity named Nikola Tesla; and an unemployed sixteen-year-old from the Rhineland, fleeing conscription in the Imperial German Army, who gave his name as Friedrich Trump. The men whose studios would define Hollywood's Golden Age three decades later had also shuffled across the fort's scuffed floors. Seventeen-year-old Carl Laemmle, later of Universal Pictures, traveled from Germany in 1884, journeying on to Chicago to join an older brother who had already settled in the Midwest. Three-year-old Lazar Meir, who would change his name to Louis B. Mayer and run MGM Studios, arrived around 1887, his parents having, like hundreds of thousands of eastern European Jews, fled the pogroms spreading across Russia. Adolph Zukor, who went on to found Paramount Pictures, landed from Hungary as a young adult in 1891. The Le Prince family's own first steps on American soil had been inside Castle Garden in the early 1880s.

Recently, however, the federal government had taken over the administration of immigration duties from the state of New York, following a series of fires and deadly epidemics at the timeworn building. A new facility was approved at Ellis Island, seven miles off Manhattan, not just to stamp out malpractice but also to facilitate more thorough medical screening and background checking of immigrants. From the spring of 1890, federal transition employees handled immigrants at the Barge Office, a smaller building erected on a wharf adjacent to the fort, and this was the building outside of which Lizzie and Mariella would stand. They made that trip often throughout October.

By early November, Richard Wilson had gained entry to Le Prince's workshop in Leeds and reported back that it did not seem as though Le Prince had returned to it since going to Dijon: his equipment was untouched, his key still in a drawer. Wilson had the building locked up and Louis's more valuable possessions—the motion picture cameras and projectors, the endless spools of paper and celluloid film—secured. From Germany, Jack Whitley requested Scotland Yard open a missing-persons investigation. Albert Le Prince wired from Dijon to announce a Détective Dougan, of the Bureau de Recherches Pour Familles, would be leading the French side of the search.

Lizzie and Mariella continued to watch the steamers. The seemingly endless parade of boats, each overloaded with people, and with their hopes and dreams. They must have known this was a pointless activity. Le Prince knew New York, and he had taken on American citizenship in the mid-1880s:[12] not only would he enter America through the office set aside for citizens, but he would know how to contact his family once he was cleared to move through. Yet they undertook it all the same, delaying the long journey back uptown. Maybe the chaos of the new Barge Office would mean Louis would be funneled through with the foreign arrivals. Maybe he was penniless—who could tell the state he might be in after these weeks of delay—or perhaps he had cause to sneak back into the country under a false name and false pretenses. These were far-fetched theories but they were preferable to visions of Louis, dead, never again to be reunited with his children.

On November 11, fifty-six days since Le Prince had last been seen in Dijon, Lizzie and Mariella finally found his name in the Barge Office's registry of arrivals. It was there, scratched hurriedly onto the page in fresh black ink: *L. Leprince*, landed the day before on the steamship *La Gascogne*, operated by the French Compagnie Générale Transatlantique (CGT), originating from Le Havre.[13] It was still berthed at the CGT's Pier 42, on the Hudson River where Morton Street met the water.

Lizzie and Mariella raced across Lower Manhattan to the piers. They interrogated the *Gascogne*'s crew; they even enlisted the help of a Board of Emigration policeman, an Irish-born detective by the name of Peter Groden. But *L. Leprince* turned out to be a stranger—a twenty-seven-year-old farmer who had left his small town and its exhausted fields for the American West, in search of more promising land to cultivate.

Soon after that disappointment, Lizzie abandoned her missions to the Battery. She and Mariella walked back to the elevated train terminal. They bought their fares and boarded the train back to Washington Heights. They returned to the old mansion on the hill—to its somber, echoing hallways, to Lizzie's ailing father, and to the anxious children.

EDISON'S NEWEST WONDER

December 1890–May 1891

■

D ecember bore on. Just before Christmas, New York was pummeled with violent winds and downpours of cold rain, whirlpools forming at street corners, and the house's old walls groaned as the gale howled and the deluge drummed the roof. The Le Prince children did their best to generate the spirit for the season, and frail old Joseph Whitley fought to retain control of his deteriorating mind. Lizzie focused her attention on taking care of him, but saw no improvement. New Year's Eve came and went. On January 12, 1891, Whitley passed away in the night. He was buried in Trinity Church Cemetery at 153rd Street. Eliza Jumel, after whom the mansion on the hill was named, was resting in the same ground.

After the service Lizzie's children hailed a coach and the family rode home in the snow, their loss and grief now doubled.

Winter turned to spring. Trees and flowers bloomed in Highbridge Park. The sun coaxed green grass out of the mud over Joseph Whitley's grave.

And then everything changed—again.

*   *   *

On Thursday, May 28, the largest headline on the front page of the New York *Sun* announced in loud, bold letters: "THE KINETOGRAPH. Edison's Latest and Most Surprising Device—Pure Motion Recorded and Reproduced." Edison claimed to be able to "reproduce the image of a living, moving, speaking human being, and not only one image but a dozen images together, or forty of them," using a "small pine box . . . [with] some wheels and belts near the box, and a workman who had them in charge."[1] The Kinetograph was a peep-show device—the pictures viewable through a pinhole in the top of the machine—but Edison predicted it could be adapted so that "a man can sit in his own parlor and see reproduced on screen the forms of the players in an opera produced on a distant stage," or each devastating blow of a prize fight, or each moment of a president's speech. It would all be available to watch on "a big screen. . . . You watch the screen, and see a picture of the stage, full size," made possible through the use in the camera of "a roll of gelatine film," as celluloid film was often referred to then.[2]

The article ran one column on the front page, two and a half columns on the first inside sheet. With every passing word, Lizzie's dread grew. Twenty-five years later, when she put her memories of the time down to paper, she wrote that she knew immediately the machine Edison was describing.

"It was my husband's invention of moving pictures!"[3]

For forty-eight hours every newspaper in America was full of praise for Thomas Edison. "Edison's Newest Wonder," exclaimed the *Evening World* in an extra edition on the twenty-eighth, "telegraphs 2,400 Photographs per Minute. . . . The Wizard Thomas A. Edison, of Llewellyn Park, waves his wand and the world marvels. . . ."[4] The *Pittsburg Dispatch* dubbed the Kinetograph "his latest and most wonderful invention."[5] The *Philadelphia Inquirer*, unable to find the right words to describe the inner workings of the machine to its readership, settled on " 'Photos' by Electricity."[6] By May 30, comparable praise appeared in newspapers in England and across Europe.

Throughout that weekend, Lizzie, still "much upset,"[7] received word, by cable and in person, from outraged friends. Henry Woolf, a decorator and friend of Louis's, had seen an early version of Le Prince's camera years earlier. "I remember seeing the pictures," he said later, and "I had grasped the manner of working the apparatus enough to know that on reading Edison's account of the Kinetoscope in the papers of May 1891, that it was an infringement on Le Prince's machine."[8] Mary Borer, who had known the Le Princes in England and now lived in Connecticut, was so "indignant" at seeing Louis's work being brought out "in Edison's name" she cut the announcement out of the *Sun* and sent it immediately to the Jumel Mansion to alert Lizzie.[9]

Each of them had read a version of the news in his or her paper of choice, and each of them expressed a version of the same sentiment: Why was Edison announcing the invention Louis Le Prince had been working on for the past five years?

Inventors toiled away at parallel ideas all the time; Le Prince had been aware of at least two rivals. And yet, with every new reported detail, the similarities between Edison's Kinetograph and Le Prince's moving picture apparatus came into sharper focus. Each device could take a great number of photographs per second, sequentially, through a single lens, powered by a hand crank. Both the Kinetograph and Louis's camera used strips of celluloid film, and both advanced that film past a single lens using sprockets that pulled it forward intermittently—the teeth clicking into a metal belt, in the case of Louis's machine, and directly into film perforations, in the case of Edison's.

"My idea was to take a series of instantaneous photographs of motions so rapidly that in the reproduction the photographic representatives become resolved into a pure motion instead of a series of jerks," Edison explained to a newspaperman. "The kinetograph takes a series of forty-six photographs in one second and keeps it up as long as desired. It starts, moves, stops, uncloses the shutter, takes a photograph, closes the shutter and starts on forty-six times a second. The result when reproduced is a pure motion."[10] The successful working of this mechanism—a strip of rollable film exposed intermittently past the camera shutter, fast enough to sustain persistence of vision—was precisely the system Louis had been perfecting in the year before his disappearance. Other rivals had used glass photographic plates, continuous movement appliances, even rotating contrivances in the shape of a gun's cylinder. What were the odds Edison and Le Prince had conceived of the exact same method of capturing and projecting images, within a year of one another, without any contact? How could the US Patent Office have permitted Edison's application for the Kinetograph when Louis held the right to the technology through a patent granted in 1888?

Joseph Whitley, in his long career as an ironmonger and engineer, had patented many innovations of his own, and spoke often, and disdainfully, of how common patent theft had become. Le Prince had admired Edison and even, in the earliest days, considered bringing his idea to the exalted genius for endorsement, as many others had and would continue to do. But Le Prince had grown increasingly secretive as he approached the achievement of his plans. Lizzie remembered how one day, shortly before Louis had left New York in 1887, she had questioned the need for him to go to England, and her husband had answered "very quietly and gravely that he had heard of 'queer' things, and that he might be 'safer away.' "[11] Was it Edison he had come to fear? Had that fear driven him back to Leeds, an ocean away from Edison's New Jersey lab, to finish his work? Edison was currently in court, defending his patent on the incandescent light bulb from competitors he asserted were infringing his rights; indeed, during the end of May, breathless eulogizing of the Kinetograph and rapt descriptions of proceedings in the US circuit court jostled for column inches almost daily.[12] Was Thomas Edison, the Wizard of Menlo Park, a patent pirate himself?

There were accounts from England that William Friese-Greene, a professional photographer from Bristol, had patented and publicly announced a "kinetoscope" device of his own conception as early as

February 1890, and that Friese-Greene had written to Edison, enclosing press clippings, for his approval. (Friese-Greene would later marvel at Edison's claiming that he had come up with the word himself.) Many businessmen accused Edison of intellectual property theft and self-aggrandizement, chief among them Edison's most vocal rival in the electrical field, George Westinghouse. It was suspicious, too, that Edison's final caveat (a form of prepatent) on the Kinetograph had been filed in the dying days of 1890, just weeks after Louis's disappearance, and that this caveat, after multiple earlier versions in which Edison's motion picture machine was of an entirely different design, suddenly bore an uncanny closeness to Louis's own patent.

Lizzie was taken by speculation—but two more events happened to tip her fancy into certainty. One morning that spring Lizzie had business in southern New Jersey; her appointments fulfilled, she boarded a boat at Atlantic Highlands to return to Manhattan. On the deck, according to her, was Thomas Edison himself, embarked on the same journey. He was hunched in close conversation with another, younger, man, whom Lizzie recognized almost immediately. William Dameron Guthrie, thirty-one, was a patent attorney with the firm of Seward, Blatchford, Griswold, and Da Costa. He was a friend of Jack Whitley's—and had briefly been Louis's own patent adviser.

The boat reached Manhattan; its passengers stepped off into the down-town streets. Lizzie, at a distance, kept her eye on Edison and Guthrie. "I followed them up Church Street as far as Broadway," she recorded, which was either their destination or the point at which she lost them.[13]

Soon after, Lizzie said, a "connection by marriage" in England by the name of Alfred Pickard[14] apprised her he had "received a visit . . . from a New York representative of Mr. Edison, who made minute inquiries about Le Prince's work and disappearance. This was at once followed by the first fan-fare [sic] in the New York papers about 'The Wizard's gift to the world' in May 1891."[15]

Le Prince had been missing for over eight months, and for eight months Lizzie had been at an impasse, without the slightest clue to his whereabouts, let alone a real lead. In the spring of 1891, when Edison's Kinetograph was announced to the world, Lizzie suddenly held on to something she hadn't had since the beginning. Her husband, on the brink of unveiling a machine that would change the world and make his fortune, had mysteriously disappeared—and then, just months later, Edison had gone public with what looked to be the same exact invention.

Until then, Louis's disappearance had been incomprehensible. Now, however, his wife saw coherence: Louis hadn't vanished, he'd been eliminated.

Lizzie had a suspect—with a motive.

A lawyer was consulted. His answers were unexpected and disheartening.

Had Louis Le Prince been confirmed dead, his family could have claimed his estate, including his intellectual property, and represented his title in court as their own. As it was—with Le Prince "only" missing—the law would continue to consider him alive until his body had been found or until a sufficient period of time, specifically seven years, had passed for it to be reasonable to declare him legally deceased. Until then, his family could not, as third parties, sue to enforce his patents.

In other words, it would be September 1897 at the earliest before the courts would even allow Lizzie to act on her husband's behalf. By then, Thomas Edison, the world's most famous inventor, fawned over by the press, financed by J. P. Morgan and the Vanderbilt family, would have exploited his legacy for all it was worth.

Lizzie burned with anger at the injustice of it all. The invention Louis had spent years of his life perfecting—exhausting himself, falling ill, throwing every penny they both made into a "bottomless well"[16]—was finally in the world, but with Thomas Edison's name on it, and it would be making Edison, who was already rich, even richer, while Lizzie and her daughters worked full time simply to make ends meet.

It was not the life she had imagined. There was no way to put it right, no way to go back in time, no matter how much she wished she could.

Time was a straight line, unstoppable and irreversible, inescapable—though Louis, for a brief few months before his disappearance, had made it something else. He had tamed time into a succession of moments, frozen on a flimsy reel—a sequence that could be rolled back at will, a simple ribbon on a spool.

PART TWO

EUROPE

1866–1880

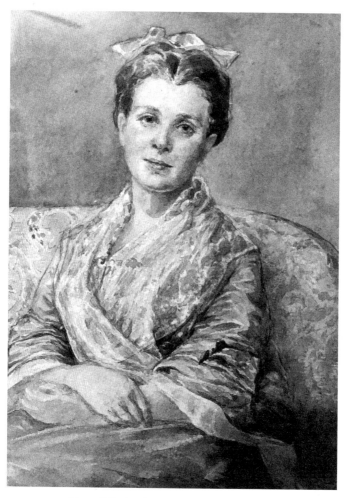

Lizzie Whitley, by Louis Le Prince (1860s).
(Private collection. Courtesy of Gwen Graves Maxwell)

LETTERS OF
INTRODUCTION

1866

L ouis Le Prince and Lizzie Whitley met in Paris. It was Jack Whitley
who had brought them together.

Sarah Elizabeth Whitley was one of dozens of young foreign women
flocking to Paris in the 1860s to study art or fashion—a brief, final
interlude of freedom before they returned to their hometowns and a life
dedicated to marriage and child-rearing. She was twenty years old and
pretty, with playful eyes, a mouth that seemed always ready to break
into a smile, and cheeks that dimpled when it did. Her arms and hands
were strong, her long white fingers nimble; she was studying pottery
under Albert-Ernest Carrier-Belleuse. Everyone knew her as Lizzie.

Carrier-Belleuse was one of the most respected and celebrated sculp-
tors in Europe. His pieces decorated the palaces at the Louvre and the
Tuileries; his marbles were the talk of the Paris salons. He was an officer
of the Légion d'Honneur and counted Louis-Napoléon and Queen Victoria as customers. In 1866 alone he was finishing a terra-cotta likeness
of Marguerite Bellanger, a stage actress and former circus performer who
was now Napoléon III's mistress; a sculpture for Napoléon's favorite
spa at Vichy; and a daring twenty-six-inch statue of a nude *Angélique*,
contorted and bound to petrified rock, which later in the year would

scandalize collectors and critics when it was shown at the Académie des Beaux-Arts' prestigious annual Salon. Nineteenth-century men liked their erotic visions pure, helpless, and gracefully chaste. The journalist Edmond About found the sculpture audacious and vulgar.[1] Her "manly and vigorous" body likewise troubled the critic Maxime du Camp: Carrier-Belleuse crafted faces and bodies so lifelike it "makes illusion impossible."[2] Equally impossible, Du Camp found, was looking away.

Naturalism was Carrier-Belleuse's trademark, and his skill was unparalleled. He kept a studio staffed with up to fifty *practiciens*, apprentices and specialists who followed the master's orders, working from drawings made in his hand to chip marble, wax plaster, and shape clay into his visions. In the running of this business, Carrier-Belleuse was greatly helped by a devoted twenty-six-year-old assistant by the name of Auguste Rodin, whose own dedicated task was usually to apply a piece's delicate finishing touches. Rodin stayed with Carrier-Belleuse nearly six years.

Gregarious and well connected, Carrier-Belleuse was adored by his pupils, whom he instructed privately or, in the evenings, at the atelier of the painter Rodolphe Julian in the Passage des Panoramas, a covered mews off rue Vivienne. Aspiring artists flocked to his classes, eager to learn how to make clay look as delicate as lace, marble as soft as cream.

Lizzie Whitley was one of these students. Julian's study rooms were especially popular with women artists, since the more prestigious Académie des Beaux-Arts had not yet opened its doors to women and would not do so until 1897. Julian, who as a young man could not afford the Académie's tuition fees, felt a kinship with up-and-coming artists to whom France's snobbish, closed art world was inaccessible. "Few artists care to have the responsibility of taking ladies into their ateliers," he explained.[3] His academy, he vowed, would be different.

Lizzie must have been one of the academy's first pupils.[4] Julian had only just opened his doors. The space was still one small room, with a stove in the center and a draped platform against a wall, on which stood the models. There was no ventilation, and in the summer, with the sun beating through the skylight, the heat was suffocating.

Lizzie adored it. She learned drawing and painting first, before moving on to the molding of clay. Female models posed nude, men in briefs. The classes were mixed then, men and women sitting and working together, though the women were few, and all foreigners. The "gentlemen" could be forward, and many of them were insulted to be sharing a studio with *mesdemoiselles*, whom they considered naturally inferior, hobbyists, where they themselves were geniuses in the making. "It was extremely awkward and disagreeable," Julian recalled, "and I soon saw that if I were to hope to get my own countrywomen to work with me, I should have to make different arrangements."[5] He finally separated the genders in 1873, and for the rest of his life he took pleasure in letting visitors and critics know the women's ateliers were "considerably more serious"[6] than the men's.

One of the trailblazers, Lizzie had to put up with the condescension, the likely advances, and the snide remarks. None of it was bad enough to sour her experience, which she remembered fondly for the rest of her days. She was smart and hardworking, though she would never be more than a proficient amateur. All the same, Carrier-Belleuse's classes cultivated her love of craft, and also gave her a framework with which to observe the world, a desire to really *see* it, in resistance to the increasing disconnection from nature wrought upon society by the industrial age. A decade later and more, when she was an art teacher herself, she would open her first class of every term by handing all her young pupils an egg and inviting them to hold it to the light, to familiarize themselves with its every detail. "I obey Nature in everything, and I never pretend to command her,"[7] Rodin once said, echoing Carrier-Belleuse's philosophy. Art was about truth, not prettiness, because truth was beauty and, added Rodin, "beauty is everywhere. It is not she that is lacking to our eye, but our eyes which fail to perceive her."[8]

Lizzie never forgot this lesson. It might have been on her mind that spring and summer in Paris when she met a tall, handsome young man who believed in the very same principles, though he expressed them not in sculpture—but in photography.

Louis Aimé Augustin Le Prince was five years older than Lizzie and everything a young Englishwoman enamored with France could have wished for in a beau. He was over six feet tall, from an esteemed upper-middle-class family, with a hint of rakish charm. He was well educated—he had just returned from the University of Leipzig, where he'd studied optics and chemistry. Before that he'd spent stints at colleges in Paris and Bonn. His passion lay in the arts and, more precisely, in the intersection of arts and technology, the science of light and its interaction with the human eye. An early photograph of Louis, likely from his student days, shows a serious young man in a sober gray work coat, white suit, and satin strap bow, his gaze direct and his posture immaculate. A portrait taken just a few years later, around the time he and Lizzie met, presents a changed man: Louis has let his hair grow and now sports a full black beard as he leans on the back of a couch or chair, his other hand in his trouser pocket. He wears a fashionable wide-lapelled overcoat over a black wool suit; the half smile on his lips has the feel of a dare or an invitation. The self-aware student is gone. In his place is a good-looking, confident Parisian bourgeois. It was as if he'd been ripped from the pages of a French romance novel, right down to his background: his father had been a soldier, his widowed mother lived on a country estate. Strangers called him Louis or Augustin. With family, he went by the affectionate diminutive of Gus.

Her brother had put Lizzie and Gus together. John Robinson "Jack" Whitley was enrolled at Leipzig in the year below Louis, studying to be an engineer. His and Lizzie's father, Joseph, was a brass founder and ironmonger, as their grandfather Thomas had been before them. Previous generations of the Whitley family had rarely even traveled to London, let alone the Continent, and Jack and Lizzie were likely the first members of the family to be afforded the benefit of an education abroad. But just as Lizzie knew she would be returning to Yorkshire to marry and start a family, so was Jack destined to come home to take over the family business. As Jack told it, he had all but left Leipzig, headed to Leeds via Paris, when he received a letter of introduction from one of his professors suggesting that, while in France, he call on a former student of the professor's by the name of Le Prince. The old teacher had a feeling Jack and Gus might hit it off.

He was right, though on the face of it the two young men could not have been more different. Jack was broad—broad of face, broad of shoulder, broad of ambition. He was the driving engine of every gathering he was a part of, a charmer and a salesman, more of an entrepreneur than an engineer. He had bold plans, for himself and for the family firm, and his will was inflexible as a steel track.

Louis, on the other hand, was a tinkerer, fascinated with the new scientific theories that attempted to explain how the world worked. He loved his books and was a keen photographer and painter. Commerce held no fascination for him—in fact he would prove time and again in life that he was a rather poor businessman when forced to try his hand at it. Where Jack had come into the world in an industrial township, his father yet to make his fortune, Louis had been born to a family that had owned money and land for generations. Where Jack was destined to join his father's trade almost from birth, Louis was afforded ample time to choose his direction in life: indeed his first, and possibly only, professional position to date had been a brief stint as an apprentice to the marine painter Augustin Delacroix. Where Jack had "none too much fear and restraint," as a biographer later described him,[9] Louis was measured. Where Jack was "not much given to abstract thought," those same thoughts were almost *all* Louis was given to.

And yet they had much in common. Both men were set on making their mark on the world, and neither was a stranger to hard work. A friend of Jack's presciently wrote of him that the "danger" in his makeup lay "in going too far rather than not far enough, of attempting to do too much rather than the reverse,"[10] and though Louis might take longer to make up his mind on a course of action, once he was decided he was equally uncompromising. They were humanists, raised to believe in progress and enlightenment. The Whitley family motto—*Fit Via Vi*, translatable as "Force Finds a Way"—echoed the battle cry of "*En*

Avant!" ("Forward!"), which was emblazoned on the coat of arms of the Boulaberts, Louis's mother's family. Jack espoused private business as a means of social betterment. Louis believed art and science could uplift a man's soul and help him understand his neighbors and the universe around him. Their tools were different, but the desired outcomes were the same. Both Jack and Louis were certain that a single man's work could benefit the entirety of humankind.

They became fast friends in the brief time Jack was in Paris. Before long he invited Louis to Yorkshire for a brief visit, though he had ulterior motives. The family firm was thriving in England, but the domestic market was saturated, and Jack's experience abroad had convinced him it needed to reach new European customers. Every town and hamlet in England had its rail station, the entirety of the island bound together by a metal network, but in France and the German states there was room for growth—growth ripe to be exploited by a firm like Whitley Partners, which manufactured machines, boilers, valves, pipes, and other sundry steam engine parts and factory floor implements. Le Prince spoke both French and German; he was a classically trained draftsman with a solid grasp of chemistry and mathematics. The more Jack got to know him, the more he saw in Louis the perfect representative for an English firm on the Continent: a modern, well-bred young man French and Prussian clients would be certain to feel more kinship toward than they did the gruff Yorkshiremen Whitley's currently had on staff. Jack, when he took over, wanted to expand. Le Prince was just the kind of man he needed to do so.

Louis had his own reasons for accepting Jack's offer of a trip to the north of England. Or rather, he had one reason.

He didn't want to say goodbye to Lizzie.

Jack hadn't taken long to introduce his sister to his new friend. Perhaps Lizzie and Louis first met at the Passage des Panoramas, after an evening class at Julian's studio: the Le Prince family owned property nearby. Perhaps it was more formal. However it happened, the timeline suggests Louis fell hard and fast for Lizzie in the spring of 1866—and the feeling was reciprocal. Lizzie was swept up by Louis's intelligence and attentiveness—writing about him decades later, out of all the qualities in him that had struck her, she would single out his "most retentive memory."[11] They could talk about art for hours. They made a beautiful but conspicuous pair: the northern lass with the distinctive Yorkshire accent, all shortened words and dropped *g*'s and *h*'s, fingertips often stained with splatters of paint, and the tall Alsatian intellectual in his suit and beard à la mode, soft spoken and well read, a rolled cigarette often cradled between his index and middle fingers.

The weather was wet and hot that entire spring and summer in Paris. Neither Louis nor Lizzie had parents present to impose propriety on them—Joseph was across the Channel, Louis's mother fifty kilometers east in Voulangis—and they seem to have made the most of it. Paris in the Belle Époque was a vibrant, sensuous city. Much of it was still a construction site, Baron Haussmann chopping and whittling the city into new boulevards, avenues, and public squares, applying the finishing touches to fifteen years spent mowing down medieval Paris's crowded, irregular houses, its enchanting but insalubrious neighborhoods, to replace them with a harmony and splendor impossible for the poor to partake or raise barricades in. Louis and Lizzie may have gone together to the Salon, which was now open, to see Carrier-Belleuse's arousing *Angélique*, or to galleries to gaze at bold new works by Monet, Manet, Cézanne, and Pissarro, whose canvases the Académie refused to show. They could have taken the short walk from the Passage des Panoramas to Printemps, the brand-new department store, with its seventeen sales counters dedicated to all aspects of fashion and interior decoration. Perhaps Louis, who was obsessive about photography, was one day so bold as to take Lizzie's picture, and if he did, perhaps the two of them spoke of the medium's limitations, of the lie a camera told in robbing life of its movement, still so far short of the naturalism Carrier-Belleuse could mold out of stone. "It is the artist who is truthful and it is photography which lies," his apprentice Rodin once declared, "for in reality time does not stop, and if the artist succeeds in producing the impression of a movement which takes several moments for accomplishment, his work is certainly much less conventional than the scientific image, where time is abruptly suspended."[12] There is a pleasing neatness in imagining Le Prince, the man who would make the world's first motion picture, seducing his future wife with fantasies of an artist's camera, one that did not have to make time stop.

One day they rode the fifty kilometers east to Voulangis, so Louis could introduce Lizzie to his widowed mother. The way of life was old fashioned there, so different from Paris. "Several members of the Le Prince family owned small farms and vineyards in this valley of the Marne,"[13] Lizzie wrote years later. "The men were well set up and notably handsome; many of them returned from college and compulsory military training in Paris to their blue blouse and home farm from sheer love of country life and freedom. It was intensive farming with them, not a yard of ground was left untilled." At the dinner table the conversation was loud and confident. "I have rarely listened to wittier talk and repartee, or more trenchant or appreciative criticism of family events and world happenings, than at that table," Lizzie remembered.[14] Money, which meant so much to the industrialists of England, left the French farmers indifferent. The celebrated painter Jean-Baptiste Corot was from the region; on a walk one afternoon Lizzie began chatting with the owner of an old farmhouse, who invited her in. There, hanging on the peasant's wall, was a painted sketch by Corot. Lizzie was flabbergasted. Works by the artist sold for nearly 5,000 francs in Paris. But when she asked the farmer if he had any idea how much the painting was worth, to her mind an entirely natural question, the man turned cold. "He stiffened a little," Lizzie recalled, "and said: 'Do you think money could buy it?'"[15]

It was a simple life, and it made Lizzie love Louis even more.

On July 1, 1869, three years after they first met, Louis and Lizzie were married—not in Paris, but in Yorkshire. Paris was enthralling, and Voulangis was charming, but Leeds was where Lizzie belonged.

And Le Prince, after his first brief visit to Leeds, had decided to stay.

GOD'S OWN
COUNTRY

1866–1869

I t was, to be fair, a city unlike any Le Prince had ever seen: so different
from Paris's wide boulevards and green parks, or Leipzig's Renaissance
marketplace and baroque trading houses.

Leeds, nestled in a valley of the river Aire and encircled by hills and
moors that seemed permanently drizzled with rain, was one of Britain's
great industrial engines—and arguably its most reviled metropolis. In
the public imagination, the city, a European leader in the textile trade,
had come to symbolize the filth and ugliness of the age. As early as
1837 one visitor had called Leeds "the vilest of the vile,"[1] an oppressive
knot of factories encrusted in "a vast dingy canopy formed by the
impure exhalation of a hundred furnaces." The German travel writer
Johann Georg Kohl crowned it "the ugliest and least attractive town
in all England."[2]

It was also, perhaps unexpectedly, a city of great wealth, a trade
hub and a mining center. While the entire West Riding of Yorkshire
was known for its textiles, Leeds was known best of all: the dressing,
cropping, and dyeing of broadcloth was a matter of local pride. There
was plenty of money to spread around—but Leeds, like the majority
of cities then, was an oligarchy. A handful of men owned the land, the

factories, and the capital. They controlled the trading markets. They possessed the most and so they profited the most, a process by which they possessed even more. Everyone else—journeymen, laborers, tailors, market stall owners, domestic servants—toiled dawn to dusk, six or seven days a week, eking out a subsistence living. The men and women of Yorkshire—"God's own country"—were known for their pride, their common sense, their work ethic, their resilience, and their stubbornness, but the system was rigged against the vast majority of them, and the Industrial Revolution deepened the injustice, demanding that huge numbers of low-skilled workers move from the countryside to crowd into squalid city streets. As they did so, they funneled unprecedented profit into the wallets of the few.

Occasionally one of the have-nots broke through to become one of the new rich—members of a novel group known as the middle class—but it took grit and luck, and the prosperity they earned was precarious, too. Downturns in the economy, which came regularly, could easily bankrupt them and send them, in the blink of an eye, back whence they had come.

Joseph Whitley was one of these men.

The Whitley family had been in Yorkshire at least a hundred and fifty years. Whitley's paternal grandfather, Thomas, was born in Halifax and his grandmother in Kirkburton. His father, also Thomas, was from Penistone. Joseph himself was born on a cold October day in 1816 in Wakefield, a market town ten miles south of Leeds, the same year Charlotte Brontë was born down the road in Thornton, which was Joseph's mother's birthplace. Local records suggest Joseph may have had as many as nine siblings, all but one younger than he was. Thomas Whitley was a brass founder and Joseph, like his brothers, was groomed to enter the family trade. In 1844, at the age of twenty-eight, Joseph took over his family's shop and incorporated it as Whitley Partners, possibly with one or more of his siblings as associates.

There was immediate pressure on Joseph to succeed. He was two years married to Sarah Robinson, a childhood friend who had grown up streets away from him, and already had a child to feed—John Robinson, nicknamed "Jack," just a year old. The family was poor. Jack was born at home, at 71 Byron Street, one of hundreds of infamous back-to-back tenements, "the pride and despair of Leeds"[3]—small houses overfilled with low-income families, built back wall to back wall by landlords looking to maximize every inch of land.

But Joseph had the grit—and he had the luck. The world's first commercial steam railway had been open in Leeds since 1812, shuttling coal wagons from the Middleton bell pits to warehouses and markets in Leeds proper, and the world's first intercity railway line, between nearby Liverpool and Manchester, had opened in 1830. The north of England was at the forefront of a transit revolution, and as Joseph entered into business the whole country was following suit. This called for coordination across a web of industries: the making of steam engines, carriages, and tracks themselves; the laying of the roads to service the stations, which also needed to be built; the digging of tunnels and the erecting of bridges. The face of England was changing day by day, literally, as vast swaths of green fields and farmland were gridded over with iron and steel. By the 1860s Leeds was the fifth-largest city in England behind London, Liverpool, Manchester, and Birmingham. Coal and iron ore were both plentiful under the West Riding moors. Engineers and metalsmiths were in high demand, and Yorkshire bred many of England's finest.

Whitley's own skill lay in the details, in the smaller mechanisms that made the whole system work: gears, gauges, valves, boilers, pumps, hackles, gills, combs, and all other kinds of engine work and machinery, which Whitley Partners provided not just to the railways but also to the local textile manufacturers, who were already beginning to replace hand labor with automated substitutes. Manufacturing these products was a sure way to a paycheck, at least as long as the boom lasted, but innovating and improving on them was the path to affluence. Take the example of Samson Fox, the son of a mill worker, who was around the same age as Joseph and, like him, had risen from the tenements to start his own businesses, the Silver Cross Works and the Leeds Forge Company. In the 1870s Fox patented a corrugated boiler flue that was such an improvement on previous designs, for efficiency and for safety both, that it was widely adopted by the British Admiralty as well as by several major steamship passenger lines, making Fox's fortune overnight. He became rich enough to fund the construction of London's Royal College of Music. Fox's life was the one all his peers in Leeds aspired to: one in which a single innovation, sprouting from years of practical experience, provided not just security but abundance for one's family for generations to come.

This was the Holy Grail Joseph Whitley pursued. He never struck upon a similar gold mine to Fox's, but he patented a wide array of successful innovations: compressed packing to improve railways, cushioning for railway wheels, proprietary stop valves, improvements in the manufacture of steel, and more. Bit by bit, sale by sale, licensing agreement after licensing agreement, he grew his earnings, one small, sensible idea at a time.

In 1851, seven years after the founding of Whitley Partners, he and his family still lived in the township of Holbeck, described by a local as "one of the most crowded, one of the most filthy, one of the most unpleasant, and one of the most unhealthy villages in the county of York."[4] Joseph and Sarah now had two children, Lizzie having arrived in 1846. They could afford a fourteen-year-old live-in servant to help with domestic tasks and at least a handful of apprentices to work a small premises in nearby Hunslet. Ten years later the Whitleys lived at 48 Bowman Lane, closer to the river in Leeds proper, but still surrounded by loud, sooty locomotive works and foundries. The servant was gone, no longer needed or no longer affordable, but now Joseph owned his own workshop—and the land it sat on—down the road at number 78. A few more years of ingenuity and toil followed, and by the mid-1860s, two decades after the founding of the firm that bore his name, Joseph was finally able to move his family to Roundhay Cottage, a multiple bedroom home in the leafy suburbs northeast of Leeds center. There the Whitleys employed a groom, a gardener, and a general servant. Their neighbors were the wealthy elite and, like their children, young Jack and Lizzie Whitley were sent abroad to complete their educations.

The train carrying Louis Le Prince to Yorkshire on that first visit in 1866, Jack and Lizzie sitting with him in the compartment, pulled into the main station at Wellington Street, on the south side of Leeds. From there the trio proceeded, by horse-drawn car, to Roundhay, a crosstown journey that took them past the factories and back-to-back tenements, redbrick walls blackened by the heavy smoke. On every day but Sunday the air was filled with the clanking and whirring of machinery.[5]

Finally, a mile and a half into the journey, the cab slowly rose onto elevated terrain. Buildings fell away, the smog thinned and then evaporated, and the countryside returned. Between tracts of farmland Leeds's affluent suburbs appeared: Chapeltown, Oakwood, Hollin Park, and finally Roundhay, home to the local oligarchs.

Roundhay Cottage, where the Whitley family lived, was a handsome country manor. The building's stones were clean, well and evenly cut; its garden was airy and filled with roses. The greatest contrast to the city center, perhaps, was to the ear: there was nothing there but silence, and not just on Sundays.

This was where Joseph Whitley, once a denizen of the cauldron, now one of Yorkshire's blessed few, had made his home.

If Joseph was apprehensive about meeting his daughter's unexpected foreign suitor, his fears were quickly dispelled. Within months Le Prince joined Whitley Partners as a draftsman and "traveler," or foreign sales agent, returning to Paris in April 1867 to represent the firm at the Exposition Universelle. Either before or after the fair he made the permanent move to Leeds, renting rooms at 27 Belgrave Street, a one-story house on a short, narrow street of single-family homes and back-to-backs just north of the city center, situated almost perfectly equidistant to the Whitley factory to the south and Roundhay Cottage to the northeast. He lived there for a year or so while courting Lizzie. It was a lively neighborhood, cleaner than the townships proper, full of pubs, shops, and churches. Two mornings a week, including Saturdays, the cloying stench of raw meat and manure from the nearby Smithfield cattle market hung over Belgrave Street. In the evenings the indigent loitered outside the two local almshouses, one just a block away from Louis's front door, and at week's end working men huddled in the street or in backyards to gamble on cockfights and bare-knuckle boxing, two of the most popular pastimes of the era. On Sunday families put on their best clothes and went to church. It was a world away from Baron Haussmann's symmetric new Paris but, by all accounts, Le Prince was taken with this new life: not only did he stay, but even when he returned to Leeds from New York in the 1880s, he chose nearby Woodhouse Lane as the place to rent a workshop.

The Whitley family welcomed Le Prince with open arms. Lizzie loved him and Jack was his comrade in business. What no one had foreseen was the bond between Joseph and Louis. The elder Whitley was a warm, affectionate man, with smiling eyes and a tousled white beard. He had the stocky build of a foundry worker and, even in his fifties, he rolled his sleeves up and eagerly made his way to the foundry most mornings by six a.m., for he valued manual work as a means toward self-improvement. Louis endeared himself to his future father-in-law soon after settling in Leeds, when, Lizzie recalled, he "took [Joseph's] advice, donned overalls, and worked all day in [the] machine shops."[6] Joseph appreciated the Frenchman's skill with his hands. The two men, though a generation apart, shared a humanistic bent. "We are fearfully and wonderfully made," Joseph once told Lizzie on the subject of humankind, and to him no men were more wonderfully made than the inventors, the engineers, and the scientists. "How god-like," he added, "are those who discover the laws that govern the phenomenon of life, and more so those who apply them to the requirements of the times through which we are passing."[7]

But, as Lizzie would comment on later, there also grew an odd dynamic between the three men around her, as if Joseph and Jack—a father-and-son pair as competitive as any—were also fighting for Le Prince's friendship. Jack was not like his father. Where Joseph seemed to take pride in raising himself from his working-class roots, Jack appeared set on concealing his. Joseph loved his *work*, and Jack loved his *business*. Louis, outwardly just the kind of urban, progressive bourgeois Jack aspired to fraternize with, turned out, after Jack had brought him to Yorkshire, to be more Joseph's type of man: happy in his shirtsleeves, more interested in patent applications than profit statements, keener to spend what spare time he had working rather than socializing. His friendship, it appeared, was a referendum of one, on the question of whose outlook on life was correct: the father's, or the son's.

This caused no rancor—yet.

The 1867 Paris Exposition was a tremendous success for France—and for Whitley Partners. Le Prince and Jack were both in attendance for much of its six-month duration,[8] and at the close of the fair Whitley's was awarded a silver medal in the Mining and Metallurgy section. Lizzie may also have returned to Paris for the occasion, as Carrier-Belleuse's *Angélique* was showing in the sculpture wing, along with four of the master's busts.

When Louis was not working, he took in the other exhibits. This was the World's Fair that first showcased electricity and how it worked. The wonder materials aluminum and petroleum captured imaginations. The photographer Nadar took paying customers on trips over Paris in a hot-air balloon, amazing hundreds with the intoxicating and stupefying experience of the world as only birds could naturally see it. Japanese art, shown at a large European event for the first time, drove at least one attendee, Vincent van Gogh, to transform his own work; demonstrations of deep-sea diving technology inspired the visiting Jules Verne to write the book that would make him famous, the science fiction epic *Twenty Thousand Leagues under the Sea*. There was Thomas Barlow's planetarium and a large-scale working model of the soon-to-be-opened Suez Canal; Samuel Morse presided over the telegraphy exhibit and Léon Edoux took volunteers up and down his hydraulic elevator. Next door in the industrial wing, between the locomotives and construction cranes, visitors could gawk at the new fifty-ton steel cannon created by the German manufacturer Krupp AG; it was the biggest the world had ever seen, and its fury would be unleashed on this very same city just three years later. The world had not yet decided whether its new discoveries and knowledge would be used for progress or for slaughter.

The year after the fair, in September 1868, when Louis's brother, Albert, was married in Dijon to a nineteen-year-old local girl by the name of Gabrielle Chevrot, both Louis and Jack were present to be his witnesses. Nine months later Louis and Lizzie themselves tied the knot in Leeds. They moved into Chapeltown, a pleasant suburb neighboring Roundhay, Le Prince invested in his father-in-law's firm and became one of the partners in Whitley Partners, and within weeks Lizzie was pregnant. Aimless just a few years earlier, Le Prince had moved abroad, married into a wealthy family, and made himself instrumental to the profitable company it owned—and now he was about to be a father.

He had his prospects neatly laid out—though distant war drums were banging closer and closer, and would soon upend his life.

SILVER AND SALT

1841–1854

War had been a constant in Louis Le Prince's childhood. He was born at 13 rue Saint-Georges in Metz, a garrison town in eastern France, on August 28, 1841, the second child of Louis Abraham Ambroise Le Prince, forty-one, a captain in the Seventh Artillery Regiment of Napoléon III's imperial army, and Elizabeth Marie Antoinette Boulabert, twenty-five, of a wealthy family of architects and builders, originally from Montpellier. Louis's only brother, Louis Auguste Albert Le Prince, was just sixteen months older than him.

Le Prince *père* had been a military man his whole life. His family was from Crécy-la-Chapelle, a small town sitting forty-five kilometers east of Paris, and his father owned and managed vineyards in nearby Voulangis. Young Louis Abraham, however, was not cut out for a life spent watching grapes grow. Soon after turning twenty-one he joined the army as a gunner, and if it was excitement he was after, he did well choosing the armed forces in the 1820s. He had opportunity to fight in Spain—to which the French king sent sixty thousand troops to help his relative Ferdinand VII take power back from a liberal revolution—and in Algeria, invaded by France in 1830 as part of the country's colonial expansion. Just two years after enlisting, Le Prince was promoted to the rank of artificier, and twelve months after that to sergeant, then sergeant-major a year after that. By 1837 Le Prince was a captain and was transferred to the Seventh Regiment, stationed at the fortress of Metz, right on the frontier between France and the German Confederation, at the heart of a sort of cold war between the two neighboring countries. France had always contended that the region between Metz and the Rhine—thirty-two thousand square kilometers, including the cities of Cologne, Bonn, Koblenz, Kaiserslautern, and Saarbrücken—was its own to govern, and had even annexed the region in 1795, only for it to be retaken by Prussia twenty years later. The cannons at Metz would be among the first to fire if, and when, the simmering conflict boiled over into war. Louis Abraham was not called to wage that particular fight—though his sons, decades later, would.

In 1839 he married Elizabeth Boulabert, a plain young woman with strong features, sixteen years his junior and the daughter of one of Montpellier's leading civil engineers. The Boulabert men were leaders in that city's public life, landlords of grape orchards and farmland, and owners of a dozen vessels rented out to various business concerns. Two months after the wedding, Elizabeth was pregnant. Two sons, Albert and Louis, were born one year after the other.

The boys were so close in age they might, as they grew older, easily be mistaken for twins. Louis remembered those early years as happy, full of "colour and movement."[1] The family spent summers either with the Le Princes in Voulangis, the children running through rows of grape vines, or with the Boulaberts on the beaches south of Montpellier, where young Louis, dazzled by the bright, frothing sea, first took up watercolor painting.

Around them the world was changing—fast. Louis and his brother were members of the first truly modern generation. Photography, the telegraph, the steam engine, anesthesia, all came into public use in the few years preceding or following their births; before they reached adulthood Charles Darwin had published *On the Origin of Species*. The very concepts of labor, trade, and leisure were transformed by new possibilities. Time itself changed: from a local reality determined by the sun—its rising, its setting, its place in the sky—it was now a national and international standard, systemized by railway time and globalization. The hour and the day, necessary parts of the factory worker's shift, became the standard units of time, replacing the farmer's seasons. These drastic shifts happened quickly—and jarringly.

Ancient interests and new longings clashed, and the old world's injustices were glaring in the promise of the new. Revolution was inevitable and it returned, to France and all of Europe, in 1848, overthrowing kings once more. The French replaced theirs with a short-lived republic, its second. Louis-Napoléon Bonaparte, nephew of *the* Napoléon Bonaparte, became the country's first popularly elected president, but within three years he abolished the republic and named himself emperor, identifying himself as Napoléon III. Through it all, Abraham Le Prince continued to serve. His duty was to follow orders, not question the legitimacy of whoever gave them. His family followed him from posting to posting: they moved from Metz to Rennes in 1844, then to Picardy in 1849. Abraham Le Prince may have sent part of that year in Italy, where the Seventh Artillery Regiment was taking part in the siege of Rome, an effort to unseat the city's own young republic, led by Giuseppe Garibaldi. In December he was made a knight of the Légion d'Honneur, France's highest military distinction[2], and the next year the Le Prince family relocated to Vincennes, on the outskirts of Paris, then in 1853 to Toulouse, near the Spanish border. In 1854, Abraham Le Prince was promoted to major and transferred back to Vincennes, to command a squadron of the mounted artillery there. It was a quiet posting, Vincennes's château little more than a stockpile of cannonballs and a training ground for new recruits. The Le Prince family estate and vineyards in Voulangis were only a few hours' ride away by coach. It seemed Major Le Prince, at fifty-five years old, had been put to pasture, to collect his pay packets and see out the rest of his career in peace.

The Le Prince family arrived in Vincennes for the second time in March 1854. The following year, just weeks before Louis's fourteenth birthday, Louis Abraham Ambroise Le Prince died.

*   *   *

The widow Le Prince, in her grief, was still expected to abide by the rules of propriety. Elizabeth, if she heeded the mores of her day, would have worn the black cap and veil of mourning, but did not attend her husband's funeral or take part in the procession. Her teenage sons, now the men of the family, would have led the cortege of grievers to the cemetery alone. Elizabeth was still young—just thirty-nine—but never remarried. She packed up her remaining belongings and moved to the Le Prince vineyards in Voulangis, where she lived for the next several years. Albert and Louis were sent off to boarding school in Bourges, two hundred and fifty kilometers away.

Though Louis was young when his father died, many of the older man's virtues showed in him as he grew older, like gifts left behind after a departure: discipline, a strong work ethic, loyalty. Shortly before he passed away, Louis Abraham had added to these values one more, final, present, one that would be particularly meaningful to Louis.

He introduced him to Louis Daguerre, the inventor of photography.[3]

When Louis met Daguerre, he was a middle-aged dandy, refined and confident, his hair carefully coiffured and his silk waistcoat spotless. He often wore the same Maltese Cross–shaped medal of the Légion d'Honneur that hung, on its red ribbon, on Louis's father's own uniformed chest. Then in his sixties, Daguerre was one of France's most famous men, a "Prometheus who disrobed the sun of its light and put it to work as his slave," in the words of a contemporary art critic, Philippe Burty.[4] He was living out his retirement in Bry-sur-Marne, seven kilometers from Vincennes, in a villa he had bought with the annual pension owed to him by his grateful country.

Somehow Louis Abraham Le Prince knew the great man. It could have happened one of several ways: though Daguerre was twelve years older than Le Prince, both were born in middle-class families in satellite towns of Paris, Daguerre in Cormeilles-en-Parisis and Le Prince in Crécy. The retired Daguerre liked to go for long walks in the park of Vincennes, where artillery squadrons marched and rehearsed their drills. The two men may have moved in similar milieux. Members of the Le Prince family later described Louis Abraham and Daguerre as "intimate"[5] friends, and Louis seemed to have shared with Lizzie childhood memories of playing on the floor of Daguerre's studio while his father visited the photographer. (Lizzie herself, who had never met Daguerre, described him as a college friend of Louis's father; Louis's daughter Mariella remembered being told they had been neighbors.) At some time during the Le Princes' first stay in Vincennes and before Daguerre's death in 1851, or during one of their earlier holidays in Voulangis, Louis Abraham took his wife and children to Bry-sur-Marne to have their photograph taken.

Daguerre's two-hundred-year-old mansion, with its private stables and dovecote, sat on two walled acres of green grass, the Marne river rolling peacefully at the bottom of its sloped garden. The photographer lived there with his wife of forty years, Louise Arrowsmith, and her orphaned niece, Félicie. Daguerre had his own experimental laboratory at home and, though he had mostly stopped taking pictures for the public, he could occasionally be convinced to snap close friends or notable guests.[6]

Daguerreotyping was a complicated affair. The Le Prince family, donning their finest clothing—the *capitaine* in uniform, Elizabeth in black, the two boys in formal tunics—stood outside to take advantage of the sunshine, the brightest light being necessary to a successful exposure. The square wooden camera stood in front of them, propped up on stout legs. Inside it was a pane of silver-plated copper, polished and buffed until it shone, then treated with iodine and bromide fumes. Before Daguerre, inventors seeking to "seize the light" and give Nature "the power to reproduce herself,"[7] as Daguerre himself described photography, had stumbled in their efforts. A photograph is fixed when light hits a certain mixture of silver and salt crystals, known as the emulsion.

This chemical reaction must happen quickly. The time during which the emulsion is lit is known as the exposure, and if it is too long, the slightest movement by the subjects in front of the lens blurs the picture.

As a result, the first experimenters in photography—or "drawing with light," from the Greek *phōtós*, meaning light, and *graphê*, meaning drawing—were chemists, not artists. Light was difficult to manipulate, particularly in the decades before electricity, so it was widely accepted that the only way to make photography possible was to come up with better emulsions—chemical mixtures so sensitive to light they would need only seconds of exposure to imprint a "drawing" of the scene in front of the camera. Researchers conducted trials with different silver chloride balances; they mixed cellulose and nitric acid and dissolved both in ether; they coated paper or glass bases in syrupy egg whites. Over time, emulsions became good enough to take pictures of still lives or empty landscapes, subjects which stood still for the hour or more required, but they were nowhere near adequate to photograph *people*.

Daguerre, a painter and entertainment entrepreneur, arrived at a solution almost accidentally, after years of trial and error. He realized that the silver plates he used as a photographic base were, within mere minutes, being imprinted with a "latent image," just the shadow of an exposure, invisible to the naked eye and undetected by all who had come before him. This impression could be coaxed out through chemical treatment, the whites of the image brightening and the darks deepening until a sharp, clear photograph appeared. The earliest daguerreotypes cut exposure times to ten minutes or so—and, soon after, to just sixty or ninety seconds, depending on how brightly the subject could be lit. Though others had taken photographs before Daguerre, his was the first process whereby pictures of people, particularly portraits, could be realized, turning a niche field for chemists and scientists into a commercially viable, massively popular technology. When, in 1839, Daguerre, rather than copyright his discovery for himself, donated it to his country, which then offered it "free" to the rest of the world, he instantly became a national treasure.

By the end of the 1840s, when the Le Prince family gathered on Daguerre's lawn, tweaks to the medium's chemistry had reduced exposure times even further, to just a few seconds, so that Louis and Albert did not, like many children before them, have to be held in place by headrests and posing clamps. All they had to do was sit still.

Daguerre, or an assistant, would have adjusted the members of the family until he was satisfied with their placement in front of the lens, then removed the lens cap. There was no need to "take" a picture—light flooded into the box as soon as the cap or other protective slide was removed—and the photographer then stood by the camera, carefully counting the requisite seconds. The boys leaned on their mother. Time stood still.

To the majority of people for whom a daguerreotype was the first, and often only, time they stood so motionless in their lives, these seconds felt unnatural. Endless.

Finally Daguerre would have snapped the lens cap back on and told his subjects they were free to move.

The photographer, possibly with the help of an assistant, would then remove the camera to his laboratory inside the house. The Le Prince family likely returned indoors as well, but to a different room, to wait: Daguerre had work to do yet, and it had to be carried out quickly. Removing the copper plate, he or his assistant would have transferred it to an airtight fuming box, inside of which was a dish of mercury. He would have lit an alcohol burner, also known as a spirit lamp, under the box, the heat drawing fumes out of the mercury, the fumes mixing with the silver salts on the polished plate, until the resulting reaction drew the latent image out. The plate was then pulled out of the fuming box and dunked in a bath of sodium thiosulfate, dissolving the silver halides on the plate and "fixing" the image permanently. Gold chloride might then have been used to strengthen the photograph's detail even further. Finally, the plate was rinsed in distilled water, dried, and immediately sealed in a glass casing to protect its fragile silver coating from scratches and oxidization. It was recommended this shell never be removed, for exposure to air could erase the picture completely: even while enclosed, many daguerreotypes suffered, after a few years, from oxygen corrosion and tarnish at the edges.

All this, in those early days, was required to make a single photograph. Only after these steps would Daguerre be able to return to the waiting Le Princes to present them with an object that still amazed and mystified: their own faces, in incredible detail but drained of color, frozen in silver and trapped under glass.

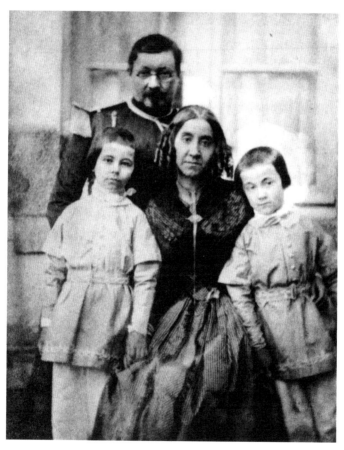

Daguerreotype of the Le Prince family, taken in the late 1840s, allegedly by Daguerre himself. Louis, about eight years old, is on the right. His brother, Albert, is on the left. (Private collection. Courtesy of Laurie Snyder.)

Many Europeans of the time were impressed by their first experience with a photographer. They described the uncanny sensation of laying eyes on one's own likeness, preserved unmoving in deep monochrome; it was like coming face-to-face with your own ghost. The daguerreotype changed people's relationship with death, and with their own sense of who they were. Many sitters were frightened of the experience, fearing exposure to either the processing vapors or "the rays of the camera"[9] might poison them. Some saw in it the work of the devil. Baudelaire feared it would put an end to art, and disconnect man from his soul.[10]

This encounter with Daguerre—the proximity to an unprecedented combination of artist and chemist who, it was thought at the time, had single-handedly transformed the world—marked the young Louis Le Prince profoundly. It was his "first impression" of the "art" of photography, he later told family, and, after they were married, Lizzie thought the adult Louis continued to emulate the famous inventor's particular "bent of thought."[8]

After both their parents had died, it was Louis, not Albert, who retained that original daguerreotype. There would be an eerie symmetry in his and Daguerre's lives. They shared a first name; they both married the daughters of English entrepreneurs; they both apprenticed as painters and worked in the same field of entertainment, the panorama, before becoming inventors late in their forties. By the time the daguerreotype of the Le Prince family was taken, Louis had likely already discovered his talent for drawing, the same skill that had set Daguerre apart as a child, and in the years after this encounter Louis took up photography, which became one of his own passions. Optics and chemistry, the subjects he read at university, were the exact disciplines required to innovate in that field. When considering his choices from this vantage point, it can feel like Le Prince, consciously or otherwise, modeled aspects of his life on Daguerre's, the most famous, and most awe-inspiring, man he met in his formative years.

He was shaped by these two men, his father and Daguerre, the soldier and the photographer—who, even after death, remained bound in that faded framed image, their presence small enough to carry in a pocket.

*   *   *

All of this—Louis Abraham Le Prince and Louis Daguerre, the past, and how one could keep its phantom alive—might have been on Louis Le Prince's mind more than twenty years later as he was back in Paris in the early days of 1871, wearing a military uniform of his own. The war his father had trained for but never fought had finally come. Paris was under siege and Prussian bombs were falling on its homes and its cafés. Louis's mother was safely in England with his wife, and the daguerreotype had probably gone with her. Le Prince, alone and away from his loved ones, surrounded by ill and dying men, was cut off from the outside world in the total, profound kind of way that most, in this modern age of telegraphy and the railroad, forgot was even possible.

It was just as good he did not have the photograph with him. Starving Parisians were robbing their fellow men for every ounce of silver they could sell for bread. Even salt, in this place, was no luxury to be wasted on memories. The men of the national guard were so hungry they had taken to boiling their shoes, in the hope they might extract, from the cracked leather, some sodium to feed their failing bodies.

WAR

1870–1871

I n 1870, when the first gunshots were fired, Louis Le Prince was still safely in Leeds, working for Joseph Whitley and celebrating the birth of his first child, Marie Gabriella, affectionately nicknamed Mariella.

Ministerpräsident Otto von Bismarck had been waging a long war of expansion for nearly a decade, with the aim of unifying all German-speaking people of Europe under one state, one ruler, and one flag. In 1864 Prussia had invaded neighboring Denmark, winning the return of the duchies of Schleswig-Holstein and Saxe-Lauenburg, and two years later it attacked Austria, securing dominion over Frankfurt, Hanover, Nassau, Hesse-Kassel, and a confederation of states north of the Main River. The time had come for the climactic fight with France, Germany's historical archenemy. At stake was the disputed territory east of the Rhine, the very land Louis Le Prince's father had prepared to defend while garrisoned at the fortress of Metz.

So, in July 1870, Bismarck provoked Napoléon III into going to war.

That summer, in the parlor at Roundhay Cottage, Louis read the bulletins from France with increasing concern. "The despatch of the French Declaration of War to Berlin is officially confirmed," blared the *Leeds Mercury* on July 20.[1] Two days later the paper reported on the amassment

61

of French troops around Metz, prepared to engage the enemy.[2] Though Bismarck had engineered the start of the conflict, exploiting a minor diplomatic incident to offend French pride, it was Napoléon who had officially declared war in response, and foreign opinion was not sympathetic to the French. "The Liberal Empire [i.e., France] goes to war on a mere point of etiquette," read the *Illustrated London News*.[3] There were rumors Queen Victoria, though officially neutral, was hoping for a Prussian victory.

Deeper, costlier humiliation was still to come. In the war against Austria, Bismarck's troops had perfected the new art of *Blitzkrieg*—swift, concentrated action intended not to annihilate hostile armed forces but to blast right through them instead. Traditional warfare, such as Napoléon was used to, saw outcomes decided in large-scale pitched battles, at the end of which one king surrendered or was captured—such as had happened at Hastings in 1066 and Waterloo in 1815. Proponents of *Blitzkrieg*, on the other hand, argued for pressure to be applied toward a target General Carl von Clausewitz called the *Schwerpunkt* ("center of gravity"):[4] the enemy capital. Bismarck, accordingly, planned to blow straight through the army of Napoléon III and march, as quickly as possible, on to Paris, sending the French troops scrambling.

Napoléon's forces were ill prepared for this new form of combat. Modern Prussian artillery guns mangled France's heavy cavalry. Muzzle-loading rifles and primitive machine guns mowed down thousands of French infantrymen before they ever got close enough to use their bayonets. And while the French army traveled slowly, lumbering forward in great numbers to predetermined points on its generals' maps, Bismarck made use of railway freight and telegram communication to organize his forces over numerous battlefields, destroying the enemy's own infrastructure as he went. It was a mass, industrial, dehumanizing war, one of the first in modern history. The Germans called it a *Millionenkrieg* ("war of the millions").[5]

Here, too, was a new world, and Bismarck was simply better prepared for it than France's sixty-two-year-old emperor. In less than three months, Prussian soldiers ripped through the French countryside, taking Metz after a brief siege and capturing Napoléon himself at Sedan in September, before continuing on to Paris. They suffered few defeats along the way.

Over the first weekend of August, English newspapers carried reports of France's first two defeats, with estimates of two thousand dead and the cavalry in desperate flight. On August 6, Le Prince would have returned home from work at Whitley Partners to learn of the "reinforced" French army's embarrassment at Wörth, near Karlsruhe, with half its men dead, wounded, or captured. Two days later, when the Monday edition of the *Mercury* arrived, it announced "a retreat along the whole line of the French army."[6] As Parisians realized Prussian troops would soon be upon them, chaos broke out in the capital. Citizens gathered at the Place Vendôme to protest the government. Scattered disturbances broke out in all four corners of the city. Confirmation that Metz was encircled, with the remainder of the army trapped inside its walls, caused further panic. Suddenly defeat seemed not just inevitable but imminent.

Louis and Albert exchanged letters while they still could. Albert's wife, Gabrielle, and their infant daughter Marie were in Dijon with his in-laws, but Albert was still in Paris, a new graduate of the École Centrale des Arts et Manufactures, where he had studied under the influential architect Eugène Viollet-le-Duc. German battalions might attempt to invade Dijon on their way to Paris from the south—in Wissenberg, one of the first towns to fall, the fighting had ended with door-to-door engagements through the streets, and the number of civilian deaths had been high. If conscripted, Albert would be unable to protect his young family. He also fretted about his and Louis's mother, Elizabeth: she lived in the Ninth Arrondissement now, in a building she had recently bought on rue Bochart de Saron. She was fifty-four years old, alone much of the time, and frightened.

Roundhay, Louis realized, was shelter. If he hurried back to France, he could, as a British resident, bring them back to Yorkshire with him to wait out the war—but he had to get to Paris before the Prussians did.

In Paris Louis found nothing but trouble. He arrived in the middle of August, about a week after the French army in the east had been forced to retreat. Within days he was caught up in the rioting. Early on the afternoon of August 14, a hot, sunny Sunday, Le Prince was at the Gare du Nord, awaiting Albert's wife, Gabrielle, who was arriving from Dijon with her baby. He had prepared his mother for departure the previous day. As soon as his sister-in-law was in Paris, they could proceed to England.

But the train from Dijon was delayed several hours, and Louis found himself with an afternoon to kill. He decided to call on a sick relative living in nearby La Villette, a working-class district outside the city center. After a brief visit, Louis's relative gave him flowers to bring back to his mother as a farewell, a bright, hopeful bunch of red and white blooms accented with forget-me-nots. It was time to return to the station; Louis, flowers in hand, made his goodbyes.

A crowd was assembled on the boulevard to watch a juggler perform near the fire station, an old building abutting the canal. Suddenly a small group of revolutionaries, concealed among the pedestrians and eager to precipitate the fall of Napoléon, cried out, "*Vive la République! Mort aux Prusses! Aux Armes!*"[7] They broke into the fire station, from which they hoped to steal weapons and ammunition, and in the struggle shot and killed a policeman and several firemen.

The insurrectionists hoped the public would rally in rebellion behind them. They called for the storming of nearby Belleville, a bourgeois neighborhood, but found no support; some of the bystanders even turned on them, confusing them for Prussian agitators. Chaos erupted. Several more gunshots rang out. Policemen seized some of the ringleaders but others escaped. Auguste Blanqui, the leader of the republican movement, tried to distribute weapons to nearby civilians, but "the population appeared dumbstruck. Attracted by curiosity, but held back by fear, they stood, immobile and silent, backed up against the houses."[8]

Le Prince, emerging from a side street, was caught in the tumult. A policeman shouted. Raised fingers pointed in his direction. "*Républicain!*" a voice barked out. Louis looked down. In his fist he held the fresh bouquet—red, white, and blue, like a revolutionary banner.

In no time policemen were upon him. He tried to explain himself, but the slight accent he could not conceal struck them as suspicious. They searched him and found English currency and tickets for international travel. The inside tag of his soft felt hat, bought while a student in Leipzig, bore the name of a German hatmaker. The police dragged Louis away with the other rioters.

When Gabrielle arrived at the Gare du Nord with her daughter, there was no one there to meet her. She made her way to her mother-in-law's home on rue Bochart de Saron.

Louis was thrown into an overcrowded jail, the air crackling with tension. The prisoners turned aggressive and some of the soldiers keeping guard, fearing a riot, fired through the cell bars to subdue them. Late at night, in the middle of "a horror of cries and suffering,"[9] Louis was removed by the guards to a separate cell elsewhere in the building. One of his jailers suggested this had to be done so Louis, who they suspected was a Prussian spy, would be ready for interrogation in the morning— and, if necessary, "execution."[10]

At some point Louis slid his watch out of his waistcoat pocket and beckoned one of the drunk guards over. He told the guard he could keep the watch—likely worth more than the guard made in weeks—if he sent two wires, one to Roundhay in England, one to Madame *veuve* Le Prince right here in Paris, asking the recipients "to come to his aid immediately."[11] The guard agreed.

The cable to Lizzie did not arrive in time. The one to Louis's mother did not arrive at all.

The guard kept the pocket watch.

The next morning, Elizabeth Le Prince, alarmed at Louis's absence, contacted *Le Temps*—the newspaper of record—and had the editor run a short missing-persons notice for her son. "Mme. Le Prince, owner, 6 rue Bochart-de-Saron, has been very worried about her son," it read, "who has traveled from England to find her and has not been seen in twenty-four hours, since she read this morning's newspaper accounts of the affair of La Villette and, she believes, recognized her son in the description of the stranger arrested and found carrying English gold and currency notes."[12]

It may have saved Louis's life. The brief article was spotted by a British journalist, friendly with Joseph Whitley, who was reporting from the French capital for the *London Daily News* and recognized Louis's name. With the help of the British ambassador in Paris, a search was put in motion, and on August 21 or 22 Louis was released, to the relief of his family, after spending a week in jail. The journalist made sure to write up and file an account of the affair, which was subsequently picked up by newspapers across Britain: the tale of the innocent bystander, "in no way mixed-up" with the fighting, arrested "with no rhyme or reason" by the French police even though he had "no connection whatever with the disturbances beyond that of a casual spectator."[13] It vindicated, in its small way, the contempt in which the British public held their neighbors across the Channel.

The incident also changed Louis. He may have been a casual spectator before his arrest, but protesting his own neutrality while surrounded by countrymen risking their lives for what they believed in made him reconsider his position. Perhaps he could not face the idea of sitting idle while his brother was called to battle, as he inevitably would be. Perhaps he read of the masses of Frenchmen living abroad who were returning home to join the fight, and was inspired by their patriotism. Perhaps he thought of his father, Capitaine Le Prince, the rosette of the Légion d'Honneur shining on his lapel, and wondered what he would have felt, watching his son run away from his country in its hour of need.

Louis made his decision. As soon as his mother, Gabrielle, and the baby were in Leeds, he would enlist and serve his country.

He had a family—Lizzie, and a baby of their own, Mariella, not yet five months old. Should she grow up without a father for the sake of pride—for an aging emperor who had overthrown the last republic, a man few Frenchmen held in true affection? Was it not more important to be present for the living daughter than to honor the ghost in the daguerreotype frame?

But Le Prince could not bring himself to choose safety. He ferried his family to Leeds and immediately returned to France, reporting for service before the end of the summer, as a volunteer with the Garde Nationale. He was assigned, as an officer, to the 120th Battalion of the Garde de la Seine.[14]

Napoléon, at the head of a reinforced army, went into battle at Sedan. It was impossible, from Paris, to be certain of the outcome, but word on the streets and in the cafés was of Napoléon's forces being routed by Bismarck's. On September 2, the War Ministry called up a hundred thousand provincial units to the capital to prepare for the arrival of the Prussians.[15] Two days later, on another sunny Sunday, throngs of angry Parisians marched on the Hôtel de Ville and the Palais Bourbon, beating drums and chanting "*A bas l'Empire! Vive la République!*" On the fifth, Parisians awoke to confirmation of the news they had awaited, with a mixture of dread and anticipation, for the entire summer. "*Napoléon III Prisonnier!*" cried the front page of *Le Gaulois*:[16] the French sovereign had been captured by the enemy.

Infighting broke out inside the legislative chambers. The emperor's Spanish wife, Eugenie, disguised in a veil, was whisked past the barricades by her American dentist, Dr. Thomas W. Evans, and taken to sanctuary in England.

A mob stormed the Palais des Tuileries shortly after Eugenie had deserted it. One civilian took chalk to a palace wall to scribble an announcement that the building was now the "PROPRIETE DU PEUPLE." The following morning the front pages of all the major newspapers opened with the same announcement: "*La République Est Proclamée!*"[17]

The Empire's days were over. France was establishing a republic instead, its third attempt at a representative system since 1789. The war, however, had not yet ended. Its worst was still to come.

The German troops marched relentlessly forward. Dijon fell. Garibaldi— whom Louis's father had fought in Rome twenty years earlier—rushed north from Italy to stand by the new French republic.

In nearby Besançon, a struggling thirty-year-old photographer by the name of Antoine Lumière packed up his house and fled south to Lyon with his wife and two sons, Auguste, eight, and Louis, six. His eldest son never forgot the sight of trains loaded with hundreds of wounded young men, their faces and limbs bandaged, their uniforms caked with dried blood.

In Bry-sur-Marne, the banks of the river Marne running amber with blood, Prussian artillery shells blew chunks out of the walls of the old Daguerre villa.

Three and a half thousand miles away in America, in a young country unburdened by the resentments and proximity of the old world, a twenty-two-year-old telegraph operator and aspiring inventor by the name of Thomas Alva Edison opened his first workshop in Newark, New Jersey. Edison was an avid reader, though he had little interest in politics or distant war—as a telegraph operator for the Associated Press, he'd preferred to work the graveyard shift, when news was slow and he could spend his time reading books and concocting scientific experiments. In 1869, he'd patented a first slew of inventions, most notable among them a printing telegraph, and in the second half of 1870—as Louis Le Prince patrolled the Paris streets, watching for Prussian artillery shells—Thomas Edison was making the beginnings of his first fortune. He called his new company the American Telegraph Works, staff: eighteen men.

A hundred and forty-five miles to the north, in Albany, New York, a growing town of breweries and lumberyards, the brothers John Wesley and Isaiah Smith Hyatt, middle-aged sons of a Starkey blacksmith, founders of the Albany Dental Plate Company and inventors themselves, registered a patent and trademark for a malleable substance of their own conception. The material, derived from gun cotton, had previously been experimented with by others, particularly in England, but no one had yet found a real use for it. The Hyatts treated the material, cellulose, with nitric acid and camphor, and made it strong, flexible, and water-proof, suitable as a cheap alternative to rubber and ivory alike. They opened a factory and advertised their discovery for use in the making of billiard balls, dental plates, hairbrushes and combs, babies' rattles, playing dice, and detachable collars and cuffs. As he drafted the patents for the manufacturing process, Isaiah Hyatt decided a proprietary name should be chosen for the material, the world's first industrial plastic.

He called it celluloid.

BURIED ALIVE

1870–1871

The Prussian army took Versailles on September 20. By the end of the next day, Bismarck's troops had Paris fully surrounded. Krupp AG's heavy artillery pieces stood at the ready. The German forces enclosed the city and waited for the people inside its walls to surrender—or starve.

Le Prince's battalion was tasked with defending Paris's "9th sector," spanning the neighborhood known as Les Gobelins, from Boulevard Arago down to the Porte d'Italie, roughly the boundaries of today's Thirteenth Arrondissement. There was restlessness within the ranks, as all the officers were, like Le Prince, from the middle and upper classes, and all the men were workers, many among them just learning they were part of a group Karl Marx had lately named the "proletariat," awakening them to the possibility they could, and should, want more out of life than poverty and hunger. Luckily, the leader of the 120th, Admiral de Challié, was a navy man with experience handling a diverse set of troops. In the middle of the night, when other officers were resting on their featherbeds, he could be found walking the streets of his sector, speaking words of encouragement to his men.[1]

At first spirits were high. The moat and forts around the city walls were reinforced, the catacombs sealed, the trees of the Bois de Boulogne chopped down and rearranged into fortifications. Museums were emptied and their masterpieces smuggled to safety or buried in secret underground chambers. The under-construction Palais Garnier, which Carrier-Belleuse had been commissioned to decorate, was turned into a military depot; theaters into hospitals; train stations into munitions factories. Hundreds of sheep brought in from outside the city walls grazed in every park and square, waiting to be slaughtered when Paris ran out of meat. The defiant attitude was best symbolized by the sixty-eight-year-old Victor Hugo, who had just returned to France after nineteen years of exile in England. Hugo was charismatic, progressive, and hugely popular, and now, "a military képi perched permanently on his head,"[2] wrote the historian Alastair Horne; he spoke for all of his countrymen in publishing public taunts to the Prussians, reminding them that *"Paris est la ville des villes. Paris est la ville des hommes. Il y a eu Athènes, il y a eu Rome, et il y a Paris!"*[3] ("Paris is the city of all cities. It is the city of humankind. There was Athens, there was Rome, now there is Paris!")

The Germans responded to the bombast with silence. Bismarck's *Soldaten* rested. They visited brothels. They sunbathed in the gardens of Versailles. French soldiers filled their own days playing cards, drinking cheap dark wine, and patrolling the southern portion of Paris's thirty-foot-high wall. "At first, it was veritably charming, veritably,"[4] wrote twenty-six-year-old Paul Verlaine, who was with the 160th Battalion of the Garde, stationed near Le Prince's at Issy, but soon "bad habits" set in: it was during these months of the siege that the poet, bored and anxious, began his destructive affair with absinthe. Rodin, Degas, and Manet were also serving in different regiments of the Garde. Manet wrote to keep his sanity. Degas found a way to continue painting, even in the darkest days of the siege, by which point at least one of his female models demanded to be paid not in useless paper money but with red meat. Rodin kept his head down. Camille Saint-Saëns, enrolled in the Fourth Regiment near L'Elysée, played concerts for the wounded.

Communications in and out of Paris were cut. Rumors spread like plague. Hoax reports of French victories led to jubilation and then, within hours, crushing disappointment. Finally the impasse was broken with hot-air balloons, bravely flown over enemy lines by aeronauts who knew full well it took just one bullet to blow them out of the sky. The photographer Nadar, who had flown a dirigible in the same 1867 exposition in which Krupp had demonstrated the artillery guns that now sat threateningly outside Paris, instituted a "Balloon Post" so the people of Paris could send correspondence out of the besieged city. (The balloons were patriotically named after national heroes; one of them was the *Daguerre*.) Inspired, the rest of France responded with a network of carrier pigeons, strapping microphotographs—another new breakthrough technology—to their scaled feet, allowing each bird to carry up to forty thousand dispatches per flight. Inside the besieged city the tiny images were projected by magic lantern, transcribed, and forwarded to their intended recipients.

It was brave, ingenious, and, in the end, mostly futile. Balloons drifted or crashed. The vast majority of the pigeons were lost or died. At Bismarck's request, Alfred Krupp designed a dedicated antiballoon cannon, history's first antiaircraft gun, which could fire three-pound grenades two thousand feet into the sky. October's damp cold replaced the warmth of September. Meat, bread, and salt were rationed and then unavailable. Temperatures plummeted. Soon November snow blanketed the city. The sheep were killed for meat, then dogs, cats, and other pets. Horses, too. Rats were hunted out of gutters.

With hunger and cold came disease. Smallpox, typhoid, pneumonia. The children and the weak died first. Occasionally, the temporary republican government ordered its regiments to breach the German blockade, but every attempt was brutally rebuffed, at huge human cost. The "Grande Sortie," a last-gasp offensive by the French at the northeastern corner of the capital, cost nearly twelve thousand lives in the last days of November. Le Prince, he later told his sons, was attached to the Garde's ambulance service as an aide to an army surgeon by the name of Dr. Demarre. The medical corps was a shambles. After every defeat, the wounded were piled in horse-drawn ambulances and on *bateaux mouches* and taken to doctors, but there were always too many casualties to look after. Countless men were left behind on the field to die. Amputation was common, painful, and often botched. Septicemia and gangrene ate through the makeshift hospitals.

One particular night, close to Christmas, black pox overran the infirmaries. Orders were given to quarantine the contaminated until they died, but Le Prince's men, "panic stricken"[5] at the thought of contracting the highly contagious disease, flatly refused even to bury the bodies. Vaccination had been introduced in France years earlier—smallpox, in fact, was the first disease human beings could inoculate against—but it was of course too late for that, and the force of the outbreak was petrifying. Le Prince, as officer, was expected to discipline his men for disobeying orders. Examples should be made, or mutiny might spread. Louis, however, understood the soldiers' fears. The dead deserved dignity, but he couldn't force the living into harm's way in the name of discipline. They had mothers, wives, children, dreams of their own.

"To spare them the penalty of disobedience," his son Adolphe wrote decades later, recording the story as his father told it to him, "[Le Prince] and a brother officer removed the bodies and buried them themselves."[6] As Louis handled the corpses, he perhaps wondered if he would be next, if within days it would be his turn to burn with fever, to vomit, to go blind, to die a death so repulsive his fellow men would refuse to bury him, too. Louis had stayed in Paris to be a soldier. Instead he'd ended up an undertaker.

He did not catch the pox.

In the New Year the Prussians began bombing the city. Krupp's new guns were unprecedented in their capacity for destruction. Each made of a single chunk of steel, they could fire thousand-pound shells over a distance of nearly four kilometers; on impact the bombs exploded into shards of shrapnel and released a cargo of up to forty hard zinc balls, which peppered in every direction at the speed of bullets fired out of a rifle. The Prussians had seventy-six such heavy guns available. On January 5 they started putting them to use.

Only Paris's southern forts and the left bank of the Seine were within reach of Krupp's cannons, and Le Prince and the 120th Battalion were stationed right in the line of fire. The bombing sprees took place overnight and at dawn, blasts suddenly setting the darkness on fire, shells streaking overhead in the gray predawn fog. Then came the screams, the confusion, the sobs, the digging of warm bodies out of ashy rubble. The Germans kept at it for twenty-three straight nights, lashing Paris with twelve thousand bombs. Though only relatively few people died, less than a hundred by some estimates, the thought of machinery—breech loaded, relentless, blind—killing so indiscriminately was unsettling. The rumble and crash of the explosives haunted every Parisian—like "the action of a steam-engine piston," remembered the writer Edmond de Goncourt.[7]

Funeral processions became a daily sight. You could usually tell how old the dead were from the size of the coffins.

Le Prince continued treating the wounded and burying the dead. He was far from the only Frenchman deeply and darkly affected by the war. At the Lycée Louis-le-Grand, near Le Prince's ninth sector, a middle-class boy by the name of Georges Méliès and his classmates huddled under their school desks, praying none of the bombs whistling through the sky would fall on their heads. In the South of France, at Le Puy-en-Velay, another future pioneer of cinema, Charles-Émile Reynaud, was assisting his uncle, a doctor, in treating the injured of France's undersize southern army, which was still trying to push the Prussians back.

The provisional government of France's green, newborn republic surrendered on January 28. By then the psychological harm of the siege had been done. Several years later a doctor specializing in nervous disorders, Lucien Nass, would conduct a pathological study of survivors and find widespread symptoms of a condition he called obsidional fever—or siege fever: anxiety, paranoia, restlessness, obsessiveness, mistrust of authority, defiance. The main cause of this fever was not the violence of war itself, but the experience of being under siege: the deep isolation in feeling "separated from the world, separated from the rest of your compatriots."[8] People were ignorant of the fates of loved ones and unable to reassure them about their own. Those who experienced the siege wrote at length of this peculiar pain. "The absence of all contact with the outside world," wrote Edmond de Goncourt, was "surprising . . . incredible . . . unbelievable."[9] At least one shop on the rue de Rivoli sold train tickets to nowhere, so customers could pretend the world beyond the city walls was still accessible to them. To be in Paris during the siege was like being buried alive—breathing shallow, useless breaths, not yet dead but no longer among the living.

In the coming years Louis Le Prince would show many signs of siege fever trauma. The senseless barbarity he had just endured challenged the accepted order. His birth town of Metz, a part of France since the sixteenth century, would soon be swallowed up into Prussia. Children born from then on in the same town he had would, when France and the German states went to war again, be fighting on the Prussian side, their allegiance decided by a clause in a treaty. Louis understood that on the ground, war was not a duel between enemies, but a tragedy of brother killing brother, neighbor slaughtering neighbor—all of them "food for cannon," as he described it later to Lizzie.[10] The Krupp gunners could end a person's life from four thousand meters away, so far removed they need never know if they had maimed a man or an infant, murdered a mother or crippled a child, or even if they had killed at all.

Artists processed the war on canvases and on the page. Each tried to find ways to make an inhuman experience human again, so people could see, and know, and understand their fellows. Manet and Degas painted; Verlaine and Goncourt wrote. Le Prince, an engineer trained in optics and chemistry, was wired differently.

It would be fourteen more years before Louis began working on a motion picture machine. But the seeds were planted in his mind, probing, taking root.

WASHED ASHORE
AT THE LIZARD

1870–1873

That winter was long and cold in Leeds, too. The house at Round-hay was crowded, the Whitleys joined by Elizabeth Le Prince, her daughter-in-law, and her granddaughter. It was then that Phoebe Eadson, an eighteen-year-old from Nottinghamshire, joined the family's service, as a general servant and nanny to baby Mariella. A newborn should have been cause for joy. Rather, it, and the fullness of the house, were both reminders of Louis's absence.

Lizzie lived in constant fear of her husband's death. "We had no direct news from him," she wrote, "only an occasional balloon letter, and in every case the contents were undecipherable: only the date and address could be read. One of these, mushed, battered and torn, was rescued from the North Sea by fishermen. It was a godsend."[1] That dispatch in Louis's handwriting was one of two hundred and fifty kilos' worth of mail carried by the balloon *Le Jacquard*, which had left the Gare d'Orléans under cover of darkness shortly before midnight on November 28 and been carried by strong southeast winds to the Irish Sea.[2] On November 30, in a night sky as black as ink, the balloon lost altitude, hit the waves, and sank. Its sole passenger was its aeronaut, Alexandre Prince, a twenty-seven-year-old seaman who had volunteered for the job despite having no experience of flight. Most of its cargo was lost, though in the early days of December fishermen working the strait off Lizard Point, on the Cornish coast, found letters bobbing on the waves, the envelopes cracked and washed out. They collected them and delivered them to the nearest rectory, from whence the local reverend resealed each missive into a clean envelope and forwarded it to its destination.[3]

This was likely the sole letter the Whitleys received from Louis throughout the entire five months of the siege, and they received it as illegible, soggy pulp. But at least it meant Louis had been alive in late November to write and send it.[4] The only other time they had news was when the reporter from the *London Daily News*, who had helped free Louis from jail in August and was still stationed in France, wrote to inform them he had seen Le Prince alive and well, leading his men outside the Paris walls to recover wounded comrades from the battlefield. That was in December. He was not able to tell them whether Louis had returned from that excursion.

Lizzie Le Prince sat in her parents' house on the hill. There was nothing to do but read the newspapers and wait.

1870: Lizzie and Mariella waited for Louis to return. They couldn't reach him. They did not know whether he would ever come home.

1890: Exactly twenty years later—Lizzie and Mariella waited, again. They couldn't reach him. They did not know whether he would ever come home.

As if the years, as they turned, folded back onto themselves.

For a week, back between Christmas 1870 and the first days of 1871, Roundhay Cottage had been snowed in, a thick white blanket covering all of Yorkshire as the year turned. The old widow Le Prince did her best to relieve the tedium and soothe the fears of her daughters-in-law; she knew all too well the disquiet of waiting for a husband to come home from war. She spun long tales as she sat by the hearth—"the old family legends"[5] of the Le Princes, as Lizzie called them, like episodes in a long-running, never-ending conflict: of her Boulabert ancestors making their fortunes in the Revolution of 1789, of her husband distinguishing himself in faraway wars of colonization, of coups and rebellions.

On January 18, Paris capitulated. Forty-eight hours later, the *Yorkshire Post* announced an armistice. The conflict was over. Days later a letter from Louis finally arrived: He was alive. Death had nipped at his heels, but it had not caught him.

Elizabeth and Gabrielle Le Prince headed back to France. Louis took up his old post at Whitley Partners. In February, Jack Whitley married Ellen Naylor, a twenty-six-year-old from neighboring Lancashire.

Life resumed, seemingly as normal.

But Louis was a different man than the one who had left England six months earlier. He sat drawing for hours, compiling a new catalog of Whitley products designed to promote the firm abroad, especially in triumphant Prussia. "His health, already impaired by the rigors of the siege of Paris, alarmed [me]," Lizzie remembered. Being driven to dedicate himself "too closely" to his technical drawings was making him worse, she thought.[6] A weariness eddied inside him.

Jack Whitley took over the business from Joseph. The new managing director had ambitious plans. Whitley Partners would expand, with a showroom in London and perhaps another on the Continent. Railways were then being built as far away as Russia, and Jack was determined to get in on fresh markets early. This required larger premises, more men—more capital. Jack went out in search of shareholders and loan partners. Optimistic as ever, he instructed his men to buy raw materials and tools on credit, and began taking new orders.

His timing was unfortunate. Otto von Bismarck, riding high on military victory, was driving the unified German empire to economic expansion. In doing so he dispensed with silver thalers and replaced them with the gold mark, moving Germany to the gold standard. Global demand for silver fell. By 1873 the speculation bubble encouraged by Bismarck's policies burst. In May the Vienna Stock Exchange crashed. In September the United States slid into crisis. Banks failed. Railroad companies went bankrupt. The New York Stock Exchange closed for business for over a week, and soon Britain sank into its own depression. Trade slumped. Investment dried up. Businesses began laying off their employees.

Whitley Partners, by then, was still £15,000 short of the financing Jack had counted on raising. Walking from bank to bank applying for exorbitant loans, forced to subcontract work out to fulfill the orders he had accepted before he had the manpower to meet them, obliged to pay a return on advance to the small group of shareholders he *had* managed to sign on, Jack drained the company's already thinning profit margins just to keep afloat. His strategy of expansion had always been boom or bust. By 1873 it was clear which one it was going to be. Whitley Partners was circling the drain, and at risk of going under.

PARENTHESIS: OCCIDENT IN MOTION

Sacramento, California, 1873

That same year, halfway across the world in Sacramento, California, another ambitious Englishman stood under a bright, limpid blue sky, preparing to freeze time. Eadweard Muybridge was tall, with burning eyes and a wild white beard. His assistants, whose wages were paid by the railroad tycoon and former governor of California Leland Stanford, were busily getting his set ready. The men had been told the Englishman was an internationally famous photographer, but he didn't look it, in his rough, weather-beaten outdoor wear and his dusty work boots. Ask about his background and you received scraps of perplexing biographical data—he'd lived in England, New York, New Orleans, and San Francisco; he'd been a publisher, a bookseller, a government employee; he'd spent time with Tlingit natives in Alaska and Modoc Indians in Oregon. He'd been some kind of a journalist, though not as a writer. It was said he'd changed his name multiple times and once went years calling himself Helios, after the Greek god of the sun. He looked much older than his forty-two years.

Most disquieting was Muybridge's manner. You never knew what to expect of him. He was boastful one second, quietly moody the next. He could be forceful to the point of intimidation. He was not unfriendly, but nor was he warm. He was so single-minded that the idea of him making small talk—carrying a conversation about the arts, politics, the news, anything other than the matter at hand—was laughable. Yet it was also common for his attention to trail away suddenly, even in the middle of a conversation. He was impatient and took offense easily, though he had no social graces himself.

It was said—and this made the man all the more fascinating—that he hadn't always been this way. A violent accident—an unfortunate, unforeseeable split second of misfortune—had smashed and rearranged his personality, as easily as a cook breaks and scrambles an egg. Thirteen years earlier the photographer had been a passenger on one of the Butterfield Overland Mail Company's stagecoaches, heading to Saint Louis. He wasn't even a photographer, then. He sold books, and was traveling to buy rare editions from European dealers on the East Coast. But he never made it. Somewhere in Texas the stage driver, who'd been whipping his horses into a sweat, realized his brakes had stopped working. The driver tried steering his horses off the path, hoping they'd slow in the thick brush, but this only alarmed the mustangs, who ran the wagon, at high speed, straight into a tree. The wooden coach splintered into pieces, throwing its passengers into the air. Two of them were killed. Muybridge woke up nine days later in a hospital bed at Fort Smith, a hundred and eighty miles away from the crash site, with stitches above his eye sockets and his mind foggy. He had double vision; he'd lost all sense of smell. When he was well enough to walk, but not to work, they sent him back to England, where he was seen by a brilliant, hardworking doctor by the name of William Gull, who, it was said, recommended time off, outdoor activity, maybe a new hobby. Muybridge stayed in England seven years. By the time he returned to America in 1867, he'd not just taken up that new hobby but mastered it. He was still erratic, but he'd turned himself into one of the best photographers in the world.

*   *   *

Muybridge had worked for Leland Stanford for about a year. Stanford loved money, himself, and thoroughbred horses. He ended up owning hundreds of them, kept on an eight-thousand-acre ranch in Palo Alto, south of San Francisco. Stanford, who'd urged the locomotives of his Central Pacific Railroad to set records for the overland crossing of North America, also frequently pitted his horses against a ticking clock. Many of his colts were record holders. Improving their performance, in the Darwinian sense, meant not just breeding them for the highest levels of performance but understanding the mechanics of their bodies as well, as closely as an engine's motorman knew the workings of its firebox and boiler. Stanford could talk about equine motion for hours, and he did, over an after-dinner cigar with his wealthy peers and with grooms and busters in the dust of his ranch. He was particularly fascinated with a horse's trot—arguably the most efficient, balanced, and elegant gait for the animal, integral to many of the harness races in which Stanford's colts took part.

The very nature of the trot was debated. Horsemen on the West Coast argued the pace included a moment of suspension—"unsupported transit," they called it—in which all four of the horse's feet were, briefly, off the ground. Breeders in the East dismissed this. One hoof, they asserted, always made contact. As a horse's movements were too fast to break down by the eye alone, Stanford decided he would settle the matter irrefutably—with a photograph. The local paper, the *Daily Alta California*, suggested he hire Helios of Montgomery Street, San Francisco's most celebrated and mercurial photographer, renowned for his technical cleverness. Helios was Muybridge's professional name.

Stanford's proposition, however, was considered impossible. Wet-plate photography had improved a little since the days of Daguerre, but it still demanded exposures of several seconds to capture a clear image; anything shorter and the resulting picture was a streaky blur. What Stanford was asking for—a photograph taken in a fraction of a second, the time a trotting horse might spend with all four hooves off the ground—could conceivably be achieved only if a blinding flood of light entered the lens, enough light to make an impression on the emulsion in such a short window of time. Even the brightest sunlight wouldn't be bright enough, and even if it had been, so much light might, paradoxically, overexpose the photograph, making any figure illuminated within it invisible. Lens caps had been invented by then, but shutters—used to control how long a lens was open to the light—had not, so the photograph would have to be timed manually, requiring phenomenal hand–eye coordination. More sensitive emulsions, which might require less light, didn't exist either.

What Stanford was demanding was an *instantaneous* photograph, one taken quicker than the human eye blinks. In 1872, to many photographers, it was all but inconceivable.

Fortunately, neither Leland Stanford nor Eadweard Muybridge feared the impossible.

Union Park Racetrack, on the outskirts of Sacramento, was booked for Muybridge's attempts. He'd given Stanford's request a first try in 1872 but had failed to capture an intelligible image. Now, a year later, Muybridge was back to give it a shot again.

The sand on the track was raked smooth. Next, the stable boys carried in yards of white linen, folded and rolled—"all the sheets in the neighbourhood of the stable."[1] They laid them flat over the dirt, end to end, and hung them like a backdrop along the side of the speedway. The bedding was needed to reflect additional light into the lens. It would also contrast with the horse—the only dark object in frame—and make it easier for the silver and salt emulsion inside the camera to arrange in a mirror image of its shape.

They brought in Occident. The "little California wonder" was Leland Stanford's first champion: a black mustang, sixteen hands high, his coat glistening from constant care, long-necked and powerful. At first he'd balked at running over the sea of white bedclothes, but his trainer, James Eoff, had nudged and persuaded him until the animal complied.

Stanford expected a photograph taken in racing conditions—anything less would be dismissed as chicanery. The boys hooked up a sulky—a one-seat cart with a big spoked wheel on either side—to Occident's harness. Eoff, who knew the mustang better than anyone, would drive him. They needed him at full speed, and Occident was a record holder, who a few months later would trot a mile in two minutes and sixteen-and-a-half seconds.[2] Muybridge stood by the side of the track, camera on its tripod. His hand was on the lens cap. There were no shutters to automate the taking of a photograph, no buttons or pull switches. At just the right moment, the photographer simply snapped the lens cap off the device, let sunlight flood through the lens, and replaced the cap to terminate the exposure. Most portraitists, whose subjects could be expected to sit unmoving, counted the seconds out loud as they waited for exposure. Muybridge did not have seconds. In a second Occident covered thirty-eight feet of track. To hold the racehorse in frame, Muybridge would have to uncover his lens for a tenth of that time.

On the first day of trials Muybridge failed to get his photograph. His hands simply didn't move quickly enough, and the developed glass plate came out an untainted white. He practiced the movement over and over, and on the second day—"with increased velocity in opening and closing" the camera—the faintest shadow was caught, but it was an inconclusive blur. Muybridge needed a mechanism faster than human motion.

Overnight he devised a solution. Instead of handling the lens cap himself, he replaced the cap entirely, substituting it with two boards meeting in front of the lens and connected to a spring. When Occident passed in front of the camera Muybridge would snap the spring, which would send the two boards briefly slipping past each other, exposing to the light a sliver of glass one-eighth of an inch "for the five-hundredth part of a second"[3] before sliding shut again.

The signal was given. James Eoff cracked his whip. Occident took off in a splash of clay dirt, the shimmering stretch of white sheet open in front of him.

Eadweard Muybridge flicked the spring.

*   *   *

The camera was taken to the darkroom and opened, the glass plate carefully removed and treated with chemical mixtures. Muybridge, with the air of an alchemist—disheveled yet purposeful, his long beard almost biblical—worked his new kind of magic. Stanford's men hovered outside his door.

An image faded up on the glass surface.

It was little more than a silhouette, the silver faint and weak, but it had clarity and it had shape. Occident hung in the air, four hooves off the ground. The wheels on Eoff's sulky were held still, their spokes as crisp as when the wheels weren't turning. It was the first time a photograph had ever been taken fast enough to freeze movement in this way, fast enough to capture reality yet strip it of motion. Fast enough to record something so elusive it was invisible to the human eye itself.

Muybridge had captured "what had always been present but never seen."[4] Wasn't that what alchemists proclaimed to do?

Leland Stanford got his proof. It was good for his stubborn ego, and it confirmed theories he believed could better train his horses. At Palo Alto, using this knowledge, he began training young trotters at high speed over short distances, developing elastic, explosive muscle strength, defying conventional wisdom that the animals should be drilled only in the gait as adults and be raced long and hard to build stamina.

The success of the experiment had blown open paths to an endless array of improvements. If Muybridge could direct even more light into the lens—if he could build an automated shutter, an improvement on his twin boards that could spring into action at the exact right fraction of a second—then nothing of life on earth would remain mysterious to humankind. Not the flight of a bird, which could be arrested by the lens; not the workings of the human body, if the camera could freeze every ripple of the muscles and every strain of the ligaments. Leland Stanford could have his horse races. Muybridge envisioned a library of natural motion, itemized and preserved, the very substance of life caught and displayed in glass, like a butterfly held up by invisible pins.

To create such a photographic record, he needed more cameras, more assistants, more horses; electrical wiring and more time on the racetrack; and more silver, glass, and mercury than most photographers before him could ever dream of purchasing. Which was to say, he needed more of Leland Stanford's money.

He got it all. Within a matter of years Muybridge would decisively "split the second," in the words of his biographer Rebecca Solnit, "as dramatic and far-reaching an action as the splitting of the atom."[5] Doing so would kick off an innovations arms race as inventors, engineers, entertainers, physiologists, and scientists jostled to stake their claims to corners of the vast world of possibilities Muybridge had opened.

But it almost didn't happen. The year after his first instantaneous photograph of Occident in motion, and before he had negotiated his way back into Leland Stanford's wallet, Eadweard Muybridge found his wife cheating on him with another man, and in his jealous rage he became a murderer.

ARTISTS

B y 1875, bankruptcy at Whitley Partners was inevitable.
Joseph and Jack fell out. There were heated arguments. For three decades Whitley Partners had existed under Joseph's stewardship, and now it looked like it would all come undone within four years of Jack taking over. He had ignored his father's warnings about guarding against the ebbs and flows of the new global economy, had dismissed the stories, delivered as cautionary tales, of thriving businesses buying splashy advertisements in the Leeds directories one year, only to be wiped off the pages by the following edition.

In July 1875 Jack stepped down as Whitley Partners' managing director and retired to a health spa in Derbyshire, claiming debilitating stomach pains. In September, the bank William Williams, Brown, and Company filed a petition for Whitley Partners to be declared bankrupt, citing unpaid debts the firm showed no sign of being able to settle. A hearing was set for October 5 in London in front of Sir James Bacon, the nation's chief bankruptcy judge—a hearing that resulted in an order to have Whitley Partners wound up by the court. William Frankland Dean, a Leeds accountant, was appointed to liquidate the company's assets.

Whitley Partners was no more. Joseph Whitley was fifty-nine. Jack wrote to his wife and asked her if she felt like spending some time in France. He had decided to stay away from Yorkshire for a while.

*   *   *

Le Prince lost a not inconsiderable amount of money in the failure of Whitley Partners. His own family was growing: his and Lizzie's first son, Adolphe, had been born in April 1872, followed by another daughter, Aimée, in January 1874 and another son, Joseph, in August 1875, named after his grandfather.

Lizzie, after spending thirty-six of the previous sixty months pregnant with one child or another, resumed her own work. With Adolphe still in swaddling blankets, she earned her certification as an art teacher from the South Kensington Science and Art Department. She was ready to return to the arts and felt her husband should do the same. So, in the year before Whitley Partners was declared insolvent, she encouraged Louis to make a momentous decision, though one that couldn't have helped things within the Whitley family: she convinced him to quit the firm. (Their son Adolphe, writing in the late 1890s, remembered the reasons for his father's resignation differently: "Some differences arising within the firm," he wrote, had motivated Louis to step away.)[1]

Louis applied for his own license to teach from the South Kensington administrators, and in early 1875 he and Lizzie opened the Leeds Technical School of Art, one of Leeds's first private art schools.

The school did well. Carrier-Belleuse's devotion to truth in naturalism guided Lizzie's curriculum. "Our art school differed from others in that it afforded its students precisely the information they required for [the] practical purposes of applied art, without insisting on every student struggling through too many cut and dried courses," she explained.[2] To supplement their incomes the Le Princes took engagements at other institutions, on one occasion traveling as far as County Durham, eighty-three miles north, to teach a private painting class. Le Prince also offered one-on-one tuition to the wives and daughters of well-to-do industrialists. He accepted portrait commissions and sold affordable oil, gouache, or watercolor copies of celebrated contemporary paintings.

In the first week of May 1875 the Yorkshire Exhibition of Arts and Manufactures opened in the city's exhibition hall, with the Duke of Edinburgh in attendance. The fair was widely advertised across England, and the halls and rooms of the hall were buzzing with guests. Louis, Lizzie, and their students had a collection of chinaware on display in the fine arts section and garnered widespread praise for their craftsmanship, boosting applications. The Duke of Edinburgh himself, second son of Queen Victoria, toured the building with Leeds mayor Henry Marsden, and singled out the Le Princes' humble cabinet for notice, shaking Louis's hand and complimenting him on the work. "In passing by a case of handsomely finished enamel, exhibited by M. le Prince, a recent French settler at Leeds," recounted the London *Standard*, "his Royal Highness noticed portraits on enamel of the Mayor and Mayoress and expressed his admiration of them. Mr. Marsden, with ready tact, asked the Duke to accept them, which the Duke did, to the Mayor's unconcealed pleasure."[3]

A commission for the Prince of Wales followed. Royal endorsement went a long way, and Louis suddenly found more elevated social circles in which to move. He and Lizzie became active members of the Leeds Philosophical and Literary Society, a humanist organization involved in all the city's cultural events and devoted to many of its social initiatives, and for which Louis also became an occasional art critic, a role he also fulfilled for a time for the Leeds Fine Art Society. The members' private collections provided much of the inventory of Leeds City Museum, and the group was also instrumental in the 1874 founding of the Yorkshire College of Science, which in time grew to become the University of Leeds.

In 1876 Le Prince also became a Freemason Brother, receiving his blue-and-white apron at the Lodge of Fidelity, on the corner of Woodhouse Lane and Saint Marks Street in central Leeds. The fraternal movement—part secret society, part mystical sect, part men's club—was enjoying its golden age, centuries after its founding. Jack had been a Freemason since 1866 but was registered at Philanthropic, a lodge on nearby Great George Street, and he did not bring Louis into the brotherhood. Instead it was Richard Wilson, a banker's clerk from Bramley, west of Leeds, who sponsored Le Prince. Wilson, a year older than Louis, was employed at William Williams, Brown, and Company, one of Leeds's five main banks and the one retained by Whitley Partners. He was intelligent, reliable, and an avid art collector, conserving every spare penny of his income to acquire furniture, decorative miniatures, and china. He was an early admirer, and purchaser, of Louis's work. As Whitley Partners unraveled in the first half of the 1870s, Wilson and Le Prince unexpectedly developed a friendship. This was an added complication to the ongoing Whitley saga: the bank was Whitley Partners' most meaningful creditor; it was the one that finally petitioned in London courts for the firm to be disbanded. Le Prince, who had already left his in-laws' business, did not see a reason to break off his growing fellowship with Wilson.

Though the Le Prince family was not wealthy, Louis's membership as a Freemason is one sign they were comfortable, since participation in the order was not cheap, with dues to be paid and regular fundraising efforts to subscribe to. The house in Chapeltown had cost them a down payment of £4,000, and there was enough spare cash left in Louis's accounts for him to buy a large tract of land just north of that home in March 1876, which he promptly carved up into plots and resold individually. With the profit, the family moved again, purchasing an elegant Georgian town house at 33 Park Square in the fashionable West End. Most of the square's residents lived in the upstairs rooms of their homes and turned the ground-floor premises into businesses: a publisher's, a tailor's, a stained glass artist, several medical practitioners. The private garden in the center of the square was neatly kept, sober flower beds livening up the green ground like flecks of color on a canvas.

The Le Prince home at number 33 was large enough to accommodate the technical school's classes, and the Le Princes hired two more live-in servants to assist Phoebe. Alice Baker was twelve, Elizabeth Beaumont just three years older. The Le Princes were only the first of a lifetime of families for whom they would scrub floors and wash kitchen pots.

Time passed, and the family prospered. At the 1878 Paris Exhibition, which celebrated France's recovery from the Prussian war, Louis showed off more of his work: "paintings on enamel, china ware, etc.; vases, dishes, slabs, tiles, etc., painted, enameled, and gilded in various styles; also miniatures, etc."[4] He won another medal. In the second half of the 1870s, Le Prince alighted upon a new method for firing photographs onto metal and porcelain, affixing vivid images onto plates, cups, and decorative fixtures. He visited with Carrier-Belleuse, now director of the porcelain manufactories in Sèvres, and took his advice on tools and base materials. The results, when glazed, were sharp and vivid, a precursor to the commemorative plates and china sets bought by so many English households to mark the coronation of new kings and queens in the twentieth century. Louis bent over these at 33 Park Square, in an extension at the back he'd built and subdivided into a darkroom and a studio, mixing and matching pigments, experimenting with daguerreotypes and calotypes, substituting glass for chinaware. On at least one occasion he drove the furnace so hard it nearly set the whole house ablaze while the children slept in their beds, though Le Prince managed to put the fire out, to Lizzie's great dismay, with the dining room's best damask tablecloth.

The young ones were not allowed in the workshop, where the fire prickled, the materials were fragile, and the chemicals poisonous, but some of Adolphe's first memories were of slipping away from Phoebe and sneaking into the "mysterious work-room"[5] when he was four or five, attracted by the undefinable mix of odors emanating from this forbidden outbuilding. From the window of the nursery, a flight higher than the shop, he often watched his father walk past the flower garden and enter his workspace, drawing a curtain of thick green baize across the double doors after he'd closed them to keep out sound. He was too small to see into the three high windows built into the side of the outbuilding.[6]

Slipping unseen into the workshop when it was unoccupied, the boy gawped at the shelves of assorted "collodions, sensitized papers, colors, lacquers," and flicked through the stacks of photographic trade journals, which Louis read assiduously. His father, he realized, was more than a teacher, and his work was more than decorating plates and cups. "Here was an amateur experimenting on as yet untrodden paths" where chemistry and art met, Adolphe wrote later.[7]

He couldn't put it in such clear terms as a boy, however. What he did in the moment, confused by the sights and smells of this private room that obsessed his father—and motivated, he admitted, by "a bad little boy's delight in destruction"—was grab every photographic plate he could find and smash it to pieces. The splintering glass, the monochrome faces on the developed plates shattering into jagged jigsaws, gave him a thrill he couldn't explain.[8]

His father, to Adolphe's surprise, did not discipline him. Even grown-ups sometimes got angry at what they couldn't understand. Instead, Adolphe said, Louis cleaned up, laid his camera and his photography tools back out, and "found time with kindly patience to give my first ideas of the art."[9] From then on, at least in the spring and summer, the studio doors remained open and the children were welcome to watch their father at work.

Louis had finally established himself on his own merits, in Leeds and beyond. His family was happy, and it kept growing—another son, Fernand, was born in 1877, followed by Jean in 1880. He had found a circle of friends separate from the family into which he had married. His new profession was anchored in art and creativity, allowed him to share his workday with his wife, and brought him a modest level of public prestige.

But there is a sense, from the course of events as well as from surviving documents, that despite all of this Le Prince was plagued by a nagging restlessness. The anxiety and obsessiveness he had brought back from war had not left him. His was a good life, but it lacked something. What that was, he didn't yet know.

THE SPARK

c. 1880

The answer—the "spark," as Louis called it[1]—flared bright and sudden at the most unexpected moment.

It must have been winter. Joseph Whitley had just bought his grandchildren a magic lantern. The toys were particularly popular around Christmas, a remnant of when they were operated by professionals in tented stalls or curtained booths during the holidays. They projected circular glass slides onto a sheet or wall, using a simple light source—originally an Argand lamp, by now most likely an arc lamp or limelight, though the latter was explosive and highly dangerous. The light was dim. Though many users projected images onto sheets, walls, or even the ceiling—children lying on their backs to take in the enchanting images—luminous taffeta offered the best results, the fabric's shine augmenting the power of the lantern.

The slides on offer were originally simple drawings. By the late 1870s, photographs, many hand-painted into color, were also available, as was movement, achieved by moving slides in front of one another to create the illusion of rudimentary animation, primarily the dissolving of one scene into another. Biurnal devices, essentially two lanterns one on top of the other, could also be purchased, and these allowed for more elaborate effects. A landscape could be shown to change from summer to fall by gliding a slide of fallen leaves over the original glass, and then to winter through the use of a piece of white cotton, wound on a roller, with pinholes punched through it, simulating snow. A hand crank was used to vary the pace of the transitions between images. The cheapest lanterns were tin varnished to a lustrous black, easily dented and hot to the touch when operated. More expensive models came in iron or metal-lined mahogany, and it was likely one of this type Whitley gifted the children, its brass lens and chimney polished to a shine.

The standard set of slides included with a lantern was a Chinese fireworks kit. A patterned wheel, placed between the light source and various colorful glass plates, was spun as the slides were changed, projecting a chromotropic, kaleidoscopic array of stars, flames, fountains, and lights. Another popular genre, sometimes called the "Life-Model Series," consisted of complete stories, each scene posed by a model like a still from a stage play, with accompanying narration to be read by the lantern's operator. Ranging in length anywhere from twelve to sixty slides, these could be adventure yarns (*The Ringing of the Bell* told of a burning ship), moralizing melodramas (*The Signal Box* warned of the danger of overwork for railwaymen), even children's spooky stories ("John could not rest," went the reading for Mary Sewell's *Mother's Last Words*, "the faintest noise made all the flesh upon him creep; He turned, and turned, and turned again, but could not get a wink of sleep . . ."). Bamforth & Co of Holmfirth, in west Yorkshire, made some of the best-selling stories of the late nineteenth century, and its products were sold across Leeds. Other, more serious slide sets made it possible for viewers to see the world, from the English seaside to the Forbidden City, without leaving the soft comfort of their couches.

"In England," Lizzie wrote decades later, "winter days are short, and the light fades early, and our children looked forward to twilight as their especial time with their father": the sky darkening outside their windows, Louis coming inside from his workshop to set up the lantern and tell them stories, from a fund "as inexhaustible as our children's appetite for them."[2] To the young ones, the lantern was a marvel. To

Louis, it was just a toy, an improvement on the centuries-old camera obscura, little more than elaborate shadow play.

And then the spark blazed, and imprinted on his mind a vision.

He was working in his studio, experimenting with compositing—the blending together of two or more photographs to create a more artful whole. The technique, along with other forms of retouching, had existed almost since the birth of medium. Wet-plate photography, with its long exposure times and sensitivity to movement, was limited in range. Group portraits could be ruined by a single participant blinking, landscapes by an out-of-focus bird, animal, or cloud. At its simplest, compositing could erase these blemishes; a more sophisticated use of it could paste old shots of now-dead relatives into new family postcards, visually reuniting people with their loved ones. At its most artful, the technique also enabled photographers to create works as purposeful and harmonious as any Renaissance painting. William Notman's mammoth *Skating Carnival, Victoria Rink* was the most famous example of this kind of work. It was a large albumen print of three hundred stitched-together photographs re-creating Montreal's annual ice skating festival with astonishing life. Notman had taken a picture of the venue, individual pictures of hundreds of carnival guests in their lavish costumes, blended the images together to his liking, and finally colored over the whole in oil paints. The end product had depth and light, detail and texture; it was as close to a canvas by a Dutch realist master as photography could then get.

Notman was internationally celebrated for his composites, which sold well in prints and postcards of all sizes. Eadweard Muybridge also made frequent and noticeable use of retouching. His overwhelming, spectacular photographs of the Yosemite Valley, of Alaska, and of the Modoc War were published in England in the 1870s—as prints, in book form, and for stereoscopic viewers. Muybridge superimposed clouds on skies previously so clear they offered nothing, on a black-and-white print, but a bland sea of negative space. He tweaked waterfalls so that they looked perfectly frozen. He applied pencil and paint to human faces to even out skin tones. He scraped imperfections away with a scalpel. Both Notman and Muybridge were regularly written about in the photographic trade journals Louis subscribed to.

Le Prince had begun using combination printing on the decorative porcelain products for which he was becoming well known. The process started with a square or rectangular piece of cotton paper, which was coated with salt and egg white—the mixture known to chemists and photographers as albumen—and then dipped in light-sensitive silver nitrate. Once the paper was dry, it was placed in a frame or immobilized in a wooden retouching desk, and exposed under a glass plate negative until the image on the glass transferred to the emulsion on the paper. Now the cotton paper was imprinted with the base structure of the final image—if Louis was making, say, a composited collective portrait of the royal family, this may have been the backdrop of a palace room, or the central portrait of Queen Victoria. Putting away this first glass plate, Louis would reach for another negative—for instance, a likeness of the late Prince Consort, the space around Albert's face and body masked or scraped away—and place this over the paper until the husband joined his wife on the photosensitive cotton paper. He would repeat this process as many times as necessary, adding in royal children perhaps, until the fusion was complete.[3] Then came retouching on the paper print, blending and erasing unwanted details and inconsistencies, and finally firing onto the enamel or china product.

On this day Louis was immersed in his work when the glass plate and the paper print beneath slipped in his hands, and to his strained, fatigued eyes the person affixed on both layers suddenly "gave a distinct impression of movement."[4] He caught the photographs, and just like that the uncanny illusion was gone—but, for the smallest moment, the image he held had come to life.

The spark was lit.

Shortly thereafter, Lizzie remembered, a birthday party was thrown at Park Square for one of the Le Prince children. After tea Louis took out the magic lantern and the slides of Chinese fireworks. As the images danced on the parlor wall, he suddenly turned to Lizzie and said: "Moving photographs will be the next invention."[5]

After the children went to bed, Lizzie and Louis sat up late in the stillness of the town house, and Louis explained what had been on his mind. "The thought took clearer shape as we remembered and talked together," Lizzie wrote. Louis told her of the incident in his workroom, the split second during which two photographs had moved between his fingers. One of them brought up the illusions they had seen at the Théâtre Robert-Houdin in Paris during their honeymoon, "the wonderful effects of transparent moving figures," as Lizzie described them, that the magician had managed to create using "reflections from numerous mirrors focussed to one point. This exhibition had greatly impressed my husband, and he visited it repeatedly"—so much so that for a while, every time Louis went out, Lizzie joked that he was going to see Robert-Houdin.[6]

They may have made other associations as they spoke, connecting information and memories, identifying a pattern. As a student in Leipzig, Louis had learned how the eye worked, how it turned what it saw into signals the brain comprehended as movement. Scientists at the time had been debating the validity of the theory of persistence of vision, according to which the retina was able to blend a series of images into one continuous image even if they were interrupted, as long as the images were viewed in very quick succession. He may have known of Muybridge's latest photographs of a horse in motion, taken in 1878 and widely written about in the press. He might have heard the news that Wordsworth Donisthorpe, the son of the textile baron George Edmund Donisthorpe and a resident of Leeds, had recently filed a patent for an apparatus to "facilitate the taking of a succession of photographs at equal intervals of time, in order to record the changes taking place . . . [and] to give to the eye a representation of the object in continuous movement"[7]—though the machine described in the document was clearly unworkable and few in Leeds had faith in Donisthorpe to follow through.

Maybe Louis even thought back to the long, cold months spent in Paris under siege, severed from the rest of the world. Maybe, in the boldest corner of his mind, he already dared to picture that darkness dispelled by a beam of light, by a lantern that could project more than dazzling fireworks. By a camera as truthful as Rodin had declared art to be: a camera that did not have to make time stop, but could capture life as it unfolded.

But taking and projecting photographs at the rate and volume necessary to re-create movement was not possible. The technology did not exist. The necessary materials did not exist. The necessary infrastructure—to print and develop and reproduce the hundreds of photographs that would make up even a few minutes of animation—did not exist. The research costs would be enormous. Photography itself was barely forty years old and still imperfect, and Louis had never designed or invented a machine of any kind in his life. Beginning with motion photography would be akin to a novice sailor setting off across the Atlantic for his maiden voyage.

The idea may have seemed impossible, but Le Prince had learned—perhaps from Daguerre, from whom Lizzie thought her husband took his "bent of thought"[8]—that much of what men called impossible was merely not yet visible, a latent image waiting to be seen.

THE NEW WORLD

The spark had flared, but it took time to ignite and grow. In the meantime, the Le Princes left England behind. It wasn't something they had planned, but Jack—who else but Jack—was back after a half decade of exile, and true to form, he had returned with a scheme.

Frederick Walton, the inventor of linoleum and a fellow Yorkshire-man, had come up with a new product named Lincrusta, a cheap and versatile wall covering made of linseed paste. Waterproof and warp-proof, Lincrusta hardened over time and could be embossed, gilded, painted, or glazed to reproduce a variety of more expensive materials and ornamentations. It could be made to look like wood, tile, leather, metal; it could be used to embellish doors, windows, mirrors, friezes, and cornices. Walton himself described it as "linoleum for walls."[1] Somehow Jack had scrounged up the cash to become part owner of Walton's patent rights in the material. Linoleum was already a smash in the United States, which was in the midst of a construction boom; imagine the money to be made if Lincrusta became as ubiquitous on Americans' walls as Walton's first invention was on their floors. Louis was unparalleled at putting together attractive catalogs and pamphlets, and he was a decent salesman; his experience decorating glass and china for the royal family would surely impress social-climbing Yankees. Jack asked him to join the venture.

Louis accepted. For all his flaws, Jack Whitley was a shrewd reader of men. That was one of the things with people like Jack. Under all the energy and optimism, you could never tell if he wanted to share something with you for your sake, or for his. After he was done passing through your life—a tornado crashing through your windows and throwing every room of your house into disarray—you were always left, disoriented in the settling dust, to wonder if what you'd experienced was a gift, or an ambush.

Even by Jack's standards, this particular gift revealed itself to be an empty box faster than usual. He and his partners had failed to set up manufacturing plants in America ahead of time, immediately setting him and Louis at a disadvantage as they hawked a product shackled with the delays and high cost of import—especially when one of Lincrusta's key selling points was supposed to be its affordability. Domestic firms, having already lost business to Walton's linoleum, did their best to take advantage of the misstep. Jack would schedule a lunch appointment between Le Prince and a wealthy New York family, at which Louis would draw up an attractive interior decoration scheme, pitching Lincrusta as a wonder material, only for the potential clients to take his proposal to a more established Manhattan decorator who would make a point of underbidding Louis's estimates. America, Jack found, was more cutthroat than Europe.

He lost interest quickly. "My brother was somewhat of an idealist," Lizzie once wrote of him, "men who accomplish things usually are"[2]— though men who fail to follow through also often suffer from the same complaint. Jack had looked forward to easy profit in a new venture in an exciting foreign land. This one turned out to be neither as fun nor as rewarding as he'd anticipated.

Luckily, he was never short of ideas. He proposed a spontaneous cross-country trip instead. "One leftover illusion of his boyhood's dreams," Lizzie wrote, "was that of finding and owning a perfect ranch in some fair southland."[3] He told Louis they might start an artists' colony in the Southwest or on the Pacific coast. Life would be cheap there. Lizzie could teach and Louis could work. At length, Lizzie remembered, "Jack persuaded my husband to take a journey with him as far as San Diego, California, traveling overland on horseback as much as possible in the hope of discovering his 'promised land.' I may add that on the way his illusions fell away piecemeal. . . ."[4] The Transcontinental Railroad, which Leland Stanford had completed in 1869, driving a ceremonial gold spike into the rail to mark the occasion, had made it possible to traverse the United States from New York to San Francisco in less than four days. But undertaking the crossing as Jack envisaged it, his eye trained on an elusive "promised land" on the horizon, could take weeks. It was grueling—and dangerous. The most direct route from New York to San Diego went through Indiana (a state of boomtowns and gas fields, the flambeaux of its flare stacks burning around the clock and turning the night sky red), Illinois (whose most populous city, Chicago, was a cacophony of rail yards and abattoirs, still reeling from the Great Fire that had killed hundreds and razed entire blocks just ten years earlier), Missouri (a state of roving vigilante gangs and political corruption, where Jesse James was then hiding out and where, in April 1882, Robert Ford raised his .44 nickel-plated Smith & Wesson pistol and shot and killed him while he was hanging a picture), Oklahoma (where cattle drivers and travelers feared confrontations with Native Americans recently relocated, by force, to the local Territories), the Territory of New Mexico (where a white English-speaking minority was struggling to wrest local power from the ethnic Mexican majority), and Arizona (where in October 1881 brothers Virgil, Morgan, and Wyatt Earp, along with Doc Holliday, shot and killed three outlaws in thirty seconds at O.K. Corral, with vendetta killings ensuing across the West in the following months). Travel by horse and stage and mud coach was hot and uncomfortable, passengers jostled and sweat-soaked on bumpy terrain. "On reaching San Diego, after passing through very unlooked-for experiences, [Jack] joyfully abandoned the project of investing in a ranch and founding a colony for his friends," Lizzie concluded.[5] Evading creditors in Yorkshire didn't seem that bad after all.

Louis, however, was enthralled by this foreign land, just as he'd been taken by Leeds. "Untried fields held fascination for him,"[6] Lizzie wrote, and in seemingly every state he found something new to fascinate him. In New Mexico he watched the local Pueblo Indians bake their pottery, polishing the damp clay with a stone and painting patterns on its surface with a plant brush, before firing the object over manure in an outdoor kiln. This final stage was carried out in the hour before sunset, as the hot air met the cooling ground. Louis was amazed by the "brilliance and translucence"[7] the images achieved by this process, which he described as a *coup de feu*. He bought several of these objects for his own collection, and within three years he would attempt to build an artificial blower to replicate the procedure, for ceramics but also for fixing photographs on glass.

The two men returned to the East Coast. Louis, though unemployed, decided to stay on in New York City. The art and industry he had seen on the cross-country journey, the energy and invention of the local people, had inspired him. He had made new friends, including William Guthrie and Clarence Seward, the patent lawyers Jack had retained for the Lincrusta business. Seward, like Louis, was a Freemason, and a nephew of Abraham Lincoln's secretary of state William Seward; Guthrie was a young attorney fresh out of Columbia Law School. Both men were helpful and generous with their time. Seward had already offered to sponsor Le Prince for admittance at the Lotos Club—a literary gentlemen's club with rooms on Fifth Avenue, which already counted among its members Mark Twain, Andrew Carnegie, W. S. Gilbert and Arthur Sullivan, Cornelius Vanderbilt's lawyer Chauncey Depew, and various politicians and newspapermen. Louis declined Seward's invitation—out of politeness or perhaps in the knowledge he couldn't afford the membership fees—but the suggestion itself was tantalizing.

Jack, disabused of his fancies but not discouraged, made plans to sell his interest in Lincrusta Walton and return to England, where he was certain to hatch a new scheme soon enough. Within a few years Walton's "linoleum for walls" would make a success, bought for use in railway carriages in England, grand staircases on Cunard liners, dining rooms and hotel lobbies around the world, and in the mansions of John D. Rockefeller and Frederick Pabst, but the fortune did not go to Jack Whitley. It flowed, instead, to Frederick Beck, an entrepreneur from Stamford, Connecticut, to whom Jack had sold his licensing stake, and who, unlike Jack, understood that the American customer did not want to save his money. He wanted to flaunt it.

Lizzie and the children left England in October to join Louis in America. There was heartache in leaving Joseph and Sarah behind—"in those days," Lizzie remembered decades later, "leaving one's country [even] for a visit to America was more of an event than it is today!"[8] The family had already said their goodbyes to Louis's mother, spending a visit with her and Albert and his own wife and children in Voulangis in the weeks before Jack and Louis sailed to New York, and already, then, Lizzie had reflected on how much she would miss "the old peak-roofed granary . . . converted into a children's dormitory,"[9] in which she had spent so many summer evenings herding little children into their beds. The house at Park Square was sold. Phoebe had agreed to come to America, the kind of adventure rarely afforded a girl in domestic service in the English counties then, though the other two servants had to be cut loose and went out to find new positions. On the night before the departure for Liverpool, Lizzie was treated to a leaving party at the Leeds Fine Art Society, during which she was the recipient of an engraved silver tea and coffee service, an engraved leather billfold probably containing a small farewell sum collected from fellow members, and many kind words.

The children had left early for Roundhay, where she would meet them. The luggage was already on Merseyside, packed and shipped ahead, on Joseph's request, by some of the boys from the old foundry.

*   *   *

There may have been other reasons for the Le Prince family to leave Leeds, and everything they knew, behind. While Louis was touring America with Jack, a letter had landed on the doorstep at Park Square, Le Prince's name marked across the envelope. Lizzie opened it. Inside was a letter from a solicitor named Nelson, inquiring when Louis intended to repay the £350 he had borrowed from his father, George, after the failure of Whitley Partners years earlier, and demanding swift repayment. It was, Lizzie alleged, the first she had ever heard of it.

She confronted her husband. Louis arranged for £30 to be sent to Nelson as a first installment toward settling his arrears. No further repayments were recorded. Within months the his family was bound for America—in search of opportunity, but also, perhaps, in the hope of leaving their problems behind.

They landed in New York and were processed through the Castle Garden immigration center on October 23. Louis had leased a house uptown, on Saint Nicholas Avenue between 169th and 170th Streets, a line of smart, neat row houses built after the Civil War.[10] Everyone was exhausted from the long voyage and happy to be reunited, "and when the children were settled for the night," Lizzie remembered, their parents "went for a stroll."[11] She and Louis walked south "through an avenue of great willow trees" for about half a mile, until they reached a big white colonial house Louis told her was called the Jumel Mansion. They "saw its beautiful portico bathed in moonlight, and through the odd branches of a row of catalpas we saw the lights of the city stretching far away below. Across the Harlem River there seemed to be only a few farms and residences, and then, returning, we crossed [Saint Nicholas Avenue] and passed along more avenues of trees, through fields and gardens, until we saw the Palisades and the Hudson River from the grounds of the Institution for the Deaf."

The school, officially known as the New York Institution for the Instruction of the Deaf and Dumb but referred to by locals as "Fanwood," sat on thirty-seven wooded acres. As Lizzie stood shoulder to shoulder with her husband, she felt "entranced by so much beauty, and full of gratitude for our safe arrival, and of hope for the future."[12] They discussed what they might do with the coming years, how they would build the framework of a new life together. "We were not rich, in money," she remembered, but the school building was huge behind them, its size a testament to the number of unfortunate children to be cared for, and they felt a desire to share their good fortune—their health, their being together, their shared way of seeing the world. They vowed, "if we ever grew rich"—the same expectant words thought and spoken by millions of immigrants to that city before and since—"to endow that school with an art department,"[13] a school like the one they'd built in Leeds, only one that would give *these* children, deaf and mute and alienated from society, fresh tools to understand and engage with it. New York City, on a cold October night at the end of the nineteenth century, felt like the kind of place such a vow might not only be made but kept.

They walked back the short distance to the house. That night they slept, exhausted and happy, together at last again.

Less than a month later, their son Jean Le Prince, not yet three years old, died of reasons unknown on Saturday, November 18. They buried him on Monday in the grounds of Trinity Church Cemetery, at 155th Street and Broadway, less than twenty blocks away from their new home.

PART THREE

TO AMERICA AND BACK

1882–1887

PARENTHESIS: WKL

1879

"Dear Mr. Eddison,"[1] eighteen-year-old William Kennedy Laurie Dickson wrote from his home in England, in a careful hand, his words packed tightly together, the letters as thin and sharp as spiders' legs. The young author was desperate to impress. He did not notice his misspelling of his hero's name—in the missive's first line, no less. If he had, he might have tossed the paper out and begun again, mortified.

"May I beg that you will not throw this letter aside," he went on, "but give it a patient reading, as my future prospects depend upon your kindly consideration. I have read a sketch of your life with the deepest interest, and the lesson it has taught me of hopefulness amid difficulties, of firm endurance and determination to vanquish apparent impossibilities, will I trust not be soon forgotten." Dickson went on:

"I have not your talents, but I have patience, perseverance, an ardent love of science, and above all, a firm reliance on God." Thomas Edison wasn't big on God, but there was no way for the young man to know that. "I have no pride," he carried on, lying a little, "and would be willing to begin at the lowest rung of the ladder, and work patiently up, if by doing so I might hope to attain independence and repay my widowed mother for the care and affection which she has lavished on me for so

111

many years. I have proved like many others that with reverses of fortune, friends fall away, and I would rather solicit the help of an utter stranger like yourself, upon whom I have only the claim of a common nationality (my mother being like your own, a Scotchwoman), than be dependent upon their aid, so coldly and grudgingly offered"—he was laying it on a bit thick now—"I am sure you will not have cause to regret holding out a helping hand to a friendless and fatherless boy."

Next he broke down his qualifications. He could speak three languages—his German was clumsy, to say the least, but he skipped that detail; he had "a fair knowledge of accounts, and [could] draw well. For all these things, I have certificates from the Cambridge Examiner," he assured, "and can give ample testimonials to my integrity and assiduity." He hadn't actually passed the Cambridge tests—the school's archives suggest he came through in a handful of subjects at best, and not enough of them to earn a diploma[2]—so his pledge of integrity would have to do. "If you will try me, I will take the lowest place in your employment, until you find me worthy of something higher, so passionately do I love your noble profession."

Dickson went on for another page or so, offering to pay his way to New York himself if Edison offered him a trial. "Believe me, Sir, yours respectfully," he finished, before signing his name to the final sheet of paper. *William Kennedy Laurie Dickson.* He underlined the four words twice.

He added one more line.

"P.S.: May I beg you to give me an early reply as"—the beginning of a word is scratched out, as if he could not bear to draft the whole thing over now—"my final decision must be made within two months."

It was February; if Edison honored Dickson's postscript he could be in New York by spring, and he would celebrate his nineteenth birthday in the New World, an employee of the Wizard of Menlo Park.

Edison took less than two months to reply. Unfortunately, the response said, he had no vacancies to fill and no jobs to offer.

Dickson booked his transatlantic crossing anyway.

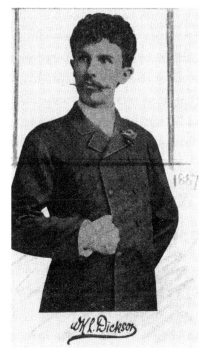

W. K. L. Dickson, 1887, in the picture he chose as his author photo in the book
he co-authored about the Kinetograph and Kinetoscope. The pencil markings and
handwritten date appear in the book as pictured. (Museum of Modern Art)

WKLD, as he would sign himself later in life, would in time become
Edison's closest collaborator in the invention of the Kinetograph and
Kinetoscope. Once arrived in New York, however, it took him three more
long years to even make it onto Edison's staff. He succeeded, this time,
by writing a more formal application to Samuel Insull, Edison's personal
secretary, after hearing Edison's companies were expanding to take on
the challenge of wiring New York City for electricity. In late March 1883
an artist by the name of Raymond Sayer, who knew both Edison and
Dickson, wrote to the former in recommendation of the latter, "a talented
young man speaking German + French fluently, & [who] has studied
electricity, [and] is very desirous of getting a position of some kind in your

establishment."[3] By September Dickson was hired.[4] In later years Dickson would variously claim Edison had hired him on the first try; that it had happened three years earlier than it actually did; and that he'd gotten the job by accosting the inventor in person and pitching him directly.[5]

But the truth was never more than a mild inconvenience to William Dickson. He told people his father, James, was a "distinguished"[6] painter, lithographer, astronomer, and linguist (he was in fact a mediocre amateur painter, a hobbyist lithographer, and neither of the latter two occupations), descended from Hogarth (he was not),[7] and that his mother, the "Scotchwoman," was directly related to the aristocratic Robertsons of Struan, "connected," Dickson boasted, "with the Earl of Cassilis, the Duke of Athol, and the Royal Stuarts"[8] (she was not; and though she had Scottish blood, she'd been raised in Chesterfield County, Virginia).[9] He claimed to have been born in the Chateau Saint Buc, in Brittany, when in fact his birth certificate shows he was born at Minihic-sur-Rance, a small town nearby. Though he painted himself to Edison as a "friendless and fatherless boy,"[10] Dickson in fact hailed, on his father's side, from a respectable middle-class professional family—his father had grown up in a large country house with its own orchard and two live-in servants—and on his mother's side from generations of wealthy Jamaica sugarcane farmers. Indeed, wrote one of his genealogists, his ancestors "held some of the largest sugar plantations of colonial Jamaica."[11] When Dickson, "friendless," sailed to America in the spring of 1879, he was not diving into the unknown, but joining his mother's family in Virginia, his two sisters and his mother in tow.

He wanted grandeur for himself. He wanted fame and respect. He tolerated being called Dickson—or, later, "Mr. D."—but never accepted any diminutives of his first name, and always credited himself as WKL, WKLD, or his full, four-worded name, eventually double-barreling the last two words in hopes of giving them some aristocratic flair.

From his first day as an experimenter at the Edison Machine Works, on Goerck Street in Lower Manhattan, Dickson saw himself as more than Edison's newest employee. He thought of himself as the Wizard's successor.

*   *   *

Young W. K. L. Dickson was not Thomas Edison's only admirer. The early 1880s were arguably the peak of the inventor's international fame and popularity—he was never more unanimously respected than in the years that followed his unveiling of the phonograph. His duplex telegraph for Western Union in the early 1870s had made him rich and well respected; his race against Alexander Graham Bell to premiere a musical telephone in 1877 had held newspaper readers in thrall for months; his demonstration of the phonograph for *Scientific American* in 1879 had made him the first overnight celebrity the United States had ever really known. Edison was bigger than P. T. Barnum, so recognizable that an envelope with just his photograph glued to the front could be accurately delivered by the Postal Service. His laboratory in Menlo Park, New Jersey, was the stuff of legends, a private complex where almost daily, it seemed, the greatest genius of the century invented a new device to challenge the accepted laws of possibility. Edison's workmanlike charm, carefully cultivated by him and by his publicity people, seemed emblematic of the American dream. Born poor, he'd worked hard to make his fortune on wits and effort alone. Even when rich—even when the Vanderbilts and the Morgans funded him—he professed to love nothing more than hard graft.[12] He wore a chore jacket and work pants, he chewed tobacco, he made ribald jokes. The average man may have been unable to explain how the phonograph or the telephone worked, but he could read an interview with their inventor and understand *him*: here was a man you'd like to grab a beer with.[13]

For a while Edison basked in the celebrity—and then the pressure began to make itself felt. Newspaper coverage fed his ego and motivated investors to continue backing him—invention, after all, was a high-risk, slow-moving business. But Edison had the bad habit of publicly overselling his results. The phonograph was announced repeatedly to be "perfect" or "perfected," though not perfect enough to be put on sale. Ditto the musical telephone, and, for a long time, this was also true of the incandescent light bulb.

Folks took notice. "What a happy man Mr. Edison must be!" one newspaper critic wrote after the latest in a string of announcements regarding the imminent completion of Edison's light bulb. "If he continues to observe the same strict economy of practical results which has hitherto characterized his efforts in electric lighting, there is no reason why he should not for the next twenty years completely solve the problem of the electric light twice a year without in any way interfering with its interest or novelty."[14] One cartoon from 1880 depicted Edison as a con man showing off his latest novelty, the "Great Invention Trick," a machine that transformed good money into worthless company stock.[15]

Once, and very recently at that, Thomas Edison had been the Wizard of Menlo Park, the "Napoleon of Invention," the "New Jersey Columbus." Now he was the butt of gossip column jokes. His eventual success with the electric light would change the public's mind again, returning him to favor, though for the last time in his life. Thereafter, he dedicated his days to chasing that high, to the pursuit of one final wonder to be adored for. He would try mining and automobile batteries, radiology and chemistry. The closest he would come to success would be with motion pictures.

He would owe much of that success to William Kennedy Laurie Dickson. The two men had less in common than WKL had suggested in that first letter. Thirteen years separated them. The mentor was self-deprecating and gruff where the mentee was unctuous and self-important. What they did have in common, however, mattered. They both worked hard. They both had oversize egos. They were competitors who liked credit, attribution, and praise more than they liked money.

"I don't care so much about making my fortune," Edison once told an interviewer, "as I do for getting ahead of the other fellows."[16] When it came to the motion picture, W. K. L. Dickson would prove useful to Edison in getting ahead of the other fellows—no matter the expense and no matter the cost.

Even if it meant brushing aside a few mild inconveniences—including the truth.

LOUISIANA
CENTENNIAL

1882–1885

N ew York had its own relationship with time, constantly leveling the past and eluding the present, living right on the line where that present became the future. Occasionally, the rest of the world paused for breath. New York did not.

The Le Princes were not immediately on pace, and faltered after Jean's death. Louis started an interior decoration business in partnership with a local by the name of Charles Pepper, with offices in Union Square. Business was not good. Within eighteen months they were forced to relocate, to 1321 Broadway in quieter, less-developed Midtown. Neither Louis nor Pepper were natural businessmen, and by 1885 their partnership was wound up. Lizzie worked as an artist, gathering commissions and administering whatever private classes she could find. She briefly took a position at the New York Society of Decorative Art, and joined the Chautauqua Institution, a Methodist teaching camp that assembled every summer on the shore of Chautauqua Lake in western New York State. The bills were not as easily paid as they were in England, but the Le Princes did not admit defeat. They made the house on Saint Nicholas Ave their own. They called it the old Belmont House, perhaps to give it some artificial history and charm. They bought a dog.[1] They found their feet. They would, over the next few years, choose to be New Yorkers; Le Prince himself was voluntarily naturalized a citizen in the mid-1880s, with his children to follow.

The Institution for the Deaf and Dumb continued to obsess Lizzie. Within weeks of arriving in New York she found a qualified way to fulfill the vow of her first night in America—by becoming the school's first art instructor. Her budget was small: to teach the children she was given only "large slates, and unlimited white chalk," as well as "charcoal clay, a few non-poisonous watercolours, and camel's hair brushes."[2] The first annual student shows out of her department were full of Lincrusta projects and leftover stock from Le Prince & Pepper, repurposed to teach the children how to decorate frames, panels, and kitchen mats. But the school was progressive and welcoming. Another Englishman, Edwin A. Hodgson, taught printing. (He was from Manchester and had had perfect hearing until the age of eighteen, when the sense was taken away from him by spinal meningitis.) The school was coeducational and believed its pupils could achieve anything: its postsecondary "High Class" program, open to children who displayed academic excellence, was unique in the country. Lizzie, who was warm and generous in her praise, fit right in. On her first day she did away with textbooks and with rote copying from lithographs. She wanted the young ones in her care to develop "forethought and precision,"[3] to think for themselves and know the world through representing it, as Carrier-Belleuse had taught her. She reminded them drawing and painting were not arts exclusively made for museums, but also skills that might make them employable. "It is not so much *fine art* as art applied to industry deaf-mute institutions require," she told fellow teachers. "We need just that kind of art training which will make a good shoemaker a better shoemaker, and of our carpenters, cabinet makers, and carvers, printers, and tailors, more expert and precise workmen." Sketching "lilies and roses" made for charming end-of-year art shows, she argued, but learning how to reproduce "the mechanism of the human foot" could help grow a child into a cobbler, and in turn help put food on his plate. She refused to lower her standards for the deaf and mute boys and girls. It would be "false kindness," Lizzie thought, to give them the impression the world would take pity on them.[4]

She was well liked by her colleagues, many of whom, impressed by Lizzie's methods but also, one assumes, her stories of having breathed the same air as Rodin, stayed at the school after classes were dismissed to take their own tutoring from Mrs. Le Prince.

Louis, seeking independent work as an interior decorator but failing to find much of it, dedicated his free time to helping out. The children were preparing a pantomime show for the unofficial 1884 World's Fair, to be held in New Orleans from December 1884 to June 1885 and thereafter known as the Cotton Centennial. Louis painted trompe l'oeil sets and guided rehearsals. The experience brought husband and wife even closer together. "Only those who have tried to teach these things to the deaf," Lizzie remembered, "can realize the intimate knowledge of detail, tact, assiduity, and patience required."[5] She watched with fondness as Louis "warmly" guided the children in the fitting and painting of scenery and walked them through each moment of performance, using a mixture of oralism (whereby the instructor made himself understood to the deaf with a mixture of lip reading and exaggerated mouthing of sounds), gesticulation, and the new American Sign Language, then being popularized by Laurent Clerc of the American School for the Deaf in Hartford, Connecticut, the only college of its kind in America older than New York's. When the delegation from the school headed south to Louisiana, Louis was by Lizzie's side on the train, shepherding the children safely to their carriages, chaperoning them as Pennsylvania and the Carolinas flew past the windows.

The School for the Deaf spent nearly $1,300 on its showing in New Orleans, a sum roughly equivalent to what it paid its art teachers every year. It was one of the minor highlights of the fair. Lizzie's and Louis's preparations were closely tracked in the educational press, the *Deaf-Mutes' Journal*. The Christmas Day edition of the paper, which separately acknowledged Louis and Lizzie's volunteer contributions to the institution's Christmas pageant, was enthusiastic: "If there is an Institution in the world which has just cause for being proud of the accomplishments of its pupils, and the efficiency of its officers and teachers, surely the New York Institution has reason to stand up and claim that distinction. The recent preparation of exhibits to be sent to the New Orleans Exposition, under the management of Monsieur Le Prince, has awakened such enthusiasm among the pupils and such interest among their superiors, that the specimens are of no end in their variations. Each department has contributed its share, and so well executed are they, that they do great credit to all concerned."[6] Louis had designed a makeshift room, entered by a narrow passageway, in which visitors would find themselves surrounded by works by students: display cases, painted screens, even a small stage on which short plays were performed, the deaf children demonstrating how they had learned the new technique of lip-reading. There were "studies from nature in charcoal, pen and ink sketches, decorative tapestries, panels for furniture, hand painted tiles, etc. . . . A fine array of printing such as was done by the pupils for the past few years, in the shape of circulars, handbills, letterheads, programmes, etc; the girls got up a fine collection of domestic and fancy sewing and knitting, representing tidies, ric-racks, mats." There were "model bureaus and writing desks" made by teenagers in the carpenter shop and "shoes of handsome make" and "suits of clothes of artistic cut" from the cobbling and tailoring shops.[7] One glass cabinet showed photographs, taken by Louis, of the children in their daily environment in New York.

Paying guests and distinguished visitors crowded the booth. One of them may have been America's most famous sufferer of hearing loss: Thomas Edison.

Edison arrived in New Orleans at the end of February 1885, two months after the opening of the fair. His name was all over the exposition— Edison Electric had wired the thirty-three-acre main building with five thousand of the Wizard's electric lamps—and he was in Louisiana on more personal business, too: the thirty-eight-year-old inventor, seven months a widower, was pursuing nineteen-year-old Mina Miller, daughter of Lewis Miller, a businessman hawking his wares in the industrial section of the exposition. Miller was a sober and public-minded man, the inventor of the first modern combine harvester, and was more than content to have America's greatest innovator woo his daughter—regardless of their age difference.

Miller was also the co-founder of the Chautauqua Institution, the Methodist organization in which Lizzie participated. Much of Miller's philanthropic work concerned itself with education, both through Chautauqua and through local initiatives in his native state of Ohio. It's conceivable he—with daughter and her suitor in tow—would have toured the pedagogical showings at the fair, particularly one managed by a new Chautauqua subscriber. Edison may have been tempted to visit those same booths. Very hard of hearing from childhood—he was nearly deaf in his left ear—he nevertheless never wore a hearing aid and preferred to see his condition as an advantage, "a blessing in disguise" that helped him focus and blocked out "the babble of ordinary conversation."[8] The matter was certainly on his mind at the time. Three weeks before departing New Orleans he'd discussed it with a journalist, arguing he would not pay $10,000 to be "cured" of his deafness, "because it prevents him hearing many things which he does not wish to hear, such as cars, carts, licensed venders [sic] in the morning, bores, telephone calls, political speeches and cats."[9]

There is no specific record of this visit, if it happened. Had the man Lizzie Le Prince eventually accused of killing her husband, stealing his work, and plunging her family into tragedy seen Le Prince's work with the deaf-mute children in New Orleans in 1885? Had he, maybe, even met Louis?

If so, Lizzie did not discuss it in her memoirs. But neither did she allude to the many summers she later spent at Chautauqua Lake with the children in the 1890s, retreats at which Mina Miller was always present, occasionally accompanied by a reluctant Edison, by then her husband.

When the fair wrapped up, representatives of the French and Japanese delegations gifted their artworks to New York's deaf and mute children as a token of appreciation for their efforts. Louis had struck up something of an admiring relationship with the Japanese artists. He appreciated the way they used color, and the refined delicacy of their ink-tipped brushstrokes. He daydreamed with Lizzie about one day traveling to Japan to learn more about the technique, in the hope of applying it to the making of color photographs.[10] In the school building back in New York, with the help of the institution's resident engineer, Joseph Banks, he'd turned a back room into a pottery room and had built a glass firing kiln of his own design, with attached blowers, fed by a steam engine, that he used to approximate the soft breeze that had fascinated him in New Mexico. He still dreamed of making moving photographs. Perhaps pulling together techniques and skills that already existed in cultures foreign to his own would help him solve the limitations that had so far prevented him from doing so.

Over five years had gone by since his exclamation, back in Yorkshire, that moving images would be the next invention. Since then he had done next to nothing to make them *his* next invention. He hadn't the funds or the resources.

He began to think that should be remedied.[11]

A GUN THAT
KILLS NOTHING

1880–1885

Whether Le Prince knew it or not, others had already started to pull ahead. Eadweard Muybridge had slowly been improving his system for taking instantaneous pictures of animals—though, when his name finally appeared in newspaper headlines in 1874, it was for entirely different reasons. He had just traveled seventy-five miles, by ferry, train, and horse-drawn buggy, from San Francisco to Calistoga, where a con man who called himself "Major" Harry Larkyns was working as a journalist at the Yellow Jacket gold mine. Muybridge had found out his wife, Flora, twenty years his junior, was having an affair with Larkyns, and that Larkyns may even have been the father of the newborn boy Muybridge had thought was his own son. Once in Calistoga, Muybridge learned Larkyns was playing cards with some of the miners at the superintendent's home, so he walked over to the house, knocked on the door, and asked for Larkyns.

"Good evening, Major," Muybridge said when Larkyns came to the porch. "My name is Muybridge. Here is the answer to the letter you sent my wife."[1] He raised a Smith & Wesson revolver and shot Larkyns through the heart. Lowering the gun, he stepped over the "Major," walked into the house, and waited for the police to apprehend him.

At trial weeks later, Muybridge's lawyers maintained he should be found not guilty on the basis of insanity, one of the earliest uses of the argument in a US courtroom, explaining that the stagecoach accident that had drastically altered Muybridge's personality years earlier also contributed to an inability to control his actions in times of emotional stress. The jury did not buy it. They did, however, believe in frontier justice—or, as they put it themselves, "the law of human nature"[2]—by which they meant a husband's God-given right to defend his honor from cuckoldry. They found Larkyns's murder justifiable and acquitted the man who had pulled the trigger. The watching audience greeted the verdict with applause.

Afterward, Muybridge returned to work for Leland Stanford, this time at the millionaire's Palo Alto ranch. There he built a new studio. A white wall was erected along the track to serve as a backdrop and divided, by black vertical lines, into sections twenty-one inches apart. Facing the wall across the track was a blockhouse, fifty feet long and incised from one end to the other with a sort of arrow slit, from which twelve Scoville cameras, also twenty-one inches apart, pointed onto the track. Thin wires ran at chest height across the track, from each camera to its corresponding section on the far white wall. As the horse trotted along the track, it hit and broke each wire, activating the matching camera's electromagnetic shutter, a mechanism designed by Muybridge, the first of its kind. The shutter released two plates obstructing the camera's lens, dropping one and raising the other, so that as they crossed they opened the lens for the briefest of instants, recording the quickest exposures ever achieved. With this system, Muybridge managed to take twelve photographs in half a second, though, of course, each camera had only to fire once. The Englishman published the resulting twelve snapshots as a series in 1878, entitling it *Sallie Gardner at a Gallop*. Over time Muybridge doubled the number of cameras to twenty-four, replaced his shutter with one that did away with the wire threads, and improved the emulsion on his photographic plates to make them more sensitive to light. The pictures thus achieved were lifelike enough for Muybridge to project them, starting in 1880, using a device he called a Zoopraxiscope, a cousin of the magic lantern in which the photographs, rather than being printed on individual slides, were reproduced along the surface of a single rotating disk. The Zoopraxiscope was not a motion picture device: its images were not from a single continuous point of view, but from twenty-four different cameras approximating the same point, and indeed the shots Muybridge projected were in fact painted re-creations of his photographs, an artist tracing over the outline of the horse and rider, so as to eliminate the inconsistencies from frame to frame. They were also cyclical. A single rotation of the disk took only a second so, when Muybridge projected his running horses for a paying crowd, he spun the same circular slide over and over, the painted animal galloping the same instant over and over again. This worked with a racehorse, which reproduced the same gait in a straight line, but was applicable to little else.

Stanford had spent upward of $40,000 on the photographer's experiments, more than a million dollars in today's money, and the results were revolutionary. Instantaneous photography had been impressive enough in itself. Now Muybridge's projector, wrote *Scientific American*, "threw upon the screen apparently the living animal. Nothing was wanting but the clatter of hoofs upon the turf, and an occasional breath from the nostrils, to make the spectator believe that he had before him genuine flesh-and-blood steeds."[3] The *Illustrated London News* called the photographer's London lecture, held at the Royal Institution in the presence of the Prince of Wales, the Duke of Edinburgh, and other royals, "astonishing . . . a magic lantern run mad (with method in the madness). . . . I am afraid that, had Muybridge exhibited his Zoopraxiscope three hundred years ago, he would have been burned as a wizard."[4]

Burned Muybridge eventually was, though not by a mob. Leland Stanford, resentful of the celebrity being bestowed on a man he thought of as an employee, published a book of Muybridge's motion studies, without crediting Muybridge on its front cover or anywhere inside its pages. Stanford had his physician and friend J. D. B. Stillman, who had had nothing to do with Muybridge's work, recorded as the author of the work instead.

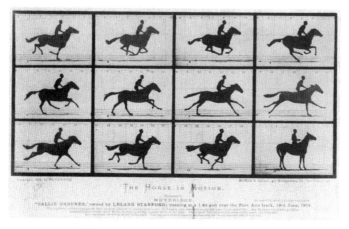

The Horse in Motion, photographed by
Eadweard Muybridge, 1878. (Library of Congress)

Muybridge found himself accused of plagiarism for exhibiting pictures he himself had taken. External funding for further photographic work was suddenly withdrawn. Muybridge sued Stanford; Stanford, the millionaire, won, as millionaires usually do. Muybridge left California, and by 1884 he was living in Philadelphia, working out of an open-air studio in the courtyard of the veterinary hall at the University of Pennsylvania. There, funded by a grant from the college, he continued to deconstruct life onto glass plates. He took approximately one hundred thousand photographs over the following twenty-four months, some focused on animals, driven over from the Philadelphia Zoo, but most of nude human bodies in action—walking, jumping, twirling, going about everyday tasks. The resulting images, printed and displayed side by side rather than projected, were fossilized fragments of life, their subjects less people than exanimate specimens in a lab.

*   *   *

Meanwhile, across the Atlantic, the French physiologist Étienne-Jules Marey also spent his waking hours consumed by a mission to measure movement. Marey was wildly creative: he'd already designed a recorder of pulse waves, strapped around the patient's wrist, that could approximately quantify the wearer's blood pressure; a system of air-filled bulbs he could insert into a man's heart to record its beats; pneumatic pressure sensors to record the footfall of horses; even an electric myograph, onto which he could strap the bodies of dead animals, such as frogs or birds, and then, by severing their tendons and hooking them to wires instead, jolt specific muscles to analyze the force generated by each contraction. There was nothing of the mad scientist to Marey, however. Already entering his fifties—he and Muybridge were born a month apart—Marey was even-tempered and collaborative, with the air of a respectable country doctor, his hair slicked back and gray at the temples, his beard neat and full. Pictures still in existence show him, somehow unchanged, over the years: the same haircut, the same length of facial hair; black suit and waistcoat over a white spread-collared shirt, black cravat. Friends described him as a "perfectionist, affable, generous"[5]—though he was equally well known for his rigor and scornful impatience for errors and dishonest work.

Marey presented every one of his discoveries to the Académie des Sciences, preferring to share them with peers rather than trademark and exploit them for personal gain. For thirty-five years he taught at the Collège de France, and starting in 1882 he operated out of a "physiological station" in Boulogne-Billancourt, on the outskirts of Paris, financed by state subsidies: the fruits of his labor would benefit his government, not a corporation.

Around the same time Eadweard Muybridge was preoccupied with horses, Étienne-Jules Marey's life was filled with birds. They were the hardest specimens of the "*machine animale*," as Marey put it, to measure and track, and the physics of their flight continued to elude him. Photography had been one of his favorite tools ever since he had used it to study the formations of the Prussian army in 1870, though the medium also frustrated him: the cameras were too cumbersome, their shutters too slow, the developing of wet glass plates a craft of its own. Marey believed in "the graphic method" as a source of scientific evidence—but the proofs created by early cameras were nothing if not questionable, their grain thick and the slightest movement a quicksilver blur.

Then came Muybridge. When Marey saw the 1878 shots of Sallie Gardner and Occident—the ones taken not with one camera, but with the bunkhouse battery of them—he wrote to Muybridge via the science magazine *La Nature*, admitting himself "impressed."[6] He asked the photographer if he might be able to apply his method to pigeons. Muybridge, unfortunately, could not, chiefly due to the impossibility of guiding a free-flying bird down a straight line on a clean white background. And Leland Stanford, who still controlled the direction of Muybridge's work, had no interest in bankrolling a study of airborne fowl.[7]

Marey was undeterred. He needed a mobile version of Muybridge's setup, one that could be pointed at the sky and moved as nimbly as a bird changed altitude and direction. His acquaintance, the astronomer Jules Janssen, had, years earlier, built a heavy photographic cannon that could take a daguerreotype every second and a half over seventy-two seconds, which he used to capture stages of Venus transiting through the night sky. Janssen suggested the method be adapted to Marey's purposes. "The principal difficulty comes actually from the slowness of our sensitive materials," Marey reported to the Académie des Sciences, "but science will certainly remove these difficulties."[8] By 1882, though Marey had not quite "removed" the difficulties, he appeared to have found an ingenious way to work around them.

"I have a photographic gun, which kills nothing,"[9] Marey wrote his mother that year to describe the apparatus he'd conceived as an improvement on Janssen's. It was a rifle, its barrel a camera lens and its cylinder loaded with circular photo plates. When Marey pulled the trigger the device shot a picture and rotated to the next exposure, an operation it could perform in 1/500th of a second. The gun held twenty-five disks of twelve apertures each. He expanded his arsenal with the construction of a small wheeled cabin on tracks, inside of which was a larger camera, with which he could take ten photographs per second on a single fixed glass plate. This he used to analyze human beings, though he reversed Muybridge's color scheme, shooting his subjects all in white, with bright studs and reflective strips on their leotards, in front of a black velvet backdrop.

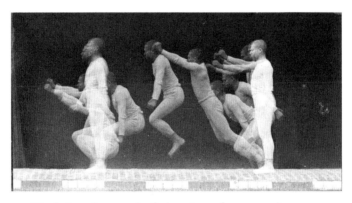

Fixed plate photograph of a long jump from a standing start, by Étienne-Jules Marey, 1882. (Collection Cinémathèque Française)

Muybridge had animated his pictures as a gimmick, to give his speaking engagements a dash of flair. Marey was not interested in projection in any form. His studies were not demonstrations but dissections, beats of time purposefully isolated and scrutinized like samples under a microscope. He called the practice chronophotography, the purpose of which was the stopping of time, not its re-creation. The Prussian photographer Ottomar Anschütz, the French researcher Albert Londe, and Marey's own assistant Georges Demenÿ augmented the field with their own modifications on Muybridge's and Marey's respective achievements. Others saw the possibility for an entirely new medium, one in which instantaneous photography was not an end in itself but a means to capture every moment of life—none of it obscured by blur or darkness—and thereby replay it at will. A soft-spoken French teacher by the name of Charles-Émile Reynaud and a dashing, charismatic young English photographer called William Friese-Greene separately tinkered with magic lanterns and zoetropes, looking for ways to turn them into projectors of long-form photographic movement. Words-worth Donisthorpe, the industrialist's son from Leeds, claimed now to have constructed a prototype of his "Kinesigraph," though it was so heavy and unwieldy a piece of machinery it was practically useless, leading Donisthorpe to abandon the project—again—for several years.

The problem, for all these men, was glass. As a base, the material was perfect for Marey. It was stable, smooth, and unbending, and its transparency made it the perfect surface on which to coat emulsions and imprint detailed tonal contrast. As a base for moving images, especially those taken through the viewpoint of a single lens, it was a torment. Even at Marey's rate of twelve photographs a second, glass plates would crack inside the projector, if they hadn't already in the camera. Shooting a twenty-second film meant lugging around a large camera and upward of two hundred plates, the entire sequence ruined if one of them splintered. It was, all things considered, not an appropriate support for moving images—but no reliable alternatives were available.

The innovators were at an impasse. They remained stuck until 1885. That year an unknown entrepreneur and photographic supplies salesman from Rochester, New York, by the name of George Eastman began marketing a replacement for glass negatives, his solution so simple, elegant, and affordable it was an embarrassment to his many competitors.

Eastman's product was a small roll of paper, divided into one hundred square exposures, each coated in sensitive emulsion. Any photographer could load a spool of it inside a camera and take a hundred pictures, advancing each frame manually, and, when the entire roll was exposed, develop and enlarge the images in the darkroom. Eastman started selling the paper-roll film and began work on a handheld camera purposefully designed for it, one that would enable anyone to take photographs without the need for training or chemical equipment.

He would call that camera the Kodak.

SHADOWS WALKING
ON THE WALLS

◼

Chaos. Soldiers screaming as cannonballs whistled past their heads to the sea. In the distance two sailing frigates were sinking, one devoured by flames; the other, tipped on its side, swallowed water from a gaping hole in its hull. Sailors swam toward the shore, dragging unconscious comrades, crawling toward the stretchers dropped into the surf by their field medical corps. Out on the waves, somewhere between the sinking frigates, two ironclad warships, squat and low on the water and almost futuristic, were firing at each other at close range. One flew the thirty-five-star Union Navy Jack and the thirty-five-state Stars and Stripes. The Confederate nine-state Stars and Bars flapped in the smoke over the other.

Louis Le Prince looked over the field. He looked at the corpses—Union men, mostly, their wool uniforms dark enough to conceal wounds and blood. He studied the green trees and the blue sea. Only up close did the paint look like paint, but no paying guest would get this near; from the viewing platform, the pigments arranged themselves into coherence, a canvas as vivid and real as a colored photograph.

The scene around him—*The Merrimac and Monitor Naval Battle, Newport News Point, 1861*—was Théophile Poilpot's newest painted panorama, an entertainment on a huge scale, and Le Prince was its manager, responsible for ensuring that every detail, down to the smallest, was believable and correct.

Outside the cold winter air blew down Madison Avenue. Christmas would be there soon, and with it would come floods of New Yorkers, the last pay packet of the year burning a hole through their pockets, eager for novel ways to entertain and educate their families.

Le Prince's show would be open and ready for them.

The Merrimac and Monitor Naval Battle[1] was one of the sensations of its New York season. The panorama—a gigantic 360-degree painting, erected in a closed circle, inside of which the public stood and took in life-size re-creations of historical events—had first been invented at the tail end of the eighteenth century but had recently made a comeback, reinvigorated by electricity and photography, spectacular tools with which to enhance the medium. This one was the brainchild of Théophile Poilpot, a Parisian painter and showman, who had hired Louis Le Prince to be the project's manager.

It's uncertain how Poilpot and Louis met. Both had served during the Siege of Paris—Poilpot in the Eleventh regiment of the Garde Mobile de la Seine. They may have been introduced by Pierre Carrier-Belleuse, the celebrated sculptor's son, who worked as a painter on the *Merrimac and Monitor* panorama and whose younger sister, Jeanne, was Poilpot's wife. Whatever the case, soon after Poilpot, already hugely successful in his native France, arrived in New York in 1885 to take on the American market, he hired Louis, who had just returned from the New Orleans Exposition—first as his interpreter and photographer, then quickly promoting him to the post of general manager of the *Merrimac* show, the first panorama Poilpot planned to open on US soil. Le Prince gladly accepted. He was hard up for cash and had done nothing since the dissolution of Le Prince & Pepper but help out at the Institution for the Deaf. Besides, panoramas, though they did not involve moving images, proved an exciting enterprise for an innovative image-maker like Le Prince. Daguerre himself had begun his career as a panorama painter, and had been led to the discovery of photography in part by those experiences.

Merrimac and Monitor depicted the Battle of Hampton Roads, one of the most significant naval engagements of the American Civil War, in which Confederate ships tried and failed to break a Union blockade of Virginia. It was the first time two ironclad warships—the titular USS *Monitor* and the CSS *Virginia*, sometimes called the *Merrimac* after the steam frigate *Virginia* had been built from—met in combat, anywhere in the world. Panorama impresarios loved Civil War subjects for their drama, scale, and newness: the Confederate surrender at Appomattox was just twenty years old.

Poilpot's own chief concern was to put on a show. His backers, like Broadway producers, got their investment back only if *Merrimac* had legs. His skill was in making the panorama much more than a painted vista: it was an immersive experience. Wheels and pulleys animated sections of scenery, gas and electric light guided the viewer's focus, wax figures and fake foreground terrain added depth and focus. A very particular set of storytelling skills was required to make the illusion work and Le Prince, as Poilpot's manager, supervised the details on which the vision depended. He'd been hired for his experience with painting and photography, and his ability to guide and instruct a team of craftsmen— be it the deaf children of the institution putting on a play, the skilled engineers of Whitley Partners, or artists installing Lincrusta Walton. A great panorama manipulated time and point of view, and engaged in the viewer a sudden suspension of disbelief: just a moment ago she stood on Madison Avenue, surrounded by concrete and the honking of traffic, yet now, blinking to adjust her sight to the darkness, it was imperative she immediately feel transported to Virginia, in the cool spring of 1862, soft grass under her feet, sea mist on her cheeks, and gun smoke in the sky.

The Battle of Hampton Roads had lasted over forty-eight hours, but *Merrimac and Monitor* compressed those two days into one view;

instead of the action unfolding over time, it was the viewer, standing at the center, who traveled through the event by turning and facing its key moments. Here was the field camp in the minutes before the first cannon shot; turn to the left and there was the *Cumberland* taking water; shuffle farther and you saw the two iron warships locked in the second day's combat, dealing each other fiery blows. The seams between each incident were smoothed over with paint and carefully thrown shadows. Depth was re-created in perspective and through the trompe l'oeil effect of false terrain built between the painting and the viewing platform. Silver clinquant added the shine of metal to weapons and uniform buttons.

According to his son Adolphe, Le Prince guided Poilpot, with a director's eye, in choreographing the "posing, grouping, and painting"[2] of the action sequence.[3] Louis's training in optics informed his decisions on how to steer the customer's vision, and his experience with a camera contributed to the realism of the figures in the fresco, which may have been painted from photographs of staged reenactments. Photographs were also used to create the preliminary "dummies," sections of the painting that were then transferred to the gigantic final canvas using either transparent prints on glass or projected slides from which the artists could trace. Poilpot was at the vanguard of making these displays three-dimensional, combining layered painted panels and miniature dioramas to enhance the main canvas's illusion.

Merrimac opened at the end of 1885 in a Midtown rotunda that had previously been used as a skating rink. (In the 1910s the building would be converted into a movie house.) It was an immediate hit and ran for nearly three years before moving to Chicago for another lengthy run. "The exhibition building is always comfortably filled," reported the *New York Times*, all the more so "in the afternoons by people who after visiting Central Park take the opportunity, while in the vicinity of the panorama, to witness the famous battle between the ironclads."[4] The men who had commanded both the *Monitor* and the *Merrimac* came in to view the attraction, as did many of their former crewmates, and "praised the mimic representation of the battle."[5] Entry was cheap, and as a result the crowd was varied. Families and groups of friends formed "panorama parties"[6] and traveled to the venue together. In the summer, huge fans had to be installed to cool down the pack of customers during their long wait up to the viewing platform. It was the first panorama of the new wave to turn a profit in America.

Le Prince seems to have canvassed the public's reactions and striven to answer them; a year after the show opened, according to the *New York Times*, he was still making "several changes and improvements."[7] Jean Aimé Le Roy, a thirty-one-year-old photographer who later made debatable claims to have been the first person to screen motion pictures, was then an assistant to a photographer, Joseph Thwaites, at his shop at 1 Chambers Street. Le Roy remembered Le Prince walking into the premises in the spring of 1884—most likely actually the spring of 1885—and placing an order "for a number of lantern slides of military scenes, that he explained were to be made to scale so that he would be able to project them without any varying sizes or proportions. It was to help him to make outline drawings on canvas to be used in a panorama of war."[8] According to Le Roy, Louis regularly returned to the little camera shop, tucked between Boss Tweed's courthouse and the brand-new Brooklyn Bridge, during *Merrimac and Monitor*'s run, to buy supplies and talk photography.

Louis couldn't stop experimenting. Here was a collective experience even more sophisticated and authentic than the magic lantern that had put Louis in mind of moving photographs. Audiences entered a darkened space and were overwhelmed by a life-size reproduction of life, itself a sequential narrative, the flow of time artistically manipulated for dramatic effect. How bowled over would they be if a similar experience could be offered with photographs, rather than a painting, and if the action truly moved—truly *lived*—instead of merely looking like it did?

Sometime during the run of *Merrimac and Monitor*, Le Prince took a back room at the Institution for the Deaf and turned it into a darkroom and workshop. His previous vision of moving images was humble: an improved magic lantern, loaded with continually moving photographs, like one of Muybridge's Zoopraxiscope projections but adaptable to any subject. Working with Poilpot had fed the fantasy. Now Louis imagined animated photographs on the scale of *Merrimac*, and as immersive and realistic, too. He described them as "a moving panorama in colour,"[9] with sound and depth: not a small circle on the living room wall but an enthralling entertainment, life-size figures thrown onto a huge screen in a darkened room.

His first attempts were relatively simple. Due to the limitations involved in the use of glass plates—George Eastman's paper roll film was not yet reliable or resistant enough to be exposed at a rate of several photographs a second—but also to his hope he might be able to capture his moving pictures in stereo to create the same sense of three-dimensionality offered by Poilpot's panorama, Le Prince built a camera first with four then with sixteen lenses, essentially concentrating Muybridge's multiple cameras into a single device. He arranged the lenses into two independent banks of eight, each of the lenses taking a picture in turn, each bank staggered in use with the other. This, Louis hoped, would make the glass plates less liable to break, since they were not required to travel as quickly through the camera to achieve the necessary frame rate to sustain persistence of vision. What this frame rate was, no one was exactly certain, just as no one was sure how genuine moving images might look. There were no supply shops, no infrastructure, no experts; no one had ever attempted the particular thing Louis and others like him were attempting.

Le Prince's widow, Lizzie, and daughter Mariella remembered Louis having some success both with the taking and the projecting of pictures as early as 1885, but this is most likely an error. Le Prince's correspondence indicates he quit working for Poilpot to focus on motion picture work only at the very end of 1885 or in the early months of 1886, after Poilpot had moved to Washington, DC, to open a new panorama, a depiction of the Second Battle of Bull Run. The first time anyone mentioned Louis's new venture in writing seems to have been in September 1886, when Lizzie wrote to her father back in Leeds to tell him about it—and, apparently, to ask him for assistance and a loan.

Joseph's response, dated October 10, is encouraging, yet wary. The new device sounded terrific, he wrote. He understood the basic concept well—the camera, Joseph wrote, was basically "an artificial retina of mechanical accuracy,"[10] and the principle of persistence of vision was sound enough, as anyone who had had the experience of looking into a bright light then closing his eyes and retaining the outline of the object viewed for a few seconds could attest. Louis's ambitions for color images and synchronized sound, however, Joseph found baffling. "We cannot understand how the sound can be retained except by a reversing phonograph machine,"[11] he wrote, alluding to Edison's audio recorder.

His past experiences dampened his enthusiasm further. He'd been crossed too many times over intellectual property himself, his inventions stolen and exploited. He wanted to help Louis but was, he said, "afraid of any partnership before [any] patents are secured." He warned against delaying and asked Lizzie to have Louis send him more details, "tracings and legal drawings and terms . . . with some [estimated] dollar margins in exchange for his own brain power, hand labor, and experiments. . . . if we can engage to make the machine for the million, we will do so." But he reiterated: patent, patent, patent—before anything could be considered Louis had to protect himself with a *patent*. Not just in America but everywhere: "If means could be got it ought to be secured in every country in the world," Joseph recommended. Until then he hoped that Louis could "keep clear of the sharks who are swarming in every part of the world to pounce upon the work of nobler minds. This fact I know to my sorrow, and of this very time while I write."[12]

The earliest surviving document in Louis's own hand in which he mentions moving image work directly is dated even later, on November 2. "My dear friend," Louis wrote Richard Wilson. "Time goes his way and finds us plenty to do not always to our liking, but there are nice bits here and there, when we can see them, and they endure and bring pleasant reminiscences." He told his old friend that, with school out for the hot months of July and August, Lizzie had gone away to a teachers' convention in San Francisco and that, in the meantime, "I stayed at home for large Panorama work which did not come, and took the opportunity to work out an idea . . . which will be spoken of when brought out. The patent will take a couple of months before issuing thro' the offices at Washington; and I shall then secure it in France, England, etc. It is in the line of Dioramas and Panoramas but with figures etc. in lifelike action; this wants keeping secret till secured. I am now making apparatus to work it practically."[13]

This work Louis carried out at the Institution for the Deaf, in the kiln room he had formerly used to fire photographs onto porcelain and clay. The principal, Dr. Isaac Peet, also granted him the use of "its large well lighted studio, after school hours and on holidays, for camera projections."[14] Two long-standing teachers, Miss Jane Meigs and Miss Ida Montgomery, "allowed some of their pupils to pose for experimental and final trials of [the] earliest machines, and were present on these occasions." Joseph Banks, the institution's maintenance man and mechanic, was fascinated with Le Prince's "large magic lantern,"[15] probably the first prototype projector, and described it in a later statement. "Near its base it had a scroll decoration cut out in the sheet iron sides, there was one lens used in this instrument," he recalled. "I know that during this said period [the mid-1880s] Mr. Augustin Le Prince was working on an invention, and that it was his custom to stay often quite late in the evening at the kiln room. . . . I made several appliances for [him] as a favor, and did such work as drilling, filing & some of the parts of the machine he brought to me. I also gave him permission to use my private work bench and tools, and he used them." Banks, like most mechanics in America in 1885, many of them inspired by Thomas Edison, was working on inventions of his own, and he and Le Prince whiled away the evening hours sharing "several talks on patent affairs." One evening Louis worked so late he was still in the building in the middle of the night and, Banks recalled, a night watchman by the name of Jacobi, mistaking him for a thief or prowler, detained him until he could be identified.

The first model of Louis's "deliverer," as he called the projector (as in, a "deliverer of images") was built by William Kuhn, a Harlem Heights tinsmith, who said he was asked to design it with "perforations for lenses, and spindles and doors to operate the lights."[16] Louis also asked Kuhn to add in gas burners, probably to fuel a light source, though he would have quickly realized the flame was not only too dim but dangerous as well.

Neither machine survives. Any plates or images created in these tests are also lost. A colleague of Lizzie's at the school, a sign language teacher by the name of W. G. Jones, remembered posing for Louis and that Louis "told me that when his machine was perfected he would photograph me in the act of telling a comic story in signs, and then . . . the pictures in rapid succession would make the audience feel as if they were really seeing me."[17]

Mariella Le Prince, then fifteen or sixteen, would often hover in the hallway near her father's workshop, intrigued by the work occupying so much of his time. One evening Lizzie asked her to fetch Louis for dinner. Mariella remembered it being "a dark night in winter," which places the memory near the end of 1886 or early 1887.

As Mariella walked down the darkened hallway, she noticed warm light dancing in the crack under the closed kiln room door. "I knew the place ought to be in darkness," she remembered, "and I went to the door to peep inside."

Mariella made to push the door open, but Louis—who had "evidently heard my footsteps"—pulled it ajar before she could.

"What do you want?" he asked.

Mariella's gaze flicked from her father's face and into the room. Behind him gray shadows were walking on the whitewashed wall. Their dim contours were the shape of human beings—Le Prince himself maybe, perhaps W. G. Jones, perhaps the deaf and mute children in

Ms. Meigs's and Ms. Montgomery's care. The phantoms were flat, their bodies did not touch the ground; and though they were faint, Mariella knew they were not the brief dissolve of a magic lantern or the simplistic painted forms of a zoetrope.[18]

She dared not interrupt, and returned to the Jumel Mansion without her father.

Lizzie returned from her summer in California with news of her own. The eleventh Convention of American Instructors of the Deaf had taken place in Berkeley over a week in mid-July 1886. Lizzie brought with her a display of exhibits recycled from the New Orleans show and gave a talk on technical art training for the deaf in which she repeated the philosophies she had learned from Carrier-Belleuse and Rodin. "Why strive to teach [a pupil] art in the abstract," she said, "instead of training eye and hand to reproduce the *things he sees as he sees them*, and his heart to take in *to the full* the beauties in appearance?"[19]

Jane Stanford, the wife of Leland, attended some of the proceedings and, according to Lizzie, was impressed by her talk and display of student artworks. She "became much interested in this exhibit and the methods of training advocated, and asked me to consider transferring our art school to the Leland Stanford University," Lizzie recorded.[20] Eadweard Muybridge's instantaneous photography had already been published to much acclaim and publicity, and he had been demonstrating the images in movement, animated by his Zoopraxiscope, for several years—but Lizzie, she wrote, was not then aware of the connection between Muybridge and the Stanford family.

Stanford University, founded in 1885, had not yet opened, but Jane and Leland were busy assembling teachers, shaping a curriculum, and taking guidance from East Coast college deans; two "bibliographers"[21] were currently on their payroll in Europe, handpicking books for the eventual university library. Leland himself was in the middle of his first term as US senator for California, while still president of the Central

Pacific Railroad, the Southern Pacific Railroad, and the Occidental and Oriental Steamship Company. (He also continued to sit on the board of Wells Fargo and Company.) The railroad business had made Stanford immensely wealthy, in no small part due, on the one hand, to sizable subsidized land grabs and, on the other hand, to the toil, in dangerous and exploitative conditions, of immigrant Chinese workers Stanford nevertheless publicly abused as a "degraded" and "inferior race," the "dregs of [China's] population."[22] The Stanford name was as synonymous with corruption as it was with wealth, even in his day, but men like Leland always evaded consequences. If anything, he was riding high. He felt untouchable enough that summer to challenge state legislature appointments on the basis of past grudges. Another one of his horses, by the name of Manzanita, was breaking world trotting records again; and he continued to boast of Muybridge's horse-in-motion photographs as if they were his own work, the courts having dismissed out of hand the photographer's claim for ownership on the basis of their being a work for hire. Last but not least, just two months before the Convention of American Instructors of the Deaf opened, Stanford's Southern Pacific Railroad had won one of the most consequential Supreme Court decisions in American history, *Santa Clara County v. Southern Pacific Railroad*, granting constitutional rights of personhood to corporations.

His wife, however, was grieving. Her only son, Leland Jr., had died of typhoid in 1884 at the age of fifteen. She'd given birth to him late, when she was thirty-nine, after years of trying to start a family, and his death was a terrible blow. Jane turned Junior's bedroom, in the Stanford mansion in San Francisco's Nob Hill, into a shrine to her son, and held séances in the hope she might establish contact with his spirit.

The university at Menlo Park—a town in northern California not to be confused with that of Thomas Edison's former residence in New Jersey—was intended in memory of her son and to be named after him. There were rumors the idea for the university had come to Leland in the night, suggested directly by his dead son, appearing to him as a ghost. Certainly Jane was as consumed with the undertaking as if it had been ordered by otherworldly forces. She was present to welcome the educators of the convention on their arrival at San Francisco and arranged for sightseeing tours for the speakers on their days off. Lizzie, who had also devoted herself to education after the loss of her own son, may have recognized Jane's pain.

Lizzie's lecture was warmly applauded by the assembled delegates. Jane Stanford's own praise, and the offer of a prestigious position at a well-funded new university, were further balm to her embattled self-esteem. There was reward in her work in New York but little prestige and little money. She'd been the family's primary breadwinner for much of the past three years and felt underwhelmed by the lack of material comfort and long-term security she had to show for it. As she remembered it, Louis, in addition to spending every available hour in his workshop, had started sinking all of their disposable income into his moving image machine. Her household budget was so tightly girdled she had recently felt it necessary to dismiss Phoebe—but luckily Phoebe had "refused to leave, offering to work for nothing until things improved."[23]

As she boarded the train back east, Lizzie was "fired with the prospect of immediate release from money cares." The trip across the country took four days. The scenery flew past in the frame of the carriage window, blurred with speed like the dissolves of an unrelenting magic lantern slide show.

When she arrived back at the house on Saint Nicholas Avenue, Louis was at his workbench. She told him about the job offer from Leland Stanford's wife, and the possibility of relocating their family to California, but it wasn't a long conversation; in fact it was almost no conversation at all. "I found my husband too deeply immersed in his experiments and model making to entertain the idea," said Lizzie. Louis reminded her that he had declined "fine salaried positions" himself for the sake of his project, including the post of manager on Poilpot's new panorama in Washington. He wasn't concerned about their lack of funds. "He was convinced, and persuaded me, that financial returns from his invention of moving pictures would far surpass them," Lizzie said. "Nothing drew him from his absorbing researches."[24]

Lizzie politely declined Jane Stanford's offer, "and another sacrifice was made for moving pictures." She was still bitter about the experience as she wrote about it thirty-five years later. Her optimism while traveling back to Manhattan was a form of self-injury, she concluded. "When Fortune leads a victim to the gates of Paradise," she wrote, "she first blindfolds [her]."

Once she was at home in Harlem Heights, her husband sitting across the room with her, Fortune showed her hand, and "my Gate of Paradise closed with a clang."[25]

THE WIZARD'S
TOWER

1884–1886

■

W. K. L. Dickson was assigned first to the Edison Machine Works on Goerck Street, a dreary band of cobblestones and factories near the Brooklyn Bridge, the neighboring ironmongers and foundries filling the air with clanging and the hissing of steam. Edison had brought incandescent light to New York—and by extension the world—in September 1882, throwing a switch that lit up J. P. Morgan's offices on Wall Street, the first building in which Edison's direct current system was installed. Posterity would remember Thomas Edison as the man who had lit a filament and brought light to a dark world, but this was not the case on the day: the news made only the back page of the *New York Times*.[1] Electric arc lighting had been available for years, and gas lights before that; the huge advances offered by the incandescent bulb—it was dimmable, it was safe, it was affordable, it was lasting, it did not smell or stain as gas fumes did—were not immediately grasped by the public. Investors understood Edison had invented not just a product, but a utility—there was a reason the launch had taken place at J. P. Morgan's headquarters—but the common customer was indifferent to the achievement. No journalists turned up in person to watch Edison turn on the lights. Commercial clients were slow to sign on. Midtown and uptown power plants were announced but not built, let alone opened, for several years.

Edison's sole power plant remained the Pearl Street Station downtown, a long, narrow, smokestacked brick building, only a few blocks away from J. P. Morgan & Co., as direct current could travel only short distances between generator and customer. The Goerck Street Machine Works, just a little farther north, was where generators and other electrical grid machinery were manufactured, and where W. K. L. Dickson was assigned to the testing room as a junior experimenter. He found the building bleak—"grim of aspect, not over clean, and located in an uninviting portion of the great metropolis"[2]—but his colleagues fascinating. There was Henry N. Marvin, a gifted mechanic who would later change Dickson's life, and Charles Edgar, an ambitious, clever young man who went on to manage Boston's Edison electrical grid. A few months after Dickson's arrival, the team grew further with the addition of an eccentric and foppish twenty-eight-year-old Serb by the name of Nikola Tesla. Dickson, who was the youngest of the crew, remembered Tesla as "unostentatious," friendly, and helpful, a man of "brilliant intellect" who already "gave strong evidence of genius."[3] All the men, with the exception of Tesla, hungered for their famous boss's attention. To his chagrin, Dickson quickly learned that Edison, who oversaw a growing empire from an office building at 65 Fifth Avenue, only occasionally made the journey down to Goerck Street. Finding himself on the periphery of his idol's business, W. K. L. strove to catch Edison's eye. He put in long hours. He came up with inventions of his own and sent them up the chain of command for endorsement. When all else failed, he returned to his pen and wrote insistent, sycophantic letters. "If only you knew how I am heart and soul in all your inventions & all you do," read one, "you would now & then stoop to assist & better my prospects."[4] Edison rarely replied. Dickson ground it out. Other experimenters quit or were dismissed. Tesla left the company after about six months, upset, he said, not to have received a financial bonus Edison had promised to pay him. Dickson stayed. In his second year at the company he finally received the word he'd been waiting for, and was transferred to Edison's New York headquarters on Fifth Avenue.

Dickson now got his first long look at the man he had admired from afar, and though his regard for the inventor did not diminish, Edison fell somewhat short of the wizard portrayed in the newspapers. Edison was then only thirty-seven but looked much older. He called his employees "muckers," and they affectionately called him "the Old Man." He was unpretentious but irritable, his manner curt and his temper short, and he resented being given advice. His habits were not healthy. He worked in spurts, sometimes as long as eighteen straight hours, skipping daytime meals and refueling on "midnight dinners" of coffee, red steak, and cold apple pie. Edison didn't drink alcohol but chewed tobacco constantly, one reporter describing one of his plugs as a "yellow cake as large as a dinner plate."[5] If he was out of bricks, he smoked cigars. When exhausted he would crash on workbenches or his desk for a nap, a newspaper or worksheet draped over his face and his arms hugged around his body, hands tucked under his armpits. All of this likely contributed to his bad moods.

His piercing gaze was also usually taken as a physical expression of his genius, though it could just as probably be put down to Edison's needing to focus on interlocutors to compensate for his near deafness. He often had to cup a hand to his ear and lean closer to hear; sometimes it was unclear whether he ignored you because of his deafness or out of rudeness. His condition could make communicating with Edison difficult. Alfred Tate, Edison's secretary in the first half of the 1880s, remembered everyone at the laboratory speaking at a high volume constantly as compensation. "My speaking voice was rather loud," he wrote, "due to my frequent conversations with Edison. He was partly deaf, and in conversing with him one's voice had to be amplified. It took years after I left him to curb this habit."[6]

When Dickson moved to 65 Fifth Avenue, in fact, there were signs Thomas Alva Edison's grip on himself was slipping. He worked hard, but he went about his tasks in a haphazard way, flitting from one project to the next, and his behavior could be that of a capricious old man instead of that of a middle-aged man at the peak of his powers. He was proud of being an autodidact and openly disparaged the trained scientists on his payroll; the richer he got, the more important it was to him to be portrayed as a working-class entrepreneur. He put daily effort into what became his personal uniform—described by one employee as "a rather seedy black diagonal Prince Albert coat and waistcoat, with trousers of a dark material, and a white silk handkerchief around his neck, tied in a careless knot falling over the stiff bosom of a white shirt somewhat the worse for wear . . . and a rough, brown overcoat," somewhere between "careless" and "slovenly"[7]—and was ill at ease spending so much time in Manhattan, wearing smarter clothes and surrounded by bankers and financiers, his days filled with board meetings and promotional efforts.

In August 1884, just weeks before the electric switch ceremony at J. P. Morgan's offices, Edison's first wife, Mary, had died at home in the middle of the night at just twenty-nine, of a condition doctors described as "congestion of the brain." Edison, immersed in his work, had ignored the debilitating nervous symptoms she'd been suffering for months, even when her physicians begged for his attention. Her death was as shocking to him as a lightning bolt out of a clear blue sky—when he told his twelve-year-old daughter, Marion, the news the next morning he was "weeping and sobbing so he could hardly tell me that Mother had died in the night,"[8] Marion recalled—and the grief may have explained some of Edison's erratic behavior.

The year after his wife's death, Edison met Mina Miller, his nineteen-year-old "maid of Chautauqua." Meeting Mina reinvigorated Edison. He took time off, traveling across the country—one of his stops was in New Orleans, to visit the Cotton Centennial. He read books, mostly romantic tomes by French authors, and briefly started keeping a contemplative diary. They married in February 1886, and more changes followed.

Drawing a line between his old life and the new, Edison and his second wife moved away from Menlo Park, purchasing a twenty-nine-room mansion on thirteen-and-a-half acres of land in West Orange, twenty miles to the north. The house's previous owner, Henry Pedder, was a department store clerk arrested for embezzling company funds, with which he'd paid for the building of the home. Edison got the property at a steal in the weeks before it went to auction, including the fraudulently bought furniture and ornate interior decoration by Pottier & Stymus, the same firm that had designed the inside of Leland Stanford's San Francisco mansion. Edison called the estate Glenmont. It had central heating, running water, and a refrigerator; underground cisterns collected rainwater from the gutters and fed it into the bathrooms so the toilets could flush. Edison installed a network of speaking tubes so he, Mina, and the staff could communicate from different rooms and different floors; he had employees bury underground cables and wire the house for direct current electricity. A cook, a waitress, a housekeeper, gardeners, and stable boys were hired, with their rooms on the third floor. From the house's widow's walk Edison and his young wife could see all the way to Manhattan.

The house's entrance hall was the grandest room of all. It was decorated with a hat rack topped with Tennessee marble, a mahogany settee, a large beveled mirror, and a mounted moose head. The lower half of the great hall's walls was wainscoted in varnished oak. Their upper half was embossed in Lincrusta Walton, darkly shaded floral patterns waxed in a metallic finish to give the appearance of bronze. The Lincrusta was original, installed for the embezzler Henry Pedder in 1881, back when the rights to the product in America were controlled by Jack Whitley and his salesman and designer, Louis Augustin Le Prince.[9]

Edison drew up plans for a new, state-of-the-art laboratory, to be erected nearby—"the largest and best-equipped industrial laboratory in the world."[10] Business and finance were not for him, he'd decided: it was time for a return to full-time experimenting. The custom-built five-building complex housed specialized laboratories, machine rooms, offices, and a darkroom. Its stockrooms and chemical stores were said to include every material and substance then known to humankind. The library was stuffed with scientific tomes and trade magazines. (On the bookshelves there were also books of press clippings Edison kept about himself, carefully collected, cut out, and glued to paper leaves by his assistants.) The complex was the perfect workshop from which to run three dozen projects at the same time with the help of a vast staff; profits would enable Edison to dot the surrounding bucolic valley with factories in which he'd manufacture the resulting inventions, keeping a bigger share of the income for himself; with the proceeds he would finance his own independent pursuits and discover more devices as revolutionary and celebrated as the phonograph and the light bulb.

He did not yet know what those devices would be, though it was important that they have commercial value. "Anything that won't sell I don't want to invent," Edison told a reporter, "because anything that won't sell hasn't reached the acme of success. Its sale is proof of its utility, and utility is success."[11] But Edison worked best when he identified existing innovations and improved on them, and in truth his original ideas were rare. His early stock tickers and multiplex telegraphs were improvements on models theretofore being publicly used and debated. He'd announced his phonograph only to obstruct Étienne-Jules Marey and C. L. Rosapelly, French inventors already working on their own recorder of human voices: after reading of their progress in *Scientific American*, he wrote to the same publication, claiming his phonograph was already "perfected"—one of his favorite words, and one he often used to cover for failures, difficulties, and delays. When Edison held a single demonstration for the editors of the publication two months later, they wrote up the experience in glowing, complimentary terms, catapulting Edison to celebrity—even though the phonograph would not be reliable enough to be marketed widely for another two decades. Direct current electricity was already being rivaled by George Westinghouse's alternative current, a system soon to be perfected—in the true meaning of the sense, this time—by Edison's former employee Nikola Tesla, whose exceptional talents had completely flown Edison by.[12] His incandescent bulb had been inspired by William Arcand's imperfect "mineral oil" lamp, which Edison had seen at work in 1878 and which he combined with the globe bulb and carbon filament invented by the Englishman Joseph Swan, announced in the American inventor's beloved *Scientific American* in October 1879, and immediately after which publication date Edison began work on a carbon filament light bulb of "his own." (Edison would consider suing Swan for patent infringement a year later but, convinced by his lawyers he was in fact in the wrong, Edison merged his British operations with the Englishman's instead. In the end, with the profits he made in the United States, Edison bought Swan's interest out entirely.) Likewise, though Edison liked to think of himself as the inventor of the telephone, he'd invented only the carbon microphone, which improved Alexander Graham Bell's original. Edison was smart enough to know Graham Bell's was one invention he couldn't altogether erase publicly: instead he frequently repeated the allegation that Bell's device was inaudible, unreliable, and basically useless. In private, he angrily dismissed his rival as just one more "pirate."

Edison was, undoubtedly, the finest inventor of his era, but increasingly his genius appeared to disserve him: combined with wealth, fame, and expectation, it generated a pressure for him to create, even where inspiration had yet to provide either a purpose or a fuel. Most great engineers and scientists who stumbled upon a world-altering invention or discovery did so only once in their lifetimes. Edison had done so—or come close—several times, and had made himself and America accustomed to the idea he would manage it again and again. The Wizard's audience, like all wonder-seekers, could be kept happy only with new tricks.

And Edison needed a new trick. He reinvigorated the close knot of assistants and helpers he leaned on most: to his right-hand man and chief experimenter, Charles Batchelor, and his lawyer Frank Dyer, he now added a general manager, A. O. Tate, and a private secretary, Samuel Insull. The Englishman "Batch" Batchelor was Edison's "hands," a skilled engineer Edison trusted to work out the details of his own visions and prototypes. Dyer was the operation's guard dog—a combative, relentless advocate who wrote Edison's patents and enforced them in court. Tate, only in his midtwenties, was the man-manager, juggling organizational structures to keep the companies running, repelling those who would exert demands on the Wizard's time, and running interference with the press. Samuel Insull, like W. K. L. Dickson, was a young man who had written to his idol from England asking for a job and sailed across the Atlantic to make his ambition happen. But Insull's ambition had more method than Dickson's. He worked his way up through Edison's London operation and campaigned for the job of private secretary specifically; before Edison had even hired him, he'd memorized the details of his boss's balance sheets, and on his first day in New York he cut nearly $150,000 from the new laboratory's running expenses. In no time, wrote his biographer Randall Stross, Edison came "to view him as indispensable. . . . He spoke well, dressed well, and made sure that everything was handled just so. Edison gave him genuine decision-making authority because Insull was preternaturally adept at management and yet, because of his youth and lack of technical background, he could never be Edison's peer, drawing public attention away from Edison."[13]

These men—Batchelor, Dyer, Tate, and Insull—would be instrumental to Edison in the years that followed. They would finance, build, market, and enforce his rights to the next great invention—as soon as Edison figured out what that would be. His ideas rarely came to him unprompted: he collected technical publications in several languages and read every issue of *Scientific American*, scouring the gray pages for new patent announcements and the letters to the editor for innovations naive amateurs gave away for free. Edison's own schemes rarely came to fruition: over the years these included concrete furniture and housewares, books printed on nickel, and an electric ray with which to carve ice. He predicted metals would be transmutable by the twenty-first century, making gold "as cheap as bars of iron or blocks of steel," ushering in a world of "golden taxicabs" and ocean liners "of solid gold from stem to stern."[14]

As protective as he was of his claims—and as quick to denounce rivals as thieves—Edison could also be candid about his working process. "I never had an idea in my life," he once admitted. "My so-called inventions already existed in the environment—I took them out. I've created nothing. Nobody does."[15]

Now Edison and his new team put their noses to the ground and tracked "the environment" for the scent of a new idea.

W. K. L. Dickson was not a part of the inner circle; in fact, he was struggling to keep his job. In May 1884, a year after he'd started at the Edison Machine Works, Sherburne Blake Eaton, the legal counsel for the Edison Electric Light Company, wrote to Edison about possibly firing Dickson. "Mr. Dickson, Testing Room, has an assistant to whom we pay $10 a week,"[16] Eaton informed his boss. "I believe you propose to shut up Goerck street in a few days. Don't you think we had better let the assistant go? I suppose we had better keep Mr. Dickson, although the shop is closed? Please give me your views." The company's payroll was "pretty large," Eaton explained. "We must see if we cannot put the knife in somewhere and reduce it." Edison's half-hearted reply, scribbled in pen on the missive for Insull to elaborate on, was to let Eaton know he'd "have to keep both for a while yet."[17] He was reorganizing his companies and was unsure how much staff he would need, though he did not single Dickson out as an asset to be held on to at all costs.

Dickson was moved around over the next few months. He was promoted to superintendent of the Edison Electric Tube Company, the firm responsible for the laying of wiring under Manhattan streets. It was a step up the hierarchy but a move away from Edison himself, the Tube Company being headquartered not in New Jersey but in Brooklyn. Doggedly, Dickson continued to emulate Edison in every way he could think of. He worked fourteen-hour days and pulled all-nighters and showed up on Sundays. By the end of 1885 the Tube Company was absorbed into the Edison Machine Works, and Dickson must have felt he was going around in circles until, eventually, he was transferred to Fifth Avenue—just as Edison retreated from Manhattan back to New Jersey.

Finally his break came. Around this time it was brought to Edison's attention that Dickson, on top of being skillful and a hard worker, was an avid amateur photographer, and it struck the inventor that a camera might not be a bad thing to have around to document his life at the new house and laboratory. He requested for the ambitious young man to come to Glenmont and take pictures of the mansion. Then Dickson was tasked with the same job around the West Orange facility. Soon he was taking staged publicity shots of Edison at work—or, sometimes, pretending to be at work—and making the camera room, in the main building of the complex, his home.

LIFE ON GLASS

1886

Photography had become a global fascination. Suddenly, it seemed, great minds everywhere were talking about its possible uses and innovations. In 1885, in *La Nature*, Étienne-Jules Marey published "Etudes Pratiques Sur la Marche de l'Homme," a detailed account over four pages of his plans to photograph individual athletes including "good walkers, good runners, agile jumpers," so that he could break down "the secret of their abilities."[1] Muybridge's *Animal Locomotion: An Electro-Photographic Investigation of Connective Phases of Animal Movements*, a collection of twenty thousand of his instantaneous photographs taken at the University of Philadelphia, was being compiled for publication in 1887. Each of the book's 781 plates was a series of twenty or so pictures breaking down a particular sequence of motion: a nude man, standing in front of a black wall divided into a grid of small white squares, swinging a small racket at a tennis ball; a young woman in a white tunic and sandals, hitting the same ball underhand; a lion; a monkey; a raccoon; two elephants walking; a cockatoo in flight, wings repeated over and over like the peaks and valleys of an electrocardiogram. Muybridge could capture horses cantering and galloping by then, a mule as it kicked, even a stag at a run. Under his bright lights the dark animals appeared mythical. His human bodies were more detailed than in any previous photographs.

Thankfully for Le Prince, no one had yet to successfully explore his avenue: that of using instantaneous photography to re-create live movement, as opposed to using it to stop and dissect it. The images Mariella had seen, that night, on the wall of the Institution for the Deaf's workshop were far from perfect. Her father's first cameras attempted to unite the pictures into a single point of view, by placing multiple lenses on the front of one camera rather than in a line stretching dozens of yards, as Muybridge had done. But the results weren't ideal. The lenses, being as far as an inch or two apart on the face of the device, captured pictures from slightly different perspectives. When Louis arranged the images into a linear sequence, the action on-screen would shudder and pop anytime a frame from one lens ceded to a frame from another. Even when a filming session went as planned—and it couldn't have done so often, the glass plates often breaking or jamming as they moved, the light almost always insufficient—Louis would have been left with a reproduction of movement that looked, to his dismay, *less* regular and realistic than Muybridge's. Any sense of immersion for the viewer was further shattered by the noise of the projector, furiously hand-cranked, cogs and springs and wheels catching and clanging inside the box.

What Louis *had* discovered, however, was a principle, and he recognized that principle immediately as a tremendous step forward. Though Louis's battery of lenses followed Muybridge's, the spirit of his camera was the opposite. Where Muybridge and Marey froze singular objects over stark backgrounds to gain greater clarity over the stages of their motion, Louis's single device retained the blurring of the stages—that was the entire point. It also created space for relative movement. Several subjects could move in different directions at the same time, both horizontally and in depth. They could travel into frame and out again. The camera itself could be moved, panning and tilting to re-create the natural movements of a viewer's eye—though at this point only theoretically, because of the machine's huge weight. Muybridge, by contrast, had to erase his backgrounds into grids and white blanks to *fake* a single point of view in his Zoopraxiscope projections; his subjects had to travel straight and flat across the row of cameras (as did Marey's); any single lens being out of alignment with the others broke the entire sequence. Muybridge and Marey captured movement in a lab. Louis, even in his "crude model camera,"[2] as his daughter described it, had stumbled across the first stone on a path to seizing life whenever, and wherever, it lived.

And so, though the invention itself was unfinished, and though its workings were rudimentary and its results insufficient, Le Prince drafted a patent application. It's unclear whether he did so out of confidence in his ability to perfect the machine quickly. He may, simply, have heeded Joseph Whitley's warnings that if he didn't commit himself to protection in law, someone else would—and possibly very soon.

"Be it known," the letter of submission began, "that I, Augustin Le Prince, of the city, county, and State of New York, have invented certain new and useful Improvements in the Method of and Apparatus for Producing Animated Pictures of Natural Scenery and Life on Glass, Canvas, or other Prepared Surfaces, of which the following is a full, clear, and exact description."[3]

Louis's application proposed an apparatus including both "a receiver or photo-camera" and a "deliverer or stereopticon adapted to throw the transparent pictures obtained by means of the said camera or receiver in the same order and time in which they were taken," so that "the transparent pictures thrown in quick succession on a finely ground plate glass or other suitable material will produce on the eye of the spectator the same effect or impression as the objects themselves when in motion in front of the 'camera-receiver.'" The camera was fitted with a focusing lever and its design specified that the film base—be it glass or another material—would be carried on perforated ribbons.[4] It could be designed with either one lens or "a system of three, four, eight, nine, sixteen, or more lenses of equal focus."

The inner workings of the machine were tortuous. ("So with the first quarter of a revolution of wheel A_4," one paragraph goes, "cogs J' will work small wheel E' one revolution, and during the first quarter of that revolution cogs D_2 will work the pinions of shutters G and H', so that G will be raised over lens-opening L, while H' comes up and closes it; but as the cog gearing on pinion of shutter H' has one, two, or three teeth less than that of shutter G . . ." and so on.) But it was the projector, or "deliverer," that was most problematic. Louis expected to be able to throw images onto a screen using only the power of "sixteen or more incandescent lights," at a continuous pace, kept steady by a set of upright slides.

This design did not work well. But Louis's plans for the projector did hint at a possible way of solving all those problems. In this "deliverer," Louis wrote, glass was best replaced by a "sensitive film . . . on a transparent flexible material," ideally "an endless sheet of insoluble gelatine coated with bromide emulsion, or any convenient ready-made quick-acting paper, such as Eastman's paper film."

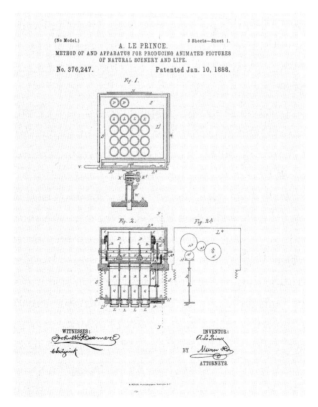

The first page of Louis Le Prince's US patent, submitted in 1886 and granted in January 1888. (U.S. Patent and Trademark Office)

Eastman paper spools fit in a person's pocket and could each carry a hundred to a hundred and twenty exposures, making it unnecessary to lug around heavy dry plates or the cumbersome chest of equipment needed to put up a temporary darkroom and prepare wet plates. It was the talk of the photographic world. In late 1886, Le Prince began experimenting with mechanisms suited for the paper-stripping film. At the same time, he tried to push the glass plates to their limit, doubling his workload.

The application was filed by Le Prince's patent agents, Munn & Co., on November 2, 1886. Then the waiting began. Patent submissions routinely took months, sometimes over a year, to process.

Munn was one of the most respected patent firms, as well as one of the largest, in America. As early as 1860, it had handled over 3,500 patents annually, about one-third of all submissions filed in the entire country. Both the agency and *Scientific American* magazine were run by Orson Munn, formerly the manager of a general store in Massachusetts, and Alfred Ely Beach, son of the founder of the New York *Sun*, two friends who had taken advantage of the technological boom sweeping through post–Civil War America to grow both the firm and the magazine. *Scientific American*'s rise was closely tied to Thomas Edison's, who told journalists that as a penniless young Midwesterner hungry for glory he had walked three miles, every week, to the nearest newsstand to pick up each new issue of the young paper. By 1886, when Louis Le Prince walked through its doors, Munn & Co. had offices not just in New York and Washington, but all over the world.

Patent law was big business. The state's responsibility for administering a patent and copyright system—"to promote the Progress of Science and useful Arts, by securing for limited Times to Authors and Inventors the exclusive Right to their respective Writings and Discoveries"—was enshrined in the US Constitution's very first article, alongside such congressional duties as collecting taxes, establishing a post office, making laws, and declaring wars. The first Patent Act required the secretary of state, the secretary of war, and the attorney general to review and approve all patent applications—making Thomas Jefferson, Henry Knox, and

Edmund Randolph the country's first patent examiners. A dedicated patent office, with its own head examiner, was created in 1836. By the 1880s the process of acquiring a claim had become difficult and arcane, and no one filed his own submission anymore. A competent lawyer, with the resources to research patent history (so as to preempt any objections on the basis of preexisting inventions) and the skill to draft clear, precise applications, was a necessity. One you could trust not to steal your idea was even better.

The Patent Office's headquarters occupied an entire city block between F and G streets and Seventh and Ninth Streets in the capital, six blocks east of the White House. Benjamin Butterworth, commissioner of patents, had five hundred examiners in his employ, who were required to comb through about forty thousand detailed applications annually—about two per week per examiner, accounting for holidays. Munn & Co. warned Le Prince it would most likely take months for his patent to be either granted, rejected, or returned with a request for modification. In the meantime there was little to do but wait, and keep on improving the device, with any modifications admissible as updates to the submission later on.

As Le Prince counted the days, he drafted a list of possible subjects suitable for filming. One reads: "B. BILL, BARNUM, SURF" as well as "HUDSON RIVER BOATS" and "BDWAY FROM OFFICE, CENTRAL PARK FASHION AND BOATING, BASEBALL, GIRL THRO' PAPER DISKS ON TIGHTROPE."[5] It's as if he knew, already, that the most sensational moving pictures would be pure entertainment: William Cody and the rough riders of his Wild West show, P. T. Barnum's "Greatest Show on Earth," New York's most scenic views. A pretty girl doing pretty tricks.

Le Prince also drew, constantly. His surviving papers are covered back and front in diagrams of machinery; sketches of possible cameras and projectors; and quick, fluid portrait doodles of one or another of his sons. On one sheet he scratched out a layout for an exhibition room: several rows of benches, arranged at an angle and facing a large screen.

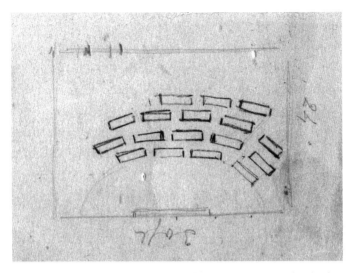

Sketch of a motion picture exhibition room from Le Prince's notebooks, late 1880s.
(Leeds University Library / Leeds Philosophical and Literary Society)

Patience was not Louis Le Prince's strong suit, and it was a particularly difficult quality to exhibit in New York, a city whipping itself headlong into the future. Five days before Louis filed his patent claim, the nation's president, Grover Cleveland, had been in town to dedicate the Statue of Liberty, a monument Joseph Pulitzer had fought to have financed and that was now being embraced by the establishment that had originally refused to pay for it. The event was picketed by suffragettes (who, after being refused tickets to the unveiling on the grounds that they were "unaccompanied women," leased a steamer to protest the hypocrisy of a woman being made a symbol of liberty in a country where women themselves weren't yet allowed to vote); mocked by African American newspapers ("shove the Bartholdi statue, torch and all, into the ocean," said the *Cleveland Gazette*, until African Americans could live in peace "without being ku-kluxed, perhaps murdered. . . . The idea of the 'liberty' of this country 'enlightening the world,' or even Patagonia, is ridiculous in the extreme")[6]; and scorned by many Chinese Americans, who four years earlier had become the targets of the Chinese Exclusion Act, the United States' first ethnically motivated immigration law.

The world felt fleeting, changing; yet Louis's attempts to snare it on glass and paper slowed as he waited for progress on the patent. His children were growing fast. Adolphe, just turned fourteen and developing his own interest in chemistry, was as curious about his father's work as he had been as a child in Leeds, when he broke into the forbidden backyard workshop. When given permission, he went along to the institution and watched his father work. "I saw a series of the four-lens deliverer projected on the screen," he wrote after his father had disappeared.[7] "It was of a man's head, he was making grimaces and moving his head about." The pictures were "about one and a half inches in diameter" and "taken on sensitive paper rolls." He remembered another sequence of "a child dancing about . . . projected onto a screen at [the] Institute." But these scenes were almost certainly disappointing: the multiple-lens cameras could not take images that were precisely equidistant, and the projections were not smooth.

While Louis waited, Jack Whitley returned. He was back in New York after some time away in the sunshine of the colonized West Indies "for the restoration of his health"[8]—how he paid for the trip is unclear—and he was full of yet another get-rich-quick scheme. He'd met some American businessmen, he said, who were hoping to "organise in London, for the following year, an Exhibition of the arts, manufactures, and products of North, Central, and South America,"[9] as a way of promoting the New World's industries to European clientele. "I had a strong desire to associate myself with them," Jack wrote, "for I felt and feel sure that Europe, with its teeming millions, already looks to the United States as the vanguard in the march of both material and moral progress."[10] He not only convinced the men to make him the project's general director, but also to modify their plans so that the exhibition would be dedicated to the United States alone. He had just toured several US cities to drum up support, and was soon on his way back to London, where a large site at Earl's Court, described by Jack as little more than "a cabbage-garden,"[11] was being readied by two thousand construction workers for the exposition's imminent opening. As unpredictable and unreliable as Jack could be, he was yet again proving his indefatigability and resourcefulness: in no time at all he had committed the Dukes of Roxburgh, Manchester, Northumberland, Wellington, and Sutherland to endorsing the enterprise; recruited the best-selling author Wilkie Collins to the event's reception committee; and booked Buffalo Bill and his Wild West show for the duration of the exposition, the first time Bill Cody and his troupe would perform on European soil. The exhibition was scheduled for the spring of 1887, the year of Queen Victoria's Golden Jubilee.

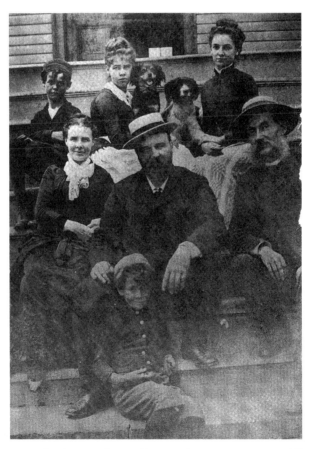

The Le Prince family around 1886. *Top*: Joseph, Aimée, Marie. *Middle*: Lizzie, Jack Whitley, Louis. *Bottom*: Fernand. (Courtesy of Laurie Snyder)

Jack was most excited about winning over Buffalo Bill. He still clung to his old dreams of the West, and Cody's acceptance of his offer delighted the Yorkshireman who had grown up reading cowboy and Indian adventures in his bedroom, while rain lashed at the roof and gray clouds hugged the moors outside his window.

Louis told Jack of his own progress and, as Lizzie and Adolphe remembered it,[12] demonstrated his crude machine to him. William Guthrie, the young lawyer, was also present. "I was shown a curious invention," he wrote years later, "but I cannot recall what the invention was."[13]

Jack's memory was clearer. "I distinctly remember that Mr. Guthrie and I were shown the apparatus by Gus at Belmont House," he wrote his sister more than a decade after the fact. "I think in 1885 or 1886, and I know that the séance took place in the studio. I remember Mr. Guthrie remarking, 'This is a most interesting scientific invention, but how are you going to make it commercially valuable, Mr. Le Prince?' "[14]

Jack himself was keen to help Le Prince answer that question. Guthrie had come along at his invitation—"I had hoped," he wrote in the same letter, "that he, and the late Mr. Clarence Seward, would give their professional assistance." Seward, Guthrie's senior partner, had already told Jack "he was ready and desirous to help Gus with the invention."[15]

Now Jack had an idea of his own. He wanted his exhibition to be a dynamic, future-facing event—not one of the fusty gatherings of engineers and artists in drafty convention halls he and Louis had routinely attended when Whitley Partners still existed. He'd later describe Cody's western show as "living and moving pictures of a fast-vanishing phase of national existence,"[16] and he wanted to add Louis's *actual* moving pictures to the exhibition's program. Could Le Prince have the camera and projector ready to premiere in time?

Louis was nowhere near ready and could not predict if he would be in nine months' time, when the exhibition was scheduled to open. He continued to struggle with both his glass plates and the paper film. His father, Adolphe later claimed, "was the first [motion picture] investigator to grasp the value and necessity of an unlimited amount of pliable film,"[17] but Eastman's product came with its own limitations, chiefly that of image size. Le Prince had reached the conclusion that recording an image on a small surface and then blowing it up to project it could only lead to a dramatic loss of image quality, as happens when a photographer prints a low-resolution snapshot onto a large canvas.

He began sketching out what a camera's interior mechanism *might* look like if adapted to a suppler base than glass—the as-yet-invented, unspecified "sensitive film [on] an endless sheet"[18] he alluded to in his patent. In doing so, he designed the first film reels, two drums at the top and bottom of the system around which the material, in long strips, would wind itself. The base would be moved up from the lower, "supply" drum in a straight, flat, vertical line, where "a clamping pad and tension device"[19] would hold each frame still behind the lens for the fraction of a second required, before it was moved on upward again, the exposed part of the material winding itself around the upper drum for storage. Louis, his son later said, dreamed of achieving "a large area of motion," one that could encompass "masses of people out of doors, on grounds sufficiently large to allow for considerable movement."[20] He imagined being able to take several cameras and several cameramen to mass events, "a number of machines registering [the] movements" of a "national game, fete, or theatricals."[21] Louis planned to tint the images, by hand or by some chemical process, and then "project these transparencies, coloured artistically, onto the immense screen of a panorama."[22] In an ideal world he would do so in 3-D—"stereoscopically," as the method was then known—so as to directly rival the panorama in spectacle and believability. This ambition was another element that set Louis apart from his contemporaries, most of whom had proceeded to motion pictures from the starting point of the magic lantern or the zoetrope—miniature, two-dimensional images projected for small groups of people, be it in living rooms, university halls, or scientific lectures like Marey's and Muybridge's. Le Prince's vision was fired by the panorama instead, by a huge, towering screen boasting of color and depth, set up in a dedicated space for the purpose of mass entertainment.

Some had tried before him. Adolphe later suggested[23] his father had studied the work of Henri Désiré du Mont, a Belgian civil engineer who, in 1861, had filed a patent for a photographic camera he hoped could take ten to twelve pictures on glass plates in a very short time—an unsuccessful precursor to Muybridge's instantaneous photography. Three years later, the Frenchman Louis Arthur Ducos du Hauron, a pioneer of color photography, had obtained a patent for a motion picture camera with multiple lenses that he hoped could record everything from "the progress of a funeral procession . . . [or] the vicissitudes of a battle" to "the grimaces of a human face" and "the movements of cloud in a stormy sky."[24] Ducos du Hauron never built a complete camera, and it would not have worked, in part because photography was not yet advanced enough in his day, and because it relied on an impracticable workflow.[25] But Louis's device, with its sixteen lenses, owes something to its design; even Adolphe's description of "a national game, fête, or theatricals" echoes Ducos du Hauron's ambition, as he puts it in his own patent, to film "a public fête, a theatrical scene, the movements of one or more people."[26]

The idea of moving images was not new in Le Prince's day, but the late 1880s—thanks to Muybridge's instantaneous photographs—were the first era in which they seemed possible. Sir John Herschel, the English polymath and genius who had coined the terms *photography*, *positive*, and *negative*, had foreseen as early as 1860 that "by adequate sacrifice of time, trouble, mechanism, and outlay" it might be "possible, and, perhaps . . . realizable" for someone to invent a machine for "the representation of scenes in action by photography."[27] Le Prince was closer to the realization of that dream than anyone had ever been before. And yet there was, paradoxically, so much left to solve. Cobbling together a tin prototype on borrowed premises had been taxing enough, financially and mentally—Adolphe calculated later that his father, between 1885 and 1887, had spent "about three thousand dollars"[28] on his experiments, roughly the equivalent of $80,000 in 2021. Designing a handsome, market-ready final product—and then constructing at least several others, so a novelty invention could become a viable business—would be an altogether different proposition, one that called for funding, expertise, and manpower beyond even Le Prince, who had taught himself to adapt so many times over.

There would be commercial hurdles after that as well. A patent, in the United States, granted its holder a right of monopoly on the exploitation of the invention for a term of seventeen years, as a recompense for his investment and risk. But there was no immediate, concrete value in holding a monopoly in a nonexistent market—as, by definition, was any field to be created by an entirely new invention. It had to be lit and kindled from scratch: the new product explained and marketed, the customers identified and persuaded, word of mouth hopefully spreading like fire. There would be stock to manufacture, cash flow to manage, distribution systems to strategize, and sales partners with whom to negotiate. None of this was Le Prince's strength.

Inventors of the nineteenth century, their papers of patent in hand, tended to follow one of three routes to create income. The first—and most common—was to found their own business, hawking their innovation in the form of a product they boasted was better or cheaper (or both) than anything yet available in the field. This required capital, often in the form of third-party investors, and so carried further risk. It was the route followed by many of the manufacturing magnates Le Prince had met in Yorkshire, who built and sold boilers, engines, valves, and cooling systems they'd patented themselves; and by the French photographer Antoine Lumière and his brilliant sons Auguste and Louis, whose family firm, Lumière & Fils, narrowly avoided bankruptcy in the early 1880s by betting on a new method of instantaneous dry-plate photography developed by the two young men. It was also the route then being taken by George Eastman in Rochester, and by the brothers John Wesley and Isaiah Hyatt, whose Celluloid Manufacturing Company, out of Newark, manufactured stiff sheets of their new plastic, celluloid, which they sold to dealers in false teeth, billiard balls, piano keys, and as a synthetic alternative to ivory and tortoiseshell. But for every business that boomed by gambling on a new invention, there were a dozen others that sank within months.

The second option open to inventors was the novelty market. It encompassed a range of public exhibition forums, from lecture halls and tours of scientific associations to fairgrounds and the theater. This method of exploitation was an imitation of the literary lecture circuit—public readings of their own works by famous authors, a marketing strategy that had lately seen the likes of Oscar Wilde and Charles Dickens crisscross the United States and Mark Twain, Frederick Douglass, and Harriet Beecher Stowe travel to speak in Europe. While orators and novelists could hope for some degree of longevity, however, inventors' tours were often short lived, fifteen minutes of fame to be made the most of before a new sensation rolled in. Muybridge toured in 1881–1882 and 1887–1888, and had to depend on sponsorship from the University of Pennsylvania to pay the bills and continue his work in the intervening years. Traveling showmen who bet on gimmicks of their own contriving, as Muybridge had with the Zoopraxiscope, lived lives of precarious popularity, never knowing which show would be their last.

The third choice available for inventors was the least easily accessible and the most fraught with pitfalls—and yet it was growing more and more popular. In this scenario the bearer of a patent simply licensed or sold his invention to a larger business, one that already dominated a relevant market, and contented himself with collecting either a one-time sales fee or seventeen years of royalty checks. This was Thomas Edison's preferred strategy: he had made his first fortune contracting in this way with Western Union, who had bought his quadruplex telegraph in 1874 for $10,000. Thereafter, he found that having the backing of an industry leader—with deep pockets, established infrastructure, and lawyers on retainer—increased his own profit, and that outsourcing manufacturing and marketing not only freed him up to spend all of his time inventing, but also led to further work-for-hire contracts with his new partners. (When Western Union decided to move away from telegraphy and into the new field of telephony, for instance, it hired Edison to invent a system that would circumvent Alexander Graham Bell's existing patent, leading to Edison's carbon-microphone telephone.) But beware the inventor who expected to contract with a large firm and be treated as anything more than an asset in a ledger. Even Edison, one of the most famous human beings in the Western world, bristled at what he felt was exploitation from the "sharps" in their Wall Street offices. Agreeing to a contract with a conglomerate was, to many, like signing a deal with the devil: use of your invention would spread, you would receive handsome payment and even some part of the credit; but you divested yourself of any oversight into the bargain. "If you can avoid it," Edison advised a fellow inventor, "don't take royalties. Sell outright. If your royalties rise to any substantial sum they will find some way to beat you out of them. They always will be able to spend more money over a lawsuit than you will."[29]

It was around this time, according to Lizzie and Adolphe Le Prince, that Louis, weighing his options, considered joining forces with Edison.[30] Edison's name was often in the newspapers. There were almost weekly updates on the progress of various companies bearing his name: Edison Electric, the Edison Illuminating Company, the Edison Lamp Company, the Edison Machine Works, Edison United Manufacturing. Colorful columns told of aspiring inventors—one an alleged "Pennsylvania millionaire"[31]—who made the pilgrimage to New Jersey to beg Edison's backing and pitch him on offers of partnership. And then there was Auguste Villiers de l'Isle-Adam's best-selling novel *The Future Eve* (*L'Ève Future*), published in 1886, which told a fictional tale of Thomas Edison inventing and building a "perfect" mechanized woman to replace a friend's gorgeous but irritating fiancée. It was science fiction before science fiction existed (the novel was the first to coin the term *android*), and it enshrined Thomas Edison in popular lore as a genius for whom nothing was impossible, an enchanter "wrapped in the robes of doctor Faustus," as one critic put it. Villiers's Edison was a mythical figure, Pygmalion and Prometheus at once. Readers lapped the fantasy up.

Edison was everywhere, and he seemed exactly the kind of man who would appeal to Louis and Lizzie: a resourceful entrepreneur, who was not just running his own companies but had founded entire public utilities bearing his name and developed technologies that promoted and enabled human progress. We have only his widow's and son's word that Le Prince seriously planned to approach Edison to interest him in partnering on his motion picture device—but Edison was one of the few men alive who had the financing, the resources, and the vision to turn Louis's imperfect idea into a reality. There is no proof Le Prince prepared a pitch for Edison—no correspondence, no drafted letters, no notes—but he would have been an outlier had the thought not occurred to him.

The plan would have been bolstered by Louis's personal connections. Clarence A. Seward, the patent lawyer who had worked with Louis and Jack on the American launch of Lincrusta Walton, and with whom Jack had discussed Le Prince's work, had just taken Edison on as a client, acting as his attorney in litigation to defend his light bulb filament and other electrical patents. William Guthrie, who worked with Seward, had seen the projector at work. In fact, the question he had asked Louis after the demonstration—*How are you going to make it commercially valuable, Mr. Le Prince?*—might logically have been answered by a partnership with Thomas Edison.

Both Seward and Guthrie were firm believers in financial might. They may have advised that a man like Louis was better off in the corner they usually represented—the wealthier, more privileged corner, the one occupied by Thomas Edison and Wells Fargo and J. P. Morgan—than competing with it. Jack Whitley agreed. Jack, Le Prince's biographer, Christopher Rawlence, wrote, "was particularly keen to involve Edison," who he also wanted to participate in the London exhibition.[32]

Le Prince could see a finish line for his work, but it was distant. It would take a lot more money to get there, and he was already exposing his family to possible ruin. Edison, on the other hand, had money, staff, and influential backers. And he had a record of perfecting innovations, seemingly overnight, that others had struggled to complete for years.

THOMAS A. EDISON
CAN GO TO HELL

1886–1887

L e Prince's patent application was almost immediately rejected. Before Christmas 1886 had even come around, Munn & Co. received a letter from Washington, informing them that, by combining three inventions—the camera, the projector, and a potential peephole device—under the umbrella of a single submission, they were breaching the Patent Office's Rules of Practice, making it impossible for the filing to be considered further. The patent examiner invited Le Prince to send in three separate applications, "properly presented," so that each of the three functions could be "examined on its merits."[1]

This caused some confusion for Louis and his agents, who thought of the camera and projector as a single system. The Munn clerk who helped write Louis's US patent applications was a young man by the name of H. A. West, who remembered Le Prince as "the finest, most charming and interesting man I have ever met."[2] More crucially, he said, speaking in 1919, that "almost everything one sees on the screen today he vividly narrated to me more than thirty-three years ago."

In the end Le Prince and West decided to hedge. In January 1887 they filed again, this time excising any mention of a peephole device. Within a month this new claim was also denied on the continued basis that capturing lifelike animated photographs and *exhibiting* lifelike animated photographs were separate innovations, to be addressed in separate filings.

Seward and Guthrie advised Le Prince not to worry: examiners, they told him, were "sticklers for the rules,"[3] and perhaps rightly so—they needed to be if the public was to trust their impartiality. Yet the rules, in this fast-moving age, could become obsolete as quickly as they were drawn up. In Le Prince's case, the Patent Office's existing classifications simply weren't ready for motion pictures: the camera portion of his camera was expected to be filed under Cameras and the projector function registered under Stereopticons. Louis, however, was proposing something entirely new: a photographic device, the purpose of which was not to take still photographs, but was intended to work in conjunction with a projector—a projector that, in itself, made no sense without a prior understanding of the camera, and that would animate images not on a spinning disk or cylinder, but on glass, paper, or even a film format that did not exist yet. Until this point no camera had been designed expressly for the taking of *moving* images, nor had any magic lantern ever been able to take photographs. William Burke, the patent examiner who was handling Le Prince's dossier, seemed unable to understand that Louis was not proposing a photographic device, but an entirely new medium.

Louis decided to go to Washington to clarify his application in person. It was a long journey by train, from New York through Philadelphia and Baltimore to the Potomac. Le Prince did not bring his prototype for a practical demonstration; not only did the Patent Office not require devices to be submitted with applications, they discouraged it due to the lack of available storage room. He had also hoped for Clarence Seward's endorsement, but a letter of support from the lawyer failed to materialize in time.[4] Le Prince told Lizzie later that when the examiner finally grasped what he explained he had looked surprised and impressed. "Good thing for you we're not still living in the age of [superstition and] witchcraft," he told Le Prince, or he'd have been first in line to be burned at the stake.[5]

All the same, the examiner could not grant the submission as Le Prince wished. A camera was a camera and a projector was a projector. If Louis wanted a US patent, he would have to abide by the US Patent Office's guidebook, whether he agreed with it or not.

Back in New York, Le Prince went to Munn & Co.'s offices and got back to work with West. They amended the wording of the patent again and sent it to Washington. It was rejected again—not on a technicality this time, but on the basis that some aspects of Le Prince's camera and projector already existed in the zoetrope patents received in 1861 and 1865 by Henri du Mont, and others in Muybridge's patent of 1883. Le Prince and West decided to remove the three claims objected to by the examiner entirely and rewrote the text describing the invention to make even clearer what a leap forward it was from both Du Mont's hypothetical zoetrope and Muybridge's magic lantern Zoopraxiscope. But now the patent examiner became hung up on Le Prince's sixteen lenses, and rejected this application yet again, notifying the Frenchman that the ferrotyper Simon Wing had already patented multiplex photography in 1868.[6]

This back-and-forth between applicant and examiner was not uncommon. The Patent Office, in truth, was loathed by most inventors. Even Edison, arguably the institution's greatest beneficiary, frequently railed against it in the press, complaining of what he felt was unfair treatment on its part. *Scientific American*—owned by Munn and Beach—had in the past denigrated examiners as "scientific men, without practical experience in mechanics,"[7] men "who never see anything new—who are always prone to regard one device as but the mechanical equivalent of another."[8] It was also clear the patent examiners, many of whom were trained academically, were struggling to keep up with the pace of technological change in the latter decades of the nineteenth century. As early as 1849 Munn and Beach had appealed in the pages of *Scientific American* for "a widening of the field of decision respecting what is new."[9]

Even after a patent was granted, inventors found a way to grumble about the lack of protections the sought-after document offered. Holding a patent granted you a legal monopoly, it was true, but in a way a patent exposed its owner more than it protected him: once accepted, a patent's contents became public, all secrecy dispelled. It was a roadmap for copycats.

"I have lost all faith in patents, judges, and everything relating to patents,"[11] Edison was alleged to have said, but the truth is he kept not only filing for his patents but litigating forcefully in court to protect them. Inventors undermined the validity of patents in general while simultaneously defending their own tooth and nail, often at great expense.

Le Prince's patent innovated on Du Mont's—whose contraption had never been realistic, with a single drum that lacked the tension that would keep each frame flat and still for exposure; and on Muybridge's—whose devices could not reproduce motion from a single point of view, or project the images he collected without their being painted or otherwise transplanted first; and on Wing's—whose photographic camera was built with multiple lenses not for the purposes of capturing movement but simply to collect several exposures on a single base plate. The manner in which Le Prince was combining the elements—the fast-moving, flexible photographic base; the multiple lenses for a unified point of view—was beyond innovative. But the patent examiners returned only to the fact that a version of each of these parts—in isolation—had already previously been thought of or used in other photographic devices. Louis could either gut his patent and see it granted, or stand his ground and, more likely than not, see himself indefinitely rejected on various technical grounds. The choice was unpleasant, but as the days passed, and as his rewritten applications kept being rejected, he found himself at an impasse.

Winter turned to spring, and Louis had still not decided what to do next.

Le Prince had always been meticulous. Hard work and a classical education had made him demanding. An artist's temperament fostered in him a tendency to perfectionism. He threw himself into everything—Whitley

Partners, Lincrusta Walton, the institution's deaf and mute children's pageant, Poilpot's panorama—with unflagging commitment. Over the years these propensities took their toll, especially when, as was the case with Whitley and Lincrusta Walton, Louis's obsessive efforts had ended in failure.

In 1886 and 1887, as he wrestled with the Patent Office, Le Prince appears to have been filled with mistrust. He became more secretive. Recalling the day Louis showed the projector to Jack Whitley and William Guthrie, Lizzie said she was surprised at how guarded her usually effusive husband had been. "I remember asking him: 'Why didn't you tell Jack and Guthrie all about what you are really attempting?' " she wrote. "And he answered very quietly: 'Just as well to wait until it is through.' "[12] On that same day, she said, she watched Louis demur as Jack "begged [him] to put his invention on the market at once as a toy, as all the others did later."[13] Lizzie noted this new aloofness in her husband, a desire to maintain "absolute freedom from noise . . . until he found" his own preferred path forward.

And if he'd been considering Thomas Edison as the exception to that rule—the only man for whom he'd sacrifice a little "freedom" in an attempt to get above all the noise—then Louis must have begun to have doubts about that, too. Lizzie and Jack recalled Louis telling Guthrie, "I've been considering taking it [the motion picture camera] to Mr. Edison"[14] in late 1886, probably in the hope Guthrie, through Seward, would offer to make an introduction. By the following year, according to his wife, Louis had decided to go see Edison himself. He was "actually on his way" to the Edison Illuminating Company building on Fifth Avenue to request an audience when, Lizzie said, "he met a friend who strongly advised the contrary."[15] Shaken, Louis returned uptown.

The story, as told by Lizzie, does strain credulity. It's serendipitous in its circumstances and momentous in its consequences. It is not *impossible* for it to have happened, however—life has a way of contributing its unlikely plot twists. New York was a smaller town, then, and Louis's frame of mind in those months lent itself to suspicion and indecision.

If he *did* meet a friend on the way downtown, and the friend had told him to steer clear of Edison, he may have heeded that advice, inaction seeming safer than any gamble.

And there were plenty of people who had trusted Edison and came to regret it. Nikola Tesla had left Edison's employ, he said, after Edison reneged on paying him a promised bonus. George Westinghouse, Edison's rival and Tesla's new employer, frequently and publicly complained of Edison's underhanded tactics and public dishonesty. And then there was Charles Sumner Tainter, an associate of Alexander Graham Bell's who, with Bell's cousin Chichester, had invented an audio recording device they called the graphophone. Tainter and Bell had approached Edison to propose a partnership, offering him a 50 percent stake in their company. Not only did Edison turn them down, but he accused Tainter and Bell of copying his phonograph, labeling them "pirates" who were attempting to steal his invention. He took them to court and smeared them in the press, crippling Tainter and Bell's American Graphophone Company until they were forced to sell it to venture capitalists. Tainter harbored a bitter grudge against Thomas Edison for the rest of his life. "Thomas A. Edison can go to Hell!" he barked once. "He hasn't got anything that he didn't steal from me."[16]

Whoever warned Le Prince—if the chance meeting Lizzie describes happened as it did—made an impression. Indeed, "for all his publicly claimed genius," wrote Le Prince's biographer, Christopher Rawlence, "Edison was known, even at that time, for less than entirely scrupulous behaviour when it came to other men's inventions."[17]

A new urgency took over. With his patent still pending, Le Prince redoubled his efforts—not just to receive legal protection as quickly as possible, but to complete his camera and projector and have them ready to be brought to market as soon as the patents came through. He could stay in New York and continue work on the devices alone, or he could take Joseph Whitley up on his offer, extended in his recent letter to Lizzie, to use the foundry and resources in Leeds. The latter option would mean leaving his family behind—it made no sense to uproot

Lizzie and the children yet again, when Louis foresaw the work taking only a matter of months—but it would relieve many of the pressures on them, as Whitley had suggested he would contribute to paying for the research and development of the motion picture devices. Jack would also be in London preparing for the opening of his exhibition, and Louis still entertained the possibility of premiering his moving images, if he was ready on time, on its grounds at Earl's Court. Perhaps he could be the first person to film Buffalo Bill and his Wild West show, one of the potential subjects he had included in the list he had drawn up the year before.

Staying in New York would mean less upheaval for his wife and young children, but it would take longer to finish the camera and projector. Le Prince, obsessive by nature and fearful someone might now pass him just as he was approaching the finish line, made his choice. After being warned about Edison, Louis told Lizzie he wanted to go to England "at once."[18] He made all the rational arguments: "He would have special facilities," Lizzie wrote, and her father's help "promised also to clear our financial horizon, which . . . loomed rather darkly."[19]

But she knew her husband; she sensed he had other reasons for the sudden change of plans. At some point in their conversations, she recalled, her husband became very serious. All he said, "very quietly and gravely," was "that he had heard of 'queer' things, and that he might be safer away."[20]

KEEPING CLEAR
OF THE SHARKS

1887

I f Le Prince harbored any doubts about leaving for Europe, a family tragedy soon accelerated his decision-making: his mother was ill.

Elizabeth Boulabert Le Prince, by then seventy-one, had been a widow for over three decades. She had moved to Paris in the late 1860s, into a five-story Lutetian limestone building she owned at 6 rue Bochart de Saron in the Ninth Arrondissement north of the Seine, a quiet, elegant residential street completed in 1860 as part of Haussmann's "renovation" of the French capital. She lived there with her brother Pierre, two years her senior. Sometime in 1887, Louis received word that her health had badly deteriorated and that it was not assured she would make it through.

Louis's older brother, Albert, was already grappling with grief of his own. On the night of January 20, 1887, around eleven o'clock, his wife, Gabrielle, had died at home. She was ten days shy of her thirty-eighth birthday. No cause is specified in the ledger recording her passing. Gabrielle's death left Albert with three children to look after—the youngest, Ernest, was only nine—and in a complicated financial situation to untangle. When he and Gabrielle married, nearly twenty years earlier, he'd been an engineer for the Charentes railway, a section chief fresh out of the École Centrale des Arts et Manufactures, still living with his mother in Paris. Gabrielle, on the other hand, was the daughter of Alfred Bénigne Chevrot, a successful Dijon architect. Himself the son of an upper-middle-class lawyer, Chevrot had designed Dijon's hospices and renovated the seventeenth-century Hospital Saint-Laurent. He taught at the École des Beaux-Arts and was a member of the Dijon Aid Society, and enjoyed abundant personal wealth. He was an imposing, opinionated figure, and he loved Gabrielle fiercely: she was all he had left of his one-year marriage to his first wife, who had passed away weeks after giving birth to her. When it came to her marrying Albert, the old architect was circumspect. Not only did he bring Albert into his firm as an employee, but he arranged a very particular marriage contract for the young couple.

There was no mystery as to which of the young newlyweds was wealthier. Albert, as recorded in the marriage agreement, owned only his clothes, personal effects, and some "mathematical instruments for personal use,"[2] in addition to which he held some stock in various railway companies, valued in total at just over 23,000 old francs. Gabrielle, for her part, declared "jewellery and gemstones"; "her piano, music books and notebooks, diamonds"; "real estate also for personal use, valued at ten thousand francs"; and an inherited three-eighths share of a family house at the Château de Vergy. Her trousseau included 3,000 francs of "clothes, linens, furniture" and another 3,000 francs in cash. As a final wedding gift, her father gave her a home at 40 rue Berbisey, in the heart of Dijon, consisting of two adjoined buildings valued at 34,000 francs.

It was agreed the marriage would be, for practical purposes, a *communauté réduite aux acquêts*—a household in which Albert and Gabrielle would remain sole owners of the property they each brought into the marriage, sharing ownership only of purchases made and income received as a couple. A complex set of clauses determined what the surviving spouse would be entitled to call his or her own in the event of one of their deaths.

And now Gabrielle had died—prematurely and unexpectedly. The home Albert lived at with the children—the gifted house at 40 rue Berbisey—moved into Chevrot family ownership, as part of an inheritance to be managed for Gabrielle's son and daughters until they all came of age. A retired banker by the name of Antoine Ernest Dunoyer was installed by the family council—controlled by the Chevrot family—as the trustee in charge of the children's accounts. The process was bruising. Albert and the Chevrots faced off in several meetings with notaries and lawyers to determine how to split the "community" of goods he and Gabrielle had acquired together. Albert had sold all the railway shares he'd owned on his wedding day, but it was agreed he could keep a share of the family cash equal to their value on that date. He was given first choice of any furniture or movable object in their home, excluding paintings and works of art, up to a value of 2,000 francs, the rest to return to the Chevrot family or to his children. Out of those children's accounts, 3,000 francs was paid out to their widowed father, to reimburse him for "various large repairs" undertaken over the years at the family home.[3] By the time this was all agreed Albert would be cash rich—if asset poor—but during the months it took to unentangle his property from his wife's, his financial situation must have been dire.

It was during these months that his and Louis's mother fell ill.

Louis made plans to sail to Paris. He would continue working on his camera and projector while there. When that situation had run its course—it's unclear whether Louis and Albert still hoped their mother might recover—he would proceed to Leeds, where he would use the Whitley foundry and resources to perfect the machines and build prototypes. He would file European patents to provide him with protection outside the United States. Lizzie and the children could join him there for a summer holiday, after the school year had ended, and if he hadn't finished work by then, it would certainly be only a matter of a few more weeks until he rejoined them in New York anyway.

He informed Munn & Co. of his plans and asked them to keep pushing Washington to approve his US patent. All that mattered was to secure the patent without bastardizing the description of the devices so much it would leave Le Prince vulnerable to imitators. He must make sure, in Joseph Whitley's words, to "keep clear of the sharks."

Letters were sent ahead to friends and family in Europe. Early on the morning of April 28, 1887, the pale dawn flecked with rain showers, Louis made his way down to Battery Park and boarded a steamship for the seven-day journey east to Liverpool.

Lizzie watched him depart with a heavy feeling in her chest. She wished she could be optimistic, or hopeful, but she didn't. Instead, she wrote, she felt "heartsick and depressed."[4]

PART FOUR

THE FIRST FILM

1887–1888

THE STARTING POINT
OF ALL MOTION

May–August 1887

L e Prince landed at Liverpool on May 5 and traveled north to Leeds by rail that same evening, arriving at six o'clock hungry and harried.[1] The next morning Joseph Whitley, who was attempting to restart his business, took him on a tour of the new Whitley Partners foundry, and then Louis dropped in on Richard Wilson at William Williams, Brown, and Company, before proceeding down to Briggate to peruse the shelves at Harvey, Reynold & Co., chemists who also dealt in surgical tools, scientific instruments, "pure chemicals," and "optical lanterns, slides, and photographic apparatus."[2] By May 9 or 10 he was traveling down to London, accompanied by his in-laws, to be present at the opening of Jack Whitley's American Exhibition. The city—in spite of the euphoria brought on by the celebration of Queen Victoria's Golden Jubilee—was as dark and chaotic as ever. The national economy had barely a pulse and unemployment was high; people without homes slept on benches on the Thames Embankment, under trees in Hyde Park, and out in the open in Trafalgar Square. The country, wrote Henry James, was "grossly materialistic," and a reckoning—"a blood-letting," as he put it—was inevitable.[3]

The American Exhibition, in its own way a celebration of materialism, had just opened. Jack Whitley—exhausted by the work and anxious for the fair's success—allowed himself a brief pause that night to have supper with his family. This rest, too, was short lived. Halfway through dinner, a Queen's Messenger arrived, "bearing," according to Lizzie Le Prince, after Louis's retelling, "Queen Victoria's commands to reserve the Exhibition for her on the next day."[4] A visit from Victoria would legitimize the event and ensure its success—even though it meant dinner would have to be cut short. In the darkness Jack returned to Earl's Court, "and through the night wires hummed and messengers hurried" to prepare the grounds for Her Royal Highness's visit. As dawn broke, Jack's couriers were waiting on the doorsteps of London's best florists, clutching orders urgently needing to be filled. Jack's reputation, his very livelihood, depended on getting the day right.

The queen arrived in the afternoon. Londoners cheered her carriage and pair—flanked by two outriders—all the way from Buckingham Palace to West Brompton. Victoria had mostly stayed out of the public eye since the death of her husband, Prince Albert, twenty-six years earlier, and it was an unexpected thrill for Le Prince—and for many British subjects—to have the chance to see her up close again. Whitley and the rest of his organizing committee, in top hat and tails, were waiting at the exhibition gate for the queen to descend from her carriage, Princess Beatrice and Prince Henry of Battenberg close behind. Jack's daughter Dorothy, thirteen, stepped forward, a bouquet of exotics clutched tightly in one hand. Dorothy's other hand was held by her uncle, Louis, whom Jack had asked to lead her forward. Reaching the queen, Dorothy curtsied and handed over the flowers, prompting the queen, as the Whitleys remembered it, to turn to the seventy-three-year-old Duchess of Atholl, her lady-in-waiting, and comment, of Le Prince and his niece: "That is one of the handsomest men and the loveliest child I have seen!"[5]

The press was initially dismissive of Jack's exhibition—the *Industrial Review* shrugging it off as "utilitarian" and the *Times* noting that not every display was yet "in complete order,"[6] "the explanation of this," added *Lloyd's Weekly Newspaper*, "being that two vessels bearing exhibits had been wrecked"[7] coming over from America—but Victoria's rare public appearance compelled visitors from across Britain to buy tickets themselves. The fanfare over Buffalo Bill—whose face was plastered on bright posters advertising the fair all across London—also captured the country's imagination, as Jack had known it would. Over the next 151 days, nearly 2.25 million people visited the exhibition, making it a smashing, unforeseen success.

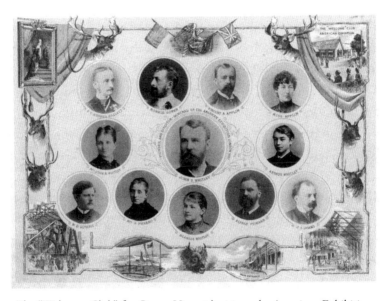

The "Welcome Club" for Queen Victoria's visit to the American Exhibition, from an album gifted to the queen by John Whitley. Jack's photograph is in the center, with his wife and son on either side; Blanche (known as "Dorothy" by her family) is directly below. (William F. Cody archive)

Just hours after the queen's visit, Le Prince was on his way to France.[8] Paris, unlike London, was bright and confident, entirely changed from the defeated, besieged ghost town of 1871. The relentless construction initiated by Napoléon III was finally slowing down, and Haussman's airy boulevards could finally be taken in in all their symmetrical glory, the polar opposite of London's higgledy-piggledy maze of dark alleys and dead ends. At night the whole city glittered like a jewel, an assortment of traditional candles, blazing yellow gaslights, blinding white arc lamps, and a few incandescent lights, brought to the Opéra Garnier in 1881 by Thomas Edison. In the Champ de Mars, the engineer Gustave Eiffel was beginning to erect the iron legs of the tower that would forever bear his name: the World's Fair was coming back to Paris, due to open in the spring of 1889. *Optimisme* was the order of the day.

But not at 6 rue Bochart de Saron. Le Prince found his mother frail and bed-bound. In addition to looking after her, he spent as much time as he could working on his camera and projector. "Since my last [letter] I have been absolutely in a turmoil," he wrote Lizzie. On May 18 he called on Théophile Poilpot, who was back in France, and met with machinists with a view to "preparing [those] parts of my apparatus that the facilities of Paris permit me to do—and thus make up for lost time."[9] The next day he met with a patent agent, visited the Directoire des Brevets, and began drafting a French description of his camera and projector.

He still thought a sixteen-lens camera using a large-format glass plate was the best way to capture the two to three dozen images per second he needed to re-create movement. He would test it in Paris, with a view to being ready to build final devices when he returned to Leeds. The work left him with precious little spare time. He wrote to Lizzie every week, almost religiously, opening every missive with affection—most often, "*ma bien chérie.*" Whenever possible he sat with his mother, who was not entirely enthusiastic about her son's obsession. A few months earlier Jack Whitley and his wife, Ellen, in France on exhibition business, had called on Elizabeth to check on her health, and updated her on the "photographic work" that had been "ripening in [Louis's] mind for the last twenty years" and finally coming to fruition. Elizabeth was pragmatic. "Let us hope he may not have worked in vain," she wrote Lizzie after Jack's visit.[10] "In any case it is no use to worry, for that helps nothing. If it is all tiring him too much," she suggested, "let him sell it and have other people do their share."

Whether Elizabeth encouraged Louis to cut his losses when she saw him in person, or whether he convinced her the toil would be worthwhile, is unknown. Sometime in those first few days she felt strong enough to go out, and so she and her son made their way north, up the hill to the top of Montmartre, where she kept a small garden.

Elizabeth took joy in her little allotment of flowers and fruits. "It is less than our painting-room but it has more plants than *our* whole garden," Louis wrote Lizzie.[11] He watched as his mother tended to the delicate greenery, forgetting her ailments for a short while. When the sky grew overcast and the air turned cool, they made their way slowly back down the hill toward the warmth of home.

"I am still here," Louis wrote his wife again on May 27, "having found a mechanic and electrician who is fitting my lenses that I count on trying in a few days with a large plate, which will decide the practical possibility of my work."[12] The next day Elizabeth Le Prince died, with her son and her brother by her side. When the city clerk, filling out the certificate of death, asked him for his profession, Louis, unsure or unwilling to explain what consumed his days, gave him the answer he'd given for most of his adult life. He was an *artiste peintre*.[13]

His mother's death, though somewhat expected, was a bitter loss to Louis. But it also cut any ties of obligation Le Prince had in Paris. He could leave for Leeds and finish his work—and, perhaps most crucially, it left him with funding with which to complete that work: Mme Le Prince's will, upon reading, revealed that she had left her sole substantial possession—the building at 6 rue Bochart de Saron—to her two sons to share.

Albert traveled north from Dijon immediately. Lizzie booked passage to Europe as soon as the news reached New York. Adolphe, fifteen, accompanied her, leaving Phoebe Eadson and the oldest of the Le Prince children, seventeen-year-old Mariella, in Manhattan to look after the younger children.

Lizzie and Adolphe traveled the longer, cheaper way—New York to Paris via the "picturesque route" of Newhaven and Dieppe. They missed Mme Le Prince's funeral in Voulangis, which took place two days after her death, but they were in Paris by late June when, on a balmy Wednesday morning, they traveled with Louis, Albert, and their uncle Pierre Boulabert to the offices of a notary, Adrien Marc, in Villemomble, a suburb east of Paris,[14] to settle the matter of their inheritance. No detailed inventory of their mother's possessions had been done after her passing, and Pierre did not challenge Elizabeth's will: all that was left to discuss was how the two brothers would handle their ownership of the building on rue Bochart de Saron. Louis needed cash, and he had little interest in sharing the rights to a Paris home he would never live in, and so it seems either he or Albert suggested that Louis sell his share of the building to his brother.

It took them a couple of weeks to negotiate the particulars, during which Louis, Lizzie, and Adolphe stayed with Pierre at Bochart de Saron. On July 15 they were all back in Maitre Marc's offices to draw up the papers, with a third meeting on September 23 to amend details further. (Lizzie's signature is on the July document, but she was back in New York by September.) Albert agreed to buy Louis's "undivided half" of the building for a price of 60,000 francs—about $700,000 in 2021 dollars—and committed to pay the sum, in full, by July 1, 1892 at the latest, roughly a five-year window from the date of signing.[15] Pierre was still owed 20,000 francs he had loaned his sister for the original purchase of the building, a sum Albert also undertook to repay. A third party, a landlord by the name of Pierre-Louis Demaison—father of one of Maitre Marc's clerks—was put forward to lend Louis 5,000 francs, at 5 percent annual interest, that Louis would repay in 1892 when his brother had paid *him*. (The sum due Demaison, by that date, would have risen to approximately 6,380 francs.)

This was not an inconsequential amount of money. "In comparison," writes Jacques Pfend, a researcher who has studied and written about Le Prince, "the average salary for a railway switchman in 1890 was a thousand francs a year for fifteen work hours a week. A newspaper cost one sou [five centimes] . . . and a litre of wine ten centimes."[16] Five thousand francs would be more than enough to pay a workman to assist in finishing Louis's motion picture devices, enough to keep his children in school and enable his and their travel across the Atlantic when necessary. It would keep him solvent until Albert had finished wrangling with his in-laws over his wife's assets.

Louis and his wife were in complete agreement, Lizzie remembered: they must "use his inheritance for patents and improvements" to the devices.[17] Let Mme Le Prince's death—and the money she had accumulated during her lifetime—be for a purpose: they would finance the world's first-ever motion pictures.

There was work to be done. Lizzie returned to New York sometime before early August. The parting was surely painful, though there was unexpected relief: it was decided, whether at Adolphe's instigation or at Louis's request, that Adolphe Le Prince would remain in Paris with his father.[19]

A MAN WALKS AROUND A CORNER

August 1887

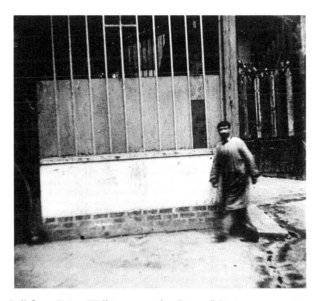

Still from "Man Walking around a Corner," Paris, summer 1887.
(National Science & Media Museum/Science Museum Group)

The US patent examiners continued to be a thorn in Louis's side. The day before he'd landed at Liverpool, he'd received word of yet another of their rejections, citing Muybridge, and they'd turned him down again later in May. "As it stands," the Washington examiner scolded, Louis's work "involves no invention, in view of the prior state of the art, shown more particularly by the patent of Muybridge already cited."[1]

The tone of Munn & Co.'s replies was, by now, equally exasperated. "Muybridge desires to produce different pictures from different points of vision," they wrote back, "while applicant produces pictures from the same point of view so that there is no interruption in the scene . . . and the effect would be natural and lifelike. Muybridge never contemplated anything of the kind."[2] In response the examiner once more denied Le Prince's submission, only this time he didn't mention Muybridge. He invoked Du Mont instead.

Munn & Co. seemed to have run out of patience for going around in circles. On June 15, 1887, they sent the Patent Office a new submission in Louis's name, informing the examiner that they had amended it to omit any and all objectionable claims. One of the items they agreed to delete was Louis's description of a camera built with one lens only.[3]

According to Lizzie, Munn & Co. had done this without Le Prince's approval. Worse, to ensure the application wouldn't be rejected on a technicality, they seemed to have faked his consent. "The signature in Le Prince's file wrapper agreeing to [the amendments]," Lizzie wrote, "is not in his own handwriting."[4]

Seemingly unaware of Munn's editing of his patent, Louis continued his experiments in Paris, now with a new partner—a Prussian mechanic by the name of Hermann-Josef Mackenstein.

Mackenstein, thirty-nine, had moved to Paris in 1872, less than eighteen months after the end of the Franco-Prussian War. He was a craftsman of an old-school sort, meticulous and hardworking, born and raised in a three-story farmhouse in the small agricultural community of Doveren on the Lower Rhine, halfway between Düsseldorf and the Dutch border. He set up as a cabinetmaker and precision mechanic in a shop on the rue des Carmes. His folding photographic camera, made in the German tradition of the *Reisekamera* ("travel camera"), which he started selling in 1884, was handsome, portable, and a reliable moneymaker; his panoramic and stereoscopic devices were equally valued by serious amateur photographers. The tiny parts inside the cameras, as delicate and precise as the inner workings of a pocket watch, were Mackenstein's specialty, and over the years he patented shutters, film roll holders, and color photography processes of his own invention.

The Prussian precision mechanic quickly became instrumental to Le Prince. It's his name—H. MACKENSTEIN, SGDC. 23 RUE DES CARMES, PARIS—that is stamped in brass on the earliest surviving Le Prince camera, a sixteen-lens device, as well as on at least one single-lens device. Louis was a clever, creative amateur, but Mackenstein was an expert with fifteen years' experience. He gutted the metal prototype from New York—fine-tuning the gearing, replacing makeshift parts with higher-quality ones, introducing new electromagnetic armatures and closers to simplify its working. It was a powerful machine. Knowing that the speed of the shutter would almost certainly rip a roll of paper film to shreds, Le Prince and Mackenstein elected to continue their trials with a glass plate, treated with gelatin emulsion.

In mid-August Le Prince and Mackenstein carried the camera to the corner of rue Bochart de Saron, where it met traffic coming off the Avenue Trudaine, and set it on its stand on the pavement. On the eighteenth, Louis sent a handful of parcels to Lizzie and the children in New York—"and within," he wrote his wife, "you will find a set of eight photos on gelatine film taken in about a quarter of a second." They were frames from the test taken just a few days earlier. "I can take thirty-two photographs, and I may take more by revolving quicker, <u>per second</u> of any moving object or objects," Louis continued; "that is quite as many as are required. The man photographed is my mechanic, he was running at the time."[5]

Almost nothing survives of this film—a handful of frames, a fraction of a second of footage, and even that only on torn paper. The original glass plate is lost, shattered or repurposed, filed away in a box in a dark corner of an attic somewhere. The moment we still have shows a man, presumably Hermann-Josef Mackenstein, "my mechanic." He takes two and a half steps as he rounds the corner out of a building—a factory or a workshop—and into the courtyard. A sliver of a carriage wheel is visible at the left edge of the frame. It's not a glamorous setting: the yard is dirty, one of the glass panes on the building wall seems to be missing. Mackenstein wears his craftsman's frock, black in patches on the front, though it is hard to tell if this is filth or shadow. His hair is dark, his chin tipped with a Mephistophelean beard. He stares straight at the lens the whole time.

The camera's ability to capture movement was the point of the trial, not any standard of aesthetic beauty. The shot isn't even level, and tilts noticeably to the left. What mattered was Mackenstein, and how the camera absorbed his walk (it cannot be described, as Le Prince did, as a run): coming out from behind the wall of the building, moving forward in depth, then laterally toward frame left. As the remaining fraction of film ends, Mackenstein is pulling up, either to stop or to change direction. Adolphe Le Prince later described his father's camera tests in Paris culminating in "a series of a man with a hammer gesticulating and moving about,"[6] which may be a description of the rest of this footage, or of another, now lost, vignette featuring Mackenstein.

The image is noisy and blotchy, though some frames are exposed so well the textures of brick and shadow in the background are discernable. The real trouble for Le Prince was in the sequence's frequency rate—the period of time that elapses between each image. He needed it to be exactly even, the gap between each frame equal to the next, for Mackenstein's walk to flow smoothly when projected. Instead—because of a misfire in the multi-lens shutter, or because of human error—the pictures were recorded at irregular intervals, resulting in inconsistent motion when played back. This was likely to happen again and again.

While shutters such as Muybridge's were fast and precise enough to engage at just the required instant, a shutter of the kind Le Prince needed—quick and smooth enough to click thirty-two times in a second in service of sixteen separate lenses imprinting on the same single plate—had never been perfected. The challenging shutter may have been *the* reason Le Prince sought out Mackenstein: the Prussian was an expert in that particular piece of photographic mechanism.[7]

And yet Louis was emboldened. This unpretentious trial had yielded the best results he had achieved so far, and he sent the frames to Lizzie to encourage her—"to show you," he wrote, "how far I have got."[8] The camera was *fast*—Louis had calculated he needed a minimum of twelve to sixteen frames a second to achieve persistence of vision, and there he found himself able to take thirty-two.[9] The emulsion was sensitive enough to record Mackenstein's walk in nothing but broad daylight, from an almost unified point of view, in the natural setting of a city street—a result leaps and bounds more realistic than Muybridge's and Marey's laboratory models moving in straight lines in front of high-contrast stationary backdrops.

The glass plate base was still unsatisfactory—Le Prince and Mackenstein would move on again to bands of Eastman's paper film—and the shutter issues needed resolving. Louis hadn't quite cracked projection either. He seems to have consulted specialists, in much the same way he had deferred to Mackenstein on issues of internal mechanics, but with less success. He wrote Lizzie, "For the second part [projection] I find I have been led astray by advisers and have to fall back to my original plan, i.e. one special light for each picture."[10] Even as he wrote, he was unenthused about his own "original plan."

And yet, when the glass plate was developed—when Mackenstein's ghostly shadow had emerged from the chemical bath—it gave images of a kind no one else in the world was known to have captured. Louis was on the brink.

"I'll keep you posted as I go," he signed off the missive to Lizzie. "I am getting nearer every day and now shall not leave it till done."

*   *   *

Headlong he rushed. Meanwhile, at his physiological station at the Parc des Princes, Étienne-Jules Marey was still photographing his birds and his gymnasts, with the help of his assistant Georges Demenÿ, a young researcher fascinated by athletes' biomechanics. Together the two men spent day after day working outdoors in the Parc, directing animal and human models in front of an outstretched black screen. Near the screen was a lookout tower, from which Marey and Demenÿ photographed birds. The two doctors were working almost exclusively with Eastman's paper film now.

Much closer to Le Prince—so close, in fact, that the two men may have passed each other on the street—was another rival. Charles-Émile Reynaud lived at 58 rue Rodier, directly around the corner from the Le Prince home on rue Bochart de Saron; it was just over a hundred-meter walk from one building to the other. Reynaud, forty-three, was perhaps the most idealistic of all the moving image pioneers—a "rather melancholy"[11] dreamer, single-minded and principled. Reynaud's father had been an engraver, his mother a schoolteacher and watercolor painter; as a boy Reynaud was homeschooled following Jean-Jacques Rousseau's philosophy: a "process of apparently autonomous discovery"[12] through which the child, rather than being taught by an authority figure, is guided to his own conclusions, through practical experience rather than books. Young Émile thus spent hours by his parents' sides, drawing and playing with tools, developing his own creative sense. Before the boy turned twelve, he was assisting his father in his workshop. At thirteen he built his first shadow puppet theater, and soon after that his first miniature steam engine. By seventeen he was taking and developing his own photographs. As Émile grew older, he continued to love machines—tinkering with them, drawing spectacle and wonder out of the right combination of tiny metal gears and parts. In 1876 he invented and patented an optical toy of his own, a zoetrope improved with tiny mirrors that reduced blur and enhanced brightness, which

Reynaud named the praxinoscope. It won an honorable mention at the 1878 Paris World's Fair.

But Reynaud was cursed with bad luck. In 1865 he'd become an assistant to Abbé Moigno, a priest and mathematician whose lectures, assisted by magic lantern, were making new scientific discoveries accessible to the public—a dream job for Reynaud, but his father died the following year, forcing him to return home to care for his mother. In 1870 he'd seen some of his illustrations published for the first time, in a scientific dictionary, only for war with Prussia to break out and for him to become a doctor's assistant, treating the wounded at Le Puy-en-Velay. Then, in 1873, Abbé Moigno called on Reynaud to join him again in Paris to assist with a series of lectures, only for the program to be quickly discontinued. Half a decade later his praxinoscope met some financial success, but not enough to make him either famous or wealthy; further modifications, including a projecting praxinoscope (a variant on the magic lantern), also failed to gain traction.

By 1887 Reynaud was married with two young sons and selling his praxinoscopes out of the workshop on rue Rodier. For the previous fifteen years, he had been working on a more ambitious version of the device, this one a humongous, double-lensed magic lantern, capable of holding up to seven hundred frames wound around two drums. His aim was to project entirely hand-drawn moving images in sequences as long as fifteen minutes—history's first animated cartoons. The machine, which Reynaud would call the Théâtre Optique (Optical Theater), was nowhere near perfect. But he had filled notebook after notebook with diagrams and ideas, and he had built and tested prototypes. He'd worked out that his drawings, to withstand the speed and pressure, would need to be created on squares of gelatin under a protective shellac coating. Most important, he'd devised a system for carrying the images through the device without breaking: perforations between every frame, pulling the pliable film forward. He'd been inspired by the sight of his penny farthing bicycle lying on its side, he said: What if he built a projector in which the images moved from one wheel or drum to the other, the same way the bicycle chain spun? Reynaud had yet to patent the machine, or to put together his first animated film—but he was less than a year away from managing both.

There is a theory of invention that argues technological advancements are culturally determined and to a certain degree inevitable—that every one of a society's discoveries lays the foundations for the next by bringing it into the realm of the conceivable. The new great innovation, as Thomas Edison often suggested, was not in the genius's mind but in the general air, waiting to be plucked by the first hand to reach it out of the many feeling for it. History bears this out: John Harrison's sea clocks and Thomas Mudge's pocket watches achieved similar levels of accuracy around the same time using different escapement mechanisms; electric telegraph systems were developed independently in the 1830s by Samuel Morse in the United States and W. F. Cooke and Charles Wheatstone in England, and a decade later Henry Fox Talbot on the one hand and the partnership of Louis Daguerre and Nicéphore Niépce on the other successfully took photographs by different methods almost at the exact same time. The telephone had been grasped at, over the course of two decades, by Alexander Graham Bell in Boston, Antonio Meucci in New York, Elisha Gray in Illinois, Johann Philipp Reis in Germany, and Charles Bourseul in France.

The road to motion pictures, in 1887, was in its endgame. Dozens of discoveries over hundreds of years—from the camera obscura and ombromanie to the discovery of silver nitrate and silver chloride, to photography, to studies of optics and flicker fusion, to the zoetrope and the magic lantern, all the way to Muybridge's instantaneous snapshots, Marey's chronophotographs, and Eastman's paper film in rolls—had dovetailed to this moment, when the invention of a machine that could capture and project genuinely lifelike moving images was no longer a pipe dream, not even just a possibility, but imminent and inescapable. Le Prince, Marey, and Reynaud were reaching for it; as was the German Ottomar Anschütz, who in March of that same year had developed what he called the Schnellseher ("Fast-Viewer"), a hand-cranked motion picture viewer using transparent chronophotographs arranged on a rotating wheel and illuminated by the spark of a Geissler tube. Anschütz struggled with some of the same issues as Le Prince—the Geissler tube's light was too weak for the projected images to be seen in any way other than through a small aperture—and would not solve these fully until 1894. But in 1887, whether they knew it or not, Le Prince, Marey, Reynaud, and Anschütz were racing each other—like explorers cleaving their separate ways through the same thick jungle, following the same partial map, hunting for a lost city of gold. As the summer turned to fall and then to winter, Le Prince had overtaken Muybridge; he was catching up to Marey. He had solved problems Anschütz and Reynaud were still grappling with and they, in turn, had made advancements Louis had yet to think of.

He was the only man in this company who had yet to be granted a moving image patent of any kind.

"INVESTIGATORS" AT WOODHOUSE LANE

January 1888

On December 22, 1887, the new US commissioner of patents, Benton Jay Hall, picked up his pen and affixed his signature to the bottom of a single-page form, addressed to Augustin Le Prince, c/o Munn & Co., New York City. The short, standardized document, typed out with spaces for the relevant details to be handwritten, read:

> Sir: Your application for a patent for an **Improvement In** *The Method of and Apparatus for Producing Animated Pictures of Natural Scenery and Life* filed *Nov. 2, 1886*, has been examined and again **ALLOWED**. The final fee, **TWENTY DOLLARS**, in the above-entitled case was received *Dec. 22, 1887*.[1]

Le Prince was by then in Leeds and staying with Joseph and Sarah Whitley at Roundhay Cottage, having wrapped up his business with his brother in France. He was feeling discouraged. "The machine is going on slowly," Louis wrote to Lizzie in early December. "It is stupefying to find the amount of forethought every detail and every point requires, and to imagine the delays required to get the required articles to be made to meet the cases as they occur."[2]

He must have received the cheering news from America—the news that he had been granted the first true motion picture patent anywhere in the world—sometime after Christmas. Joseph Whitley was preparing for sleep late on the night of December 28 when Le Prince burst into his room, flush with excitement. After Louis had left, Whitley pulled out his pocket diary and wrote, in a crisp, exhilarated hand: "1.06am. 28 Dec. 1887."

And then:

"M. Le Prince came to my bedside and told me that 'I have done it!'"[3]

Le Prince's American patent was officially granted on January 10, 1888, and numbered 376,247. It did not cover any single-lens version of the camera. On the same day, Louis filed his application for a British patent—this one including a provision for a one-lens device. The next day, his Paris patent agents, the Cabinet Thirion, offices 95 Boulevard Beaumarchais, filed his French submission, which also described a single-lens version of the camera. As with Munn & Co. in the United States, Le Prince had chosen prestigious firms to represent him in Europe. Charles Thirion was one of France's most esteemed experts in intellectual property, and Thompson & Boult were equally established in the United Kingdom. In the coming years the firm would represent John Boyd Dunlop, inventor of the pneumatic tire, and John Logie Baird, one of the pioneers of television.

Fifteen-year-old Adolphe had followed his father back to England and, after spending Christmas in London with Jack Whitley and his children, would return to Leeds to help Louis set up a workshop. The holiday was Adolphe's first on his own or, as his father described it, his "first big journey."[4] Louis fretted and fussed, drilling his fifteen-year-old son on each step of the rail itinerary. "It will be hard to leave him," he wrote Lizzie, "but it will be for the best."

There is a lonely tone to Louis's letters over the final period of 1887. He was tired and "getting sick of these delays."[5] He took comfort in the familiar surroundings of Roundhay. "It is a great help to me to be with dear Grandpa and Grandma," he wrote Lizzie, but he missed her. He insisted he was doing the right thing being away: "Matters would be much worse in America, both for time, cost, and quality." He sent Christmas presents. For Lizzie he also picked "a little pansy just freshly bloomed in the bed on the east side of the house, a bit of jessamine from the west side, and a holly leaf, ditto." The winter had been mild in Yorkshire, with little snow. Aimée had written to Adolphe to wish him a happy Christmas and told him New York was not very cold either. "I hope that with care you will escape all those dreadful fevers and throat complaints," Louis wrote Lizzie.

"Bye bye, my darling," he signed off. "I try to keep patience and temper. You all do the same and be jolly and helpful."

To counter the melancholy, Le Prince redoubled his efforts at work. He leased a workshop space at 160 Woodhouse Lane in the industrial heart of Leeds, a fifteen-minute walk north of Park Square, where he and Lizzie had once opened the Leeds Technical School of Art. The building was adjacent to Blenheim Baptist Chapel on the corner of Blenheim Terrace, a row of flats parallel to the main road, and faced a Society of Friends meetinghouse.

It was a working-class neighborhood, the old Woodhouse Moor paved over with redbrick back-to-backs to accommodate Leeds's growing population. The shops and businesses around Louis's new workshop were family owned and varied: coach builders, surgeons, ironmongers, butchers, linen drapers, grocers and fruiterers, tobacconists and confectioners.

The expense of a lease underlined Louis's seriousness. More notable still was his hiring of an entire team of specialists to help him build the final camera and projector. He contracted with Rhodes Brothers of Wakefield, makers of machine tools, to construct new models of each device. He was so impressed with one of their employees, a twenty-nine-year-old mechanic named Jim Longley, that he convinced him to leave Rhodes and join him at Woodhouse Lane. Longley was a working-class laborer of the kind Leeds was famous for and proud of, born among the factories of Holbeck and living there still with his young wife, dedicated to self-improvement and, in the meantime, picking up work wherever he could. He had worked at the Whitley foundry for a time, along with at least one of his cousins, and Joseph Whitley's factory manager, a Mr. Horsman, vouched for his work ethic and trustworthiness, as had Richard Wilson.[6]

Longley quickly became Le Prince's right-hand man. He was a skilled metalworker and, like Mackenstein before him, had a flair for building reliable moving mechanisms. Aside from his work at Rhodes Brothers, in 1885 Longley had invented and patented the world's first coin-operated ticket machines, which were later installed on all Leeds omnibuses, at the city's Leamington Athletic Ground, and at theaters and music grounds across England, including the Theatre Royal in London's Haymarket and the Gaiety Theatre on the Strand. He was also working on an automated matchbook dispenser. These devices were examples of a set of components advancing an item (a ticket, the matches) regularly and reliably to a desired outcome—as Louis needed his film base to do inside both the camera and the projector. All the same, Le Prince never fully confided in Longley. Lizzie, who met the mechanic on a later summer visit to Leeds, wrote that "his own fellow workmen respected him highly," but also that, while honest and loyal, Longley was also known to be affable and perhaps overly trusting—the kind of man who "might talk too much."[7]

Five doors down from the shop on Woodhouse Lane were the premises of William Mason & Sons, joiners. The Masons were Quakers and regularly met for worship at the Society of Friends across the way. The men of the family had been carpenters for at least three generations, and the Mason household, according to a descendent, was "austere"[8] and self-disciplined, in keeping with the values of their faith. One of Mason's sons, Frederic, was working in the timber yard one day when Le Prince walked in, looking for him. Fred was a creative, industrious young man, gifted with a saw, lathe, and plow plane, and also much admired in his family for his watercolor painting. Mason later told the *Yorkshire Evening*

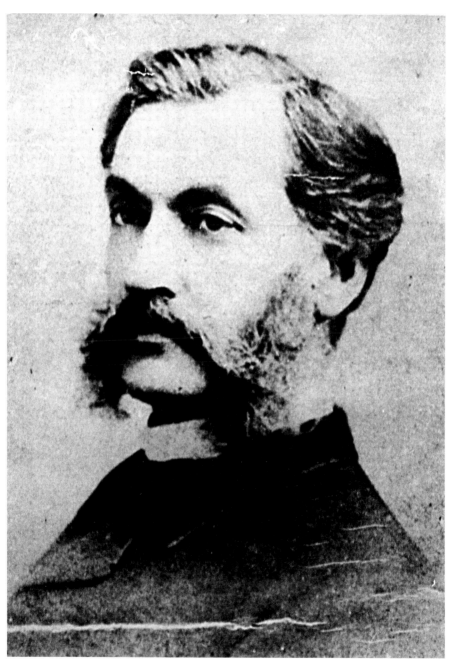

Louis Le Prince, c. 1880. (*Courtesy of Laurie Snyder*)

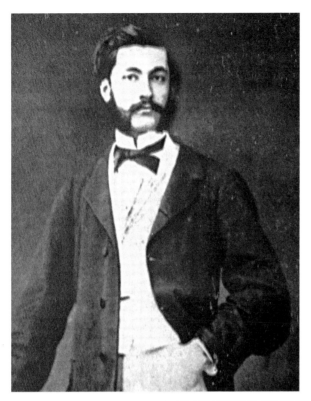

Louis Le Prince, early 1860s.
(*Courtesy of Laurie Snyder*)

Louis Le Prince, c. 1866.
(*Courtesy of Laurie Snyder*)

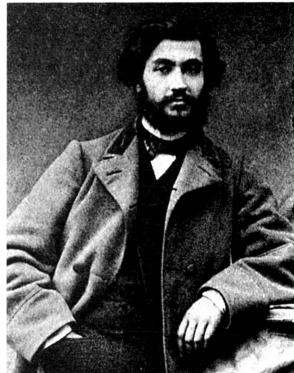

ENGINEERING INVENTIONS.

A rail joint has been patented by Mr. George H. Williams, of Nashville, Tenn. This invention covers a novel construction and combination of parts to secure a perfectly rigid joint, as solid as the rail itself, in which the jarring and joling of cars passing over the joint is prevented and the wear of the meeting points reduced to a minimum.

A railway tie has been patented by Mr. Joseph W. Smith, of Mount Carmel, Penn. The invention covers a novel construction and combination of parts to provide a secure fastening for the rails, and which, while holding the rails securely in position, will be sufficiently elastic to admit of rapid traveling without injury to the rolling stock or discomfort to passengers.

A car coupling has been patented by Mr. Charles G. Crouse, of Sun Prairie, Wis. The coupling hook is automatically thrown into engagement with a link or bar brought to bear against it, and is uncoupled therefrom by means of a mechanism connected to the hook and extending to the car, the device being also applicable for coupling a pole or shafts to a carriage.

A car coupling has been patented by Mr. Jonathan Hendenhof, of Evelyn, West Va. By this invention the drawhead of the car is provided with a vertically swinging member, having at its free end a downwardly projecting coupling lug, which, after the entrance of the coupling link, may be locked against upward movement by a block sliding in the top of the drawhead.

A mechanical movement has been patented by Mr. James F. Hanley, of Charleston, S. C. A double crank shaft is combined with a vibratory lever pivoted coincidently with the centered axis of the shaft, the lever being connected upon opposite sides of the shaft by links and rocking arms, and also connected with a rotary shaft, making a compact, evenly balanced arrangement of parts to facilitate running at high speed, and apply power in both directions.

AGRICULTURAL INVENTIONS.

A cotton chopper has been patented by Mr. William T. Clark, of Elberton, Ga. This invention covers a novel construction and arrangement of parts whereby, as the main wheel revolves while the machine is being drawn forward, a gear is operated to work a chopper with revolving knives, but such gear...

pecially adapted for the water supply pipe of a locomotive, and is designed to filter the water before it passes to the injector, and also to provide means for preventing the cock from freezing up in cold weather, and for quickly and conveniently cleaning it.

A washing machine has been patented by Mr. George F. Dunning, of Deep Water, Mo. It is designed to afford a simple and effective machine, to be operated with economy of time and labor, and is arranged to give easy access to all its parts for handling the clothes or washing fluid, and for cleaning the machine when the work is finished.

A liquid measuring faucet has been patented by Mr. Herman M. Nye, of Corydon, Ind. It is a combined supply and discharge faucet, in connection with an intervening reservoir, on which is marked a measuring scale, with various novel details, making a faucet whereby liquids may be measured as drawn from a cask or receptacle.

A combination tool has been patented by Mr. James Angus, of St. Catharines, Ontario, Canada. The body of the tool is of malleable iron or steel, and it is made of few and simple parts, to be used as a saw set, stove cover lifter, pot hook, can perforator and can opener, screw driver, corkscrew, tack puller, wrench, and a sad iron holder or plate stand.

A method of and apparatus for producing animated pictures of natural scenery and life has been patented by Mr. Augustin Le Prince, of New York City. Combined with a photo-camera and stereopticon adapted to show pictures in the order and time in which they were taken, in quick succession, on a finely ground plate glass, to produce the effect of the objects themselves in motion.

A carburetor has been patented by Mr. François J. Lottammer, of Paris, France. Combined with a compressed air reservoir and its supply pipe is a carbureting chamber within the reservoir, a valved pipe leading from the reservoir into the chamber near its bottom, a hydrocarbon receptacle surrounding the chamber, a heating chamber, and various other novel features.

An automatic device for shutting water cocks, etc., has been patented by Mr. James W. Brook, of Lynchburg, Va. This invention covers a novel combination and arrangement of parts whereby dripping water, as it freezes in cold weather, will operate a balanced mechanism to close a valve in the service pipe, or the device may be used to open or close a pipe...

are treated by themselves, and introduce the subject of molecular physics. Here Professor Osborne Reynolds' new and celebrated experiments in distancy are described in science, so that any child of intelligence can perform them successfully. Capillarity is fully treated, some entirely new examples and experiments being presented. The illustration of the constitution of a water drop, and the formation of bubbles of metallic mercury, are two specially interesting experiments. Soap bubbles come next, and an exhaustive series of illustrations of the phenomena of films, all performed with almost no apparatus, except a few pieces of wire, affords probably the fullest treatment of the subject accessible. Formulæ for various soap bubble solutions are collected and given here. Heat, sound, and light follow, with a quantity of experiments, and a chapter on scientific lecturing closes the work. In this last portion the suggestion is made that science lectures should be made a feature of home amusement, so as to take the place of charade and dramatic performances. This certainly opens up a new field for the energies of the young lover of science. The work is beautifully bound in ornamental cloth gilt, and is very fully illustrated with nearly one hundred cuts, and has an extensive table of contents and index. It is emphatically what its title indicates, a manual of experiments. The publishers send free to all who apply by letter, a large illustrated circular, giving the full scope of the work, with samples of the cuts. It will be supplied by mail post free to any address by Munn & Co. or by the publishers on remittance of the price.

SCIENTIFIC AMERICAN BUILDING EDITION.

JANUARY NUMBER.

TABLE OF CONTENTS.

Special.

AN UNPUBLISHED AND UNRECORDED RECORD.

"Really, how well you look! You are much stouter, and look ten years younger than when I saw you a few years ago. Then I did not think you were long for this world." "No," my friend replied, "four years ago I little expected to be in the land of the living at this time. It had for many years seemed unavoidable that I should have a sick spell in the latter part of January. So regularly had this been the case that my family looked for it. Four years ago an attack of pneumonia in January was followed in February by an attack of neuralgia of the heart. So violent and sudden was the attack, that although within forty rods of my house I was unable to reach it, and was carried into a neighbor's house bleeding. I soon rallied and was carried home. No life succeeded by two lighter attacks. After recovering so I could be about, I was taken down with three successive attacks of renal calculi. Recovering from these, I was prostrated with a long siege of diarrhœa, from which the attending physician had little hope of my recovery. I had little strength left; little vitality; recuperative powers seemed gone; felt completely prostrated. No life, no ambition, no power. I then commenced the Home Treatment. In a few weeks I was able to try work again, although quite feeble and not able to endure severe or much labor. I resorted to the Compound Oxygen more regularly, and to my surprise all the old bad feelings gradually disappeared. Life assumed a different aspect. Strength and the elasticity of youth in a great measure returned. And now, though of threescore and four years, I feel younger, brighter, and more active than I did twenty years ago. To Compound Oxygen I attach the credit; and I would recommend all chronically afflicted to try it. Tell all such for me that it will be greatly to their interest if they will call at the office of Drs. Starkey & Palen, 1529 Arch Street, Philadelphia Pa., and get their advice upon their special case, which is given free.

A volume of two hundred pages on "Compound Oxygen—Its Mode of Action and Results," will be mailed free to all on receipt of address.

Business and Personal.

The charge for insertion under this head is One Dollar a line for each insertion; about eight words to a line. Advertisements must be received at publication office as early as Thursday morning to appear in next issue.

A Link Belt Testimonial
from...

Announcement of Louis Le Prince's patent in *Scientific American*, January 28, 1888, p. 58. Thomas Edison read the magazine religiously, and in turn he was the editors' favorite subject. His name appears five times in this issue alone, all on the subject of electricity. (Scientific American)

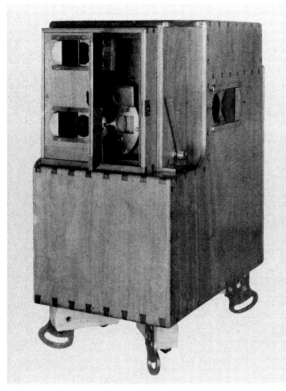

The front and back of Le Prince's single-lens camera, built in 1888 and described as the "Mark II," as it is considered to be the second single-lens camera he built. It is the camera thought to have been used to film *Roundhay Garden Scene* and Leeds Bridge sequence. (*National Science & Media Museum/ Science Museum Group*)

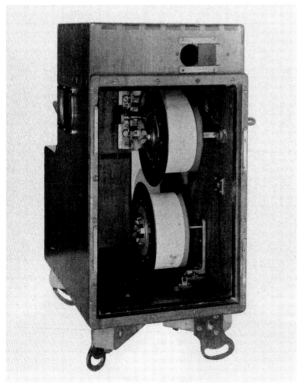

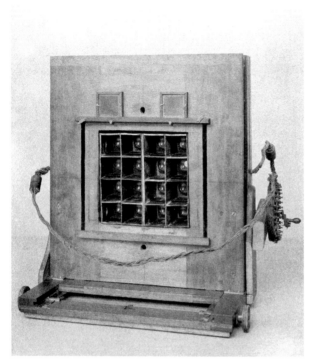

The front and back of
Le Prince's sixteen-lens
camera, built in 1887 in
Paris with Hermann-Josef
Mackenstein. (*National
Science & Media Museum/
Science Museum Group*)

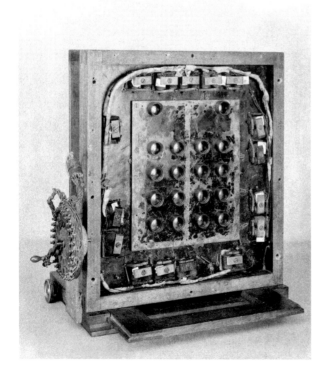

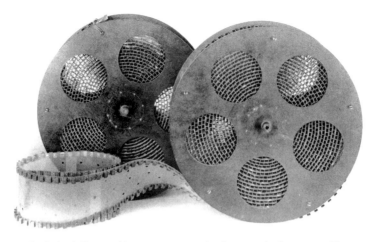

Two spools of celluloid film used by Le Prince, with silver-notched margins. These were used for developing film, not for shooting or projecting it. (*National Science & Media Museum/ Science Museum Group*)

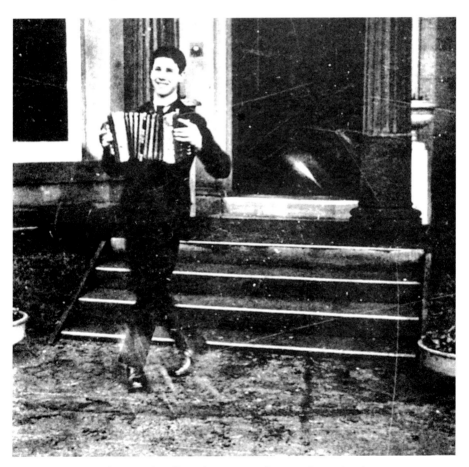

Adolphe Le Prince, from the first film taken at Roundhay, Leeds, on October 14, 1888. (*National Science & Media Museum/Science Museum Group*)

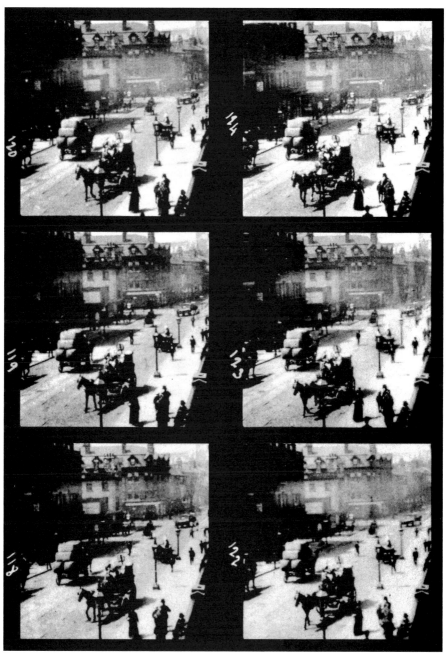

Stills from *Traffic Crossing Leeds Bridge*, filmed by Louis Le Prince in October 1888. (*National Science & Media Museum/Science Museum Group*)

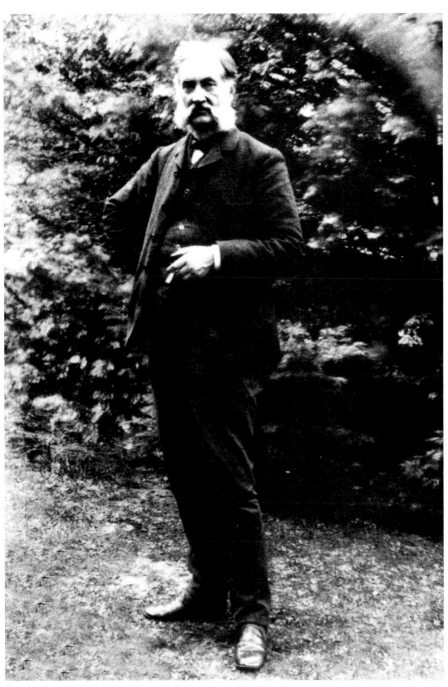

Louis Le Prince, in 1889 or 1890. (*Courtesy of Laurie Snyder*)

Post that Le Prince had "somehow discovered that I, then a youth of twenty, was extraordinarily skilled in using wood-working tools,"[9] and had come to his shop to ask him to build "all the many wood parts and all the patterns for the metal parts of [some] experimental machines," specifying that each part "must be very accurately made."[10] Not quite sure what he was getting into, Frederic, who was "near the end of my apprenticeship,"[11] agreed. He would spend close to three years working for Le Prince.[12]

That brought the team to four: Le Prince, the mechanic Longley, the woodworker Mason, and Adolphe. His son would be the only assistant Louis could totally trust—and Adolphe would have the chance to put his growing love of chemistry into practice.

The four men worked five- and six-day weeks in the Woodhouse Lane shop. Others came and went, as needed. Arthur Wood, one of Joseph Whitley's engineers, put together the heavy metalwork for the projector—"such as the pedestal, gears, chains, etc.," Wood remembered.[13] Hicks Brothers, Ironmongers, provided an oxyhydrogen lime-light for the projector.[14] When Le Prince saw the limes were not only too weak but also dangerous—the open flame blistering the film and threatening to catch fire—he ordered a set of arc lamps from the Wilson Hartnell Volt Works, a local manufacturer of dynamos and electric lights. Over the course of 1888[15] and 1889[16] several of Hartnell's engineers came by Woodhouse Lane, first to provide Le Prince with a battery-operated carbon lamp and, later, to install electrical wiring. John Vine, a local engineer, was contracted to build "special burners"[17] for the projector lights.

The Woodhouse Lane studio was a single long room on the ground floor of the terrace building, and described by one of the Hartnell men as more of a "laboratory"[18] than a workshop. Workbenches and tables were set up at one end of the space, and a "large white sheet" hung over the brick wall at the other end. The heavy camera and projector were usually sat on one of the tables, rather than on tripod stands. While Le Prince's whole team knew, in vague terms, that they were building moving picture devices, each of them was privy only to the detail relevant to his own workstation. Longley refined the moving machinery, Mason measured and cut the wooden frames in which each developed picture would be mounted before projection, Wood put together gears and chains. The Rhodes Brothers men worked away from Woodhouse Lane, building to Louis's specifications; the Volt Works men delivered their lights and installed their wires and asked intrigued questions that Longley could answer only in the most general of terms. Everything, Mason recalled, "was constructed to scale drawings made by Mr. Le Prince; he was a very clever draughtsman."[19] Only Louis saw the full picture.

And yet the younger men—Louis was nearly twenty years older than Longley, the eldest of his assistants—quickly grew fond of their manager. They were working-class Yorkshire lads, Louis a middle-class Frenchman of the previous generation, and he could be silent and secretive. But Le Prince, Mason recalled, was "most generous and considerate and, although an inventor, of an extremely placid disposition which nothing seemed to ruffle." He came to think of him, he said, as a "very extraordinary man," whose "inventive genius . . . was undoubtedly great."[20] Mason agreed—Le Prince was "genial and ingenious," he remembered, "a gentleman."[21] E. Kilburn Scott, one of Hartnell's engineers and a friend of Longley's, remembered Le Prince as "the most creative" of men, impressive in his "alert ability and adaptableness."[22] Writing later, Adolphe would describe his father and his men—including himself—not as inventors, innovators, craftsmen, or engineers, but as "investigators":[23] not high-mindedly applying some form of genius but striving to bring something undiscovered into the light. Everything "evolved from [Louis's] brain," Adolphe wrote. "He had no other experts to lighten his task; these men and myself were his tools, and sufficed."[24]

Long after everything went wrong—after Le Prince had suddenly disappeared, and the Woodhouse Lane workshop was left empty—Mason, Longley, and Scott continued to speak up, until the end of their lives, for the value of Le Prince's work, penning letters to newspaper editors and even, in Scott's case, authoring a pamphlet and lobbying elected officials. Longley, though he was in ill health later in life, offered to travel to the United States to testify on Le Prince's behalf in patent lawsuits. There would be no grudges, no recriminations; none of the collaborators ever claimed or demanded a larger part of the credit.

Day in, day out, they gathered at the Woodhouse Lane shop, starting early on the cold, damp mornings and going until teatime or later, the sky purple overhead, the surrounding pubs already crowded and noisy. They settled in to the jangling and rattling of metallic parts, the chipping and scraping of Mason's saw, the whirs and clunks of the machines as they ran, the arc lamp burning hot and bright. They got used to Le Prince's silences, and to their breaking when Louis had an idea and suddenly "opened his mind," in the words of one electrician, Walter Gee.[25]

The first stage of the work involved Le Prince rethinking the number of lenses on the camera. The sixteen used in New York and Paris had had some success in taking pictures, but they could not play smoothly in the projector. He and Longley discussed changing the number of lenses—to three, or one—and debated doing the same in the projector. Some of their early projection tests seem to have used a copy of Muybridge's photographs, as Arthur Wood, the Whitley Partners engineer, remembered the first film he saw being, "if my memory holds good[,] of a horse galloping."[26] Though Muybridge's shots had been taken with multiple cameras, they played back believably, at least in the Zoopraxiscope; by contrast, Louis's film of Mackenstein walking around a corner, though shot with one camera, skipped when projected.

Each step was slow. If a test on the projector proved successful, then the camera had to be remodeled to match. If the camera was modified, then the projector had to be redesigned to be compatible. Whenever the emulsion was changed, so did the mixture of chemicals in the developing baths. Every problem crossed off Louis's to-do list seemed to engender three more. "Each step seems to cost an infinity of tests and trials," he wrote Lizzie, "but also each step confirms me in the assurance of an early success both excellent and practical."[27]

The Sisyphean dimension of inventing was to be expected. Thomas Edison, writing to his employee Theodore Puskás, an inventor in his own right, admitted it was true even for him. To "have the right principle and [be] on the right track" was a beginning, not an end. "It has been just so in all of my inventions. The first step is an intuition and comes with a burst—then difficulties arise."[28]

Yet just as Edison couldn't stop himself prematurely declaring success, as he had with the phonograph and the light bulb, so Le Prince was unable to refrain from setting unrealistic deadlines for himself. At Christmas in 1887 Louis wrote his wife that he would have the devices ready to "take some winter views—of sleighing, skating, etc. in New York on the bright winter days," suggesting he would be back in America before spring. "I shall know latter end of next week what time may be required, and, if my present attempt is successful, I'll send a telegram." The telegram is lost, if it was ever sent, but Louis did not return to New York before the spring. Over and over, he declared the machine almost perfected, without managing to see it through. His secretive way of working—managing multiple suppliers, compartmentalizing their work—caused delays. The Rhodes Brothers were "very slow,"[29] Louis reported, and when they delivered their work he found it didn't fit the lenses to be mounted by Whitley Partners. "I am at last getting near my result," Louis announced in a letter to Lizzie in late January 1888.[30] "I have everything or nearly so in fair order and will have the test machine going tomorrow or Tuesday." He now thought he could have the system ready to unveil at Jack Whitley's upcoming Italian Exhibition, a follow-up to the American Exhibition scheduled for later in 1888, though Louis admitted "time is getting short . . . it will go like the wind." By February 2, he was admitting temporary defeat again. "I have succeeded in producing the movement of a man walking," he reported to Lizzie, "but I still have violent shocks in the machine, and I am working to reduce them. I have satisfied myself that the effect will be absolutely natural, but it is hard to pull off."[31]

Two years into his work, it was clear that capturing life, and locking it inside the heavy wooden box of the camera, was the easy part. Releasing it back into the ether, to move and dance for the viewer's entertainment, was the seemingly insurmountable challenge.

THE MUYBRIDGE
LECTURE

February 1888

E adweard Muybridge was on tour again. The aging photographer, about to turn fifty-seven, had taken to the road to promote *Animal Locomotion: An Electro-Photographic Investigation of Connective Phases of Animal Movements*, his 1887 book presenting the results of the motion studies conducted over three years at the University of Pennsylvania, 781 photographic plates spread over eleven volumes. In a departure from Muybridge's previous instantaneous photographs, this book heavily featured human beings—more than five hundred of the plates showcase men and women as subjects—though the photographs were much like the pictures of Sallie Gardner at a trot that had won Muybridge fame: all shot in a dedicated outdoor studio, in front of stark backgrounds, taken with the formal eye of a physiologist. The quality and the detail of the images were unprecedented, however, and they attracted more controversy than those of Stanford's horses: in his rigorous quest to capture human movement in the same way he had that of animals, Muybridge had had many of his models pose nude, an affront to the sensibilities of many Victorians.

Muybridge's new lecture tour ran, on and off, for nearly three years, from early 1888 to the summer of 1891, taking in cities across the United

States and Europe. Standing at the front of packed rooms with a long presentation stick in his hand, dramatically lit by the beam of light projecting his lantern slides, he challenged his audiences to embrace a new standard of realism: his own.

The junket began humbly two days after Christmas 1887, with a preview at the Pittsburgh art studio of Thomas Shields Clarke, a young up-and-coming painter and sculptor who, like Lizzie, had studied at Rodolphe Julian's Académie in Paris's Passage des Panoramas. Early reviews of *Animal Locomotion* followed, and were largely enthusiastic, and *The Century* magazine, a hugely popular outlet that had published the first excerpts of Mark Twain's *Adventures of Huckleberry Finn*, signed a contract to publish a selection of Muybridge's photographs. *The Nation* magazine, in January 1888—right around the time Le Prince's American patent was issued—even published a piece imagining the feasibility of a daring new machine, one that would combine Muybridge's photographs and Edison's phonograph to reproduce life with "startling verisimilitude."[1]

Some critics, however, challenged Muybridge's description of his pictures as "instantaneous." Members of the Photographic Society of Philadelphia gathered around a print, taken by one of their members, of "a projectile being fired from a dynamite gun," and found that the shell was "blurred about one-half its length,"[2] proof that truly *instant* photography had yet to be achieved. In truth, Muybridge had had to heavily manipulate his pictures to achieve the desired results. His battery of cameras often let him down, the electromagnetic shutters failing to go off, the glass plates fogging and cracking. In approximately 40 percent of the final plates, by the estimation of Marta Braun, a historian and an expert on Muybridge, the images Muybridge claimed were "synchronous" were in fact assemblies of images rearranged and edited, some phases of movement removed, some photographs repeated, backgrounds cropped to match.[3]

But almost no one noticed. And Muybridge, who admitted in the book's foreword only to the odd gap in a motion sequence due to "the loss of negatives during manipulation,"[4] did not make his process clear.

The press, on the whole, was admiring. No longer did anyone question his work for Leland Stanford. Few mentioned his decade-old murder trial or the verdict of justifiable homicide. In early February 1888, flush from his positive notices, Muybridge continued with two lectures in New York City. There, too, the reception was enthusiastic.

His fourth outing, on the evening of Saturday, February 25, was at the invitation of the New England Society, in Orange, New Jersey.

It had been a mild, overcast day, though in the air there was the smell of rain coming off a fresh easterly wind. In the evening six hundred local people filed into the music hall's auditorium, a standing-room-only crowd. Among them was Thomas Edison.[5]

At the back of the room were two men, and in front of the men was a table, roughly six feet by four. On top of it sat a wood-and-brass box: Muybridge's Zoopraxiscope. Its lens was pointed at the white screen hanging behind Muybridge—sixteen feet square, two feet away from the wall and four feet off the ground. On the table next to the Zoopraxiscope were a series of glass disks, sixteen inches in diameter. On each of them, the phases of a particular sequence of motion—an animal running, a man jumping—had been hand-drawn in high-contrast black and white, the illustrations traced from Muybridge's pictures but carefully elongated, because the Zoopraxiscope projector squeezed the perspective of the photographs. Connected to the Zoopraxiscope were two cylindrical canisters. One contained hydrogen, the other oxygen.

Muybridge came out onto the stage. The gaslights dimmed. The two men behind the Zoopraxiscope opened the valves on their canisters and lit a flame. The gases mixed over a bed of lime, which in turn burned and glowed "white hot,"[6] creating a portable limelight behind the lantern's projector. A circular beam of light was thrown onto the screen. The correspondent for the local Orange *Chronicle* recalled what followed.

"Mr. Muybridge began with the horse," his column read a few days later, "analysed the walk, the trot, the amble, the rack, the canter, the gallop and the jump, demonstrating the possibilities of each, and proving by comparison with photographs from Bonheur, Landseer, Meissonier and other celebrated painters not one of them had correctly drawn their subjects, in most cases the positions in the paintings being almost impossible."[7] This was much the same material as Muybridge's Stanford lectures. But soon the program moved to the new photographs. There were images of birds, and animations of a more exotic kind: lions, camels, kangaroos. Finally came the sequences of human beings. There were murmurs along the stalls as the naked bodies, male and female, flickered on the screen, the same brief motions repeated over and over again—as the Zoopraxiscope disks ran only a few seconds—or frozen still in lantern slide prints, the nudity seeming all the more indelicate for being held unmoving to be stared at.

Thomas Edison was not outraged, but intrigued. After the show, he made arrangements for Muybridge to visit his West Orange laboratory the following week.

On Monday Edison eagerly returned to work. The sky was cold and clear. He dropped in on his experimenters in their individual rooms, signed correspondence typed up for him by his private secretary, Samuel Insull, and worked on a design for a new "pyrochemical generator."[8] He drafted a six-page letter to his patent lawyers, complete with simple diagrams, detailing the progress made by W. K. L. Dickson on an iron ore–separating machine. At some point in the day, a coach was heard pulling down the path to the main building. Eadweard Muybridge had arrived.

Edison preferred to entertain guests in the library, an impressive room filled with hundreds of bound volumes—general-interest books, scientific and technical journals, a nearly exhaustive collection of recently published patents. Four fluted columns of brown stone rose to the high ceiling, and a fireplace roared on the north wall. It was a room as ostentatious as any owned by Leland Stanford.

The conversation quickly turned to moving images. Perhaps inspired by the article in *The Nation*, Muybridge suggested a collaboration. "We talked about the practicability of using the Zoopraxiscope in association with the phonograph, so as to combine, and reproduce simultaneously, in the presence of an audience, visible actions and audible words," he remembered.[9] Edison, speaking to a reporter soon after the meeting, agreed it was the photographer who had "proposed . . . [the] scheme."[10] It was a wildly ambitious concept—synchronized-sound movies decades before their time—and one neither man was ready to tackle. Edison, his public declarations notwithstanding, was nowhere near constructing a perfect phonograph, and Muybridge, by his own admission, had only "contemplated"[11] the many improvements this would require to his Zoopraxiscope. But Edison recognized a marketable idea when he heard one. Consider, he told the press afterward, an "appliance by which [one] would be able to accurately reproduce the gestures and the facial expression of [any speaker] making a speech" and then project the images "by means of a magic lantern upon a screen."[12] The examples Muybridge conjured in the meeting were compelling: they could record the great Shakespearean actor Edwin Booth playing Hamlet, or Lillian Russell singing the finest operettas, and offer all American citizens the chance to experience these in the comfort of their own home, as immediate and lifelike as if they had been there themselves. If they joined forces, the Englishman said, Edison's phonograph "could produce . . . the tones of the voice," and Muybridge "would furnish the gestures and facial expression."[13]

Edison asked Muybridge to send him the catalog of *Animal Locomotion* photographs: he was keen to order one of the books for the library, or prints of some of the plates to put on the walls. The meeting ended without a formal agreement; no immediate follow-up letters discussing a partnership exist in the West Orange archives. Muybridge returned to New York and then continued on to Boston, the next stops on his speaking tour. Edison's own plate was full. He drew his focus back to the phonograph, his ore separator, and his legal wrangling with George Westinghouse.

The idea, though, stayed with him. The real experimental work in electricity had been done; the ore-separating idea, which Edison hoped would one day revolutionize the mining industry, was still in its early stages and a long way from yielding profit. Combining moving images with the phonograph must have seemed, at the very least, a marvelous way to promote the latter device. It must have appealed to his innate curiosity, too: he was never the kind of man who could hear of a technical impossibility without longing to solve it himself.

Several things came to light in the weeks following Edison's meeting with Muybridge. He learned that Muybridge, who had patented his electromagnetic shutters and batteries of cameras, had somehow failed to patent the Zoopraxiscope itself. When the pamphlet for *Animal Locomotion* arrived in the mail, Edison ordered fifty plates, telling Insull to let Muybridge pick which fifty to send. The gigantic prints, twenty-four images to each sequence, were hung around the library, for Edison to see every time he walked in and out of his corner office. He told a New York *World* reporter that Muybridge's idea had "met with [his] approval," but that he would "perfect it at his [own] leisure."[14]

It is the last interview in which Edison acknowledged Muybridge's role in the project. From that day forth he denied that Muybridge had suggested any such "scheme," denied any discussions on those lines had taken place whatsoever, and insisted he had begun work on a motion picture device a year earlier, in 1887.[15]

He never saw Muybridge in person again.

HAGGARD MILES OF HALF-BURIED HOUSES

March 1888

A dreadful blizzard hit New York City in March, burying the city under twenty-two inches of snow over three days. The pilot boat captains at Sandy Hook were the first to see it coming. They felt it in the air—a mass of cold Arctic air from the north coming to meet an equally powerful system of warm air roaring up from the Gulf of Mexico. The two forces met, hard, crashing and intermingling to give birth to the "Great White Hurricane." The winds shifted and roared. The water rippled. Standing on their small wooden vessels, the sailors felt the soft rain turn to snow, the flakes sharp as they hit their faces, like so many razor blade cuts. Out at sea, fifteen-foot waves had already turned larger ships over.

Overnight, from a Sunday to a Monday, the whiteout battered the city. Eighty-mile-per-hour winds howled down the avenues, ripping down telegraph and electric wires, the dangling copper webs live with deadly current. Gas lines froze. Fifty-foot snowdrifts pushed against the walls of buildings, blocking second- and third-story windows. Two hundred people died, many of them found only days later, when the snowbanks melted. The thaw brought flooding. The torn electric wires caused fires.

Men in snowshoes ventured out on salvage missions. At Castle Garden, exhausted families overwhelmed the shipping offices. They screamed as they were told the steamers out in the Long Island Sound, those on which their loved ones were passengers, had been wrecked or sunk.

Nature reminded the city how helpless it could make it, no matter how miraculous the telephone and the electric bulb were. It hard turned the metropolis into a "sepulture," the New York *Herald* later wrote, and its civilized streets into a "ghostly . . . dark wilderness": "so white, strange, picturesque and grandly terrible as the ugly sky frowned upon the pulseless, haggard miles of half-buried houses."[1]

Lizzie Le Prince and the children stayed indoors through the storm. There was no way to get a letter or cable to Europe to let Louis know they were safe, though it would have been unnecessary: for the same reason private communications couldn't make it *out* of New York, the people of Leeds did not even learn of the horror that had hit America's Eastern Seaboard until much later in the week.

On March 18, Louis, still unaware of the blizzard, wrote his wife that he was canceling a planned return to New York in the spring. "I'm afraid I shall not be coming for some time," he apologized, "'tis hard, for I long to see you all. . . . The machine is progressing—I mean the large projector—but every step is slow and wants personal watching."[2] The "large projector" was fifteen feet long and twelve feet high, Fred Mason later estimated, as Louis attempted to reduce the vibration and breakage during projection with larger parts and heavier stabilizers. Perhaps a cabinet, bigger than the man operating it, was more realistic than a tabletop or tripod-propped box. It would prove to be a failure, though Louis did not know that yet.

"I do not want to raise your expectations too much, though I understand that after such a length of time you must be very impatient—and so am I," Louis wrote his wife.[3] "I have had very difficult problems and experiments and got through them all. . . . It cannot be long now—tho' from past experience I cannot tell to a week or two—something unforeseen often turns up, and means more changes."

Lizzie believed in her husband's work—she wrote later that "as [an] artist, scientist, and mechanician, he had the trained eye, hand, and brain needed to bring into harmony every phase of his invention"[4] and he "knew the dramatic value of his invention."[5] But, in the same recollections, she alluded repeatedly to how difficult she had found the years 1887 to 1889—her sadness when Louis had left, her struggle with so much "unforeseen waiting,"[6] her exhaustion from days spent teaching "four to five hundred pupils a week in the school for the deaf and elsewhere; and writing for art magazines until far into the night, to make ends meet; and incidentally mothering and schooling our five active boys and girls."[7] She hadn't been in England to meet Queen Victoria, or in France to be with her mother-in-law when she died.

Her replies to Louis, sent to him during the time he spent in Leeds, are all lost. But those years were undoubtedly a trial—with only Phoebe for regular adult company, never knowing for certain whether the bills could be paid; going to an empty bed every night, living alone through blizzards and children's birthdays.

The world Le Prince was born into in 1841 had been one of gaslights, horsepower, backbreaking manual labor; of illnesses thought to be caused by miasma and treated by bloodletting, change of air, and prayer. Forty-seven years later, rail networks gridded the countryside and electric and telephone wires crisscrossed city skylines. Heavy machinery made factory systems and mass manufacturing possible. Invisible germs were found, cataloged, vaccinated against. Europeans could reach the Americas by steam liner in a week—with electricity, running water, and fine food on board. War was waged with bombs and cannons. An age of exponential growth—described by the historian Eric Hobsbawm as an "age of capital"—had begun.

Muybridge (born 1830), Marey (born 1830), Le Prince (born 1841), and Edison (born 1847), each in their own ways, were men of their time. The world had become exponentially smaller and yet, somehow, harder to keep up with. It was a noisy and frantic, and their respective attempts at creating motion pictures were one way of trying to tame it into coherence. In the midst of such restless, relentless movement, capturing each moment was a triumph and a subversion.

They all had different motivations. Muybridge was an exceptional artist—solitary, exacting, ill at ease in the company of fellow human beings. His instantaneous photographs broke and reassembled time in a manner as influential as that of the Cubists and Futurists who would later break and reassemble perspective. Marey, the scientist, saw moving images as just another tool in an ever-growing box. Edison was an entrepreneur, who directed a research-and-development staff toward the creation of *products*, to be marketed and sold.

For all of them, however, moving images were a means to an end. For Le Prince, they seem to have been an end in themselves. Motion pictures would entertain—he once told Adolphe of plans to film fictional scenes, either "out of doors" or on "a stage indoors adequately lighted," featuring actors "suitably costumed" and taking part in "theatricals."[8] Motion pictures would educate—as Le Prince had discussed with teachers at the Institution for the Deaf. They would connect the people of the world, communicating human experience and transferring empathy—Lizzie remembered Louis predicting that the medium of film would put an end to "the divine right of kings and much needless priestcraft."[9] He knew, as indicated by his patents and technical drawings, that motion pictures needed to be longer than snippets of action; he had sketched floor plans for a space that is recognizable today as a screening room, and which he and his wife discussed as a "people's theatre."[10]

Louis wanted life—history—captured on his "ribbons,"[11] to be replayed, rewound, reexperienced at will.

There had been nothing like it, nothing as transformative and momentous, since the printing press four hundred and fifty years earlier.

A SEWING MACHINE, MULTIPLIED BY THREE

Spring and Summer 1888

The ribbons kept catching fire. The projector would be running and smoke suddenly seeped out of its corners—or a bright red flame would lick up in front of the arc lamp—or the Eastman's paper roll, taut and hot, would snap, the images on the blank screen cutting out to white. Louis would call for the arc lamp to be shut off at once and the film cooled down. Mason or Longley would open the projector and pull out the faint black-and-white images, cockled and blistered like charred skin. The air inside the studio was sweltering and acrid.

Sometime in the spring of 1888, as he wrestled with burning film, torn paper, breaking glass plates, jamming mechanisms, and the mealy shadows that shuddered and jumped on the Woodhouse Lane screen, Le Prince made two pivotal decisions. The first was to concentrate on a camera and projector with a single lens each—though he kept exploring devices with multiple lenses, in the hope his dream of a stereoptic, three-dimensional experience could be achieved. As Adolphe Le Prince later recalled, it was in March or April 1888 that his father and his team "began to build a one lens camera which acted in much the same manner as the 16 lens camera, but the shutter in front of the lens had to revolve 15 times more to make up for having 15 lenses less, and there was of course only one set of supply and wind-up drums" rather than two.[1] Lizzie Le Prince remembered the one-lens device being conceived first as a smaller, simpler machine, designed for expediency and put "on the market to make money."[2]

The second decision was to abandon the use of glass plates altogether. For months Louis had struggled with the projector in particular. Though the camera was not perfect, he and Mackenstein had imprinted a reasonable number of images onto glass plates—but transferring those pictures to the projector and replaying them at nineteen or more frames per second proved much more difficult.

After considerable tinkering, Le Prince came to see that the problem was less to do with the projector than with what he put inside it. Describing this period later, Adolphe wrote that the real problem continued to be the base material—what he called the "film vehicle."[3] Neither plates nor paper rolls were sturdy or sensitive enough for the high speed and high temperatures inside the camera and projector, which made filmmaking, Adolphe wrote, "much more difficult and manipulations . . . correspondingly more tedious."[4]

The problem was that no alternative existed. Photographers were still thrilled with the novelty of paper film, and only a handful of experimenters—Le Prince, Muybridge, Marey, Anschütz, and, soon, Edison—needed something sturdier for high-speed use. They were the only market for it, and they were no market at all. Adolphe and Louis experimented with making a stripping film of their own, using paper substitutes including mica, gelatin sheets, and collodion sheets, all without success.

They were back to trying to improve the machines, so that they might compensate for the fragility of the film. Longley designed metal picture belts, threaded with eyelets, to gird the paper film. These led to the "large projector" Le Prince referred to in a letter to Lizzie on March 18, the same projector Frederic Mason remembered being "fifteen feet long and twelve feet high." It was so heavy that, according to Louis, it vibrated with "violent shocks"[5] whenever it was turned on. It emitted such an ungodly rattle—and the images on the screen were so blurred by the shaking—that it was unusable.

Work began on a smaller model. This posed its own challenges. "The actual size of each picture . . . in both my father's 16 lens and one lens cameras was a square 2⅛ by 2⅛ inches," Adolphe wrote.[6] "There was no experimenting with pin point pictures or one inch pictures; my father in 1887 at once used successfully a large sized picture, which of course has great advantages for screen projection." But nineteen or more frames a second, each approximately four and a half inches square, multiplied over several minutes, made for a compact, restrictive interior, congested and delicate to travel through. It also placed the paper film very close to the arc lamp lighting it, making fires more likely. Miniature mechanisms coped less well with the pressure and velocity required of them. By the time Louis, Longley, and Mason had got the small projector to work, it, too, vibrated and roared, the mass of small gears convulsing inside the box.

A three-lens projector was considered. More lenses, more supply reels and spooling drums: perhaps the movement would be smoother. Problems persisted. "With us it was only a question of size of drum and lengths of film,"[7] Adolphe wrote of the Woodhouse Lane period. According to him, had Le Prince wanted to exhibit the kind of views Muybridge and Anschütz had demonstrated—short scenes only a few seconds long—or even those Edison would later sell with the Kinetoscope, twenty to twenty-seven seconds in duration—then he could have done so. But real life did not happen in twenty to twenty-seven seconds. Immersion was not possible, in twenty to twenty-seven seconds.

The men went back to the drawing board.

As the work progressed, Louis was in continual contact with his patent agents, updating and amending his pending applications. He scribbled notes in pencil over previous drafts, stressing one modification or another. He wrote Lizzie weekly and sent money whenever possible.[8]

The camera, unlike the projector, was being improved every day. By June or July, in Adolphe's memory, the one-lens version was ready to be tried with "blanks,"[9] and the test was successful enough for Louis to turn his mind to live shooting. That he made absolutely sure the camera worked first may be an indication of how fast Louis was burning through his money, and how little he could afford to waste even a cartridge of Eastman's film.

There were two possible ways to safeguard the integrity of the film as it moved through the camera and the projector. One was to strengthen the film itself—something Le Prince had no means to do. The other was to stabilize its movement, protecting it from the strain placed on it by the mechanism.

In early 1888, Le Prince wrote again to Thompson & Boult in London. He had another modification to make to his British patent—specifically, the projector—and he implored them to have it drawn up: it was vital, he said, to "lay stress upon the <u>intermittent</u> character of the projection."[10] He was overhauling the machines so that each frame of film was now brought forward to the lens, held for exposure or projection, and then moved on. Until then, most pioneers, including Louis, had assumed that continuous movement of the film in front of the projector's light was necessary for continuous movement of the action on the screen. In fact, Louis discovered, intermittent movement delivered better results. Instead of the frames blurring as they flew past the lens without stopping, the brief stop behind the glass gave the human eye time to register each image clearly, and then—as long as the pictures followed each other fast enough, at least twelve or thirteen a second—persistence of vision led the eye to read intermittent movement as continuous, unbroken action. The same movement protected the film from tearing, because every time a frame was held in place at the lens, it briefly relieved the tension placed upon the whole roll.

The studio at Woodhouse Lane was surrounded by fabric mills and small tailoring shops, particularly in the Leylands, less than a kilometer to the east, notorious for its airless, unsanitary sweatshops, and walking through the neighborhood or even along its edges, as Le Prince did hundreds of times, he would have heard the clanking and punching of dozens and dozens of the sewing machines, the steady *chunka chunka chunka* of needles punching through fabric, the machine's mechanism intermittently moving the cloth forward, stopping it for each stitch, driving it onward for the next. Later, in a letter to Lizzie, Louis would write of a projector prototype that "works almost as easily as a sewing machine multiple by three."[11]

Adapted to Louis's devices, intermittent movement would regulate the action of separate bands of film in the three-lens projector and sixteen-lens camera, but, Louis wrote Thompson & Boult in another letter, he expected it to work in machines with "any number of lenses as well as [only] one."[12]

This was an undeniable innovation. Along with the length of the films Louis hoped to shoot—scenes far longer than those achieved by any magic lantern or Zoopraxiscope—it described a system of a novelty impossible for any patent agent to reject.

"The intermittence and duration of the successive projections," Louis wrote, "are a most important feature of the method."[13]

Mason and Longley gutted the camera and projector and started from scratch. Edgar Rhodes, the engineer, remembered this happening "during the early part of the year 1888."[14] Longley installed "pins" in the drums inside the machines, Rhodes said, and "the edges of [the picture belts] were perforated with holes to correspond." The film was mounted inside the belts, and then "carried over" vertically past the lens "with an intermittent motion." Later in the year, according to Rhodes, Le Prince abandoned the picture belts entirely, and began punching the perforations directly onto the film, one "in each corner" of every frame.[15]

At first, the new alternative moment was uneven, and the images on the screen quivered worse than ever. But the basis of the mechanism would work—Le Prince was sure of it. "I know my principle is right and practical," he wrote Lizzie in March.[16] The problems were not fundamental; they were "bugs," as Edison called them,[17] needing to be smoothed out. After nearly two years of trying, he was on the verge of figuring out the projector.

The dreaded machine was finally going to work.

A YORKSHIRE
SUMMER

Summer 1888

L izzie Le Prince readily admitted her husband was not always the easiest of men. "[He] was reflective and reticent by nature," she remembered after his disappearance, "and not a little proud and self-contained."[1] He could be combative and impatient when disagreed with; as Lizzie put it, he "found it difficult to let a point lie in abeyance as soon as he had proven its feasibility."[2]

Those years were particularly demanding for her, living an ocean away, teaching at the institution and looking after the children, watching every penny disappear down the sinkhole created by the motion picture experiments. It could not have helped that Louis was in Leeds, living in her childhood home, with her parents nearby, while she missed it all. It was "faith" that carried her through, she wrote later[3]—faith that Louis's machines would not just be a new technology but "a new world power," as influential as Edison's electrical empire. Faith that his "pre-vision of the far reaching value of moving pictures" would come to pass. In the meantime, she accepted that her lot was to share "the day to day struggles."[4]

At last, in the summer of 1888, Lizzie and the younger children visited Leeds, the first time she'd been home since the death of Elizabeth Le

Prince the previous spring. It was an odd vacation, joy difficult to come by. The sun shone; Lizzie had a chance to tend to her beloved flowers behind the Roundhay mansion. There was Fernand's eleventh birthday to celebrate in July, Joseph's thirteenth a month later. Jack Whitley had just launched his second annual exhibition at Earl's Court, this one in celebration of Italy, its opening marked on June 6 by a banquet dinner at which Oscar Wilde and other intellectuals were present. "The indefatigable Mr. Whitley," as the newspapers had taken to calling him,[5] had come a long way from the bankruptcy of Whitley Partners. He understood what many impresarios and curators of the late nineteenth century were still resisting: industrial growth was turning *everyone* into a member of the leisure class, driven to consume, eager for diversion and entertainment. He specialized now, he said, in the "vivid and picturesque." By the time the Italian Exhibition closed in the fall, over 1.7 million visitors had passed through its entrance gates.

There should, in short, have been cause for celebration and pride that summer, but it is not hinted at in later correspondence, or described in Lizzie's memoirs. The newspapers told of international tensions, of labor strikes and socialist cells. Lizzie found her mother looking older, her hair white and her body overweight, and her father still struggling to resurrect the Whitley firm to its former glory.

There were tensions in the family, too. Three decades later, as an elderly Lizzie drafted her memoirs, she was still angry at the doubts expressed about Louis's work. She abstained from naming names but remembered that "some of our friends thought us 'cranks,' and were quite angry to have us 'waste money' on inventions."[6] Elsewhere she wrote of the "many of [Louis's] friends and relatives [who] did their utmost to belittle and prevent what they considered a foolish expenditure of time and money in research, and a waste of his other rare talents and natural gifts."[7] In the face of their doubts, Le Prince, she wrote, simply "fell into a habit of reserve . . . and went quietly about his work saying the least possible."[8] She may have been referring to Jack, who might have grown tired of Louis breaking repeated promises to premiere his pictures at one of his exhibitions. She might also have been writing about Louis's own brother, Albert, whom Louis met regularly in France and who, still owing Louis money from their shared inheritance, might have felt he was bankrolling a selfish, heedless folly.

In the end it was a bittersweet vacation, somber one moment and the source of joyful memories the next, as changeable as the Yorkshire skies. It was, as far as records indicate, the last time Lizzie Le Prince saw her husband in person, or her younger children their father.

ROUNDHAY
GARDEN SCENE

October 8–14, 1888

■

Following the approval of his American claim—dated January 10, 1888—and the granting of his English provisional specification on the same day, Le Prince obtained patents in Belgium (February 15), France (March 23), Italy (March 29), and Austria-Hungary (July 5). The patents accelerated his timeline for two reasons. Maintaining them cost money—a hundred francs annually in France, thirty francs per annum in Belgium, forty lire every year in Italy. And while they were technically licenses granting Louis a monopoly on his invention in their respective jurisdictions, their publications also made that work public, meaning his detailed descriptions of the devices were now available to anyone who might desire to look them up—or copy them.

On the legal front, Louis was well ahead of any rivals, with the exception of Marey. Charles Reynaud worked only with illustrations, not photographs, a crucial distinction—animation was life manufactured, not life reproduced. In any case, Reynaud's French patent on the Théâtre Optique would be granted by French authorities only on December 1, eight and a half months after Louis's own claim had been approved. Edison had yet to submit any paperwork on a patent of his own; he hadn't even begun work in the field. Other pioneers—William

Friese-Greene, Wordsworth Donisthorpe—would not apply for patents on their own versions of a motion picture device until the following year. The young Lumière brothers, then in their late twenties, were running the manufacture of photographic plates and equipment established, and nearly bankrupted, by their father. They were over five years away from expending even a second's thought on motion pictures.

As the British summer made way for a wet, mild autumn, Le Prince finally felt himself close to genuine success. He wrote again to Thompson & Boult on September 22, enclosing copies of his French and Italian patents and asking them to ensure the final British complete specification—the full patent grant in the United Kingdom—was in line with their "most complete" descriptions of his devices. He asked them to set aside, for the time being, any mention of a stereoscopic device, "which will be the subject of a special [separate] Patent" in future. He signed off, "Please let me know what amount I am to remit to you to cover expenses and fees, and believe me yours sincerely—A. Le Prince."[1]

Thompson & Boult worked on the document for a few days and sent it back to Le Prince for approval, to which Louis replied meticulously and insistently on October 4—make sure, he said, to "strengthen and specify" the description of the "absolutely automatic simultaneous intermittent action of the shutters and drum carrying the films (in the receiver as well as in the projector)," and to specify the machine could be powered "by hand or power (of any kind)" and to repeat and emphasize wherever possible that the devices were "capable of operating successively any number of lenses as well as one." This point was important enough for Louis to repeat it later in the letter, imploring his agents a second time to ensure the patent "be secured for any number of lenses including one." He offered to board the next train down to London if they preferred him to be present for the rewriting and asked them to urgently "wire whether I am required [in person] or not."[2] Misplacement of even a single word might find his application in interference with another party's patent or, worse, make him vulnerable to future copycats.

Thompson & Boult cabled a few days later as requested, notifying Louis they would not be needing him in London. They filed the complete specification to his exact demands, making clear the camera "sometimes may be . . . provided with only one lens" and "correspondingly in the deliverer,"[4] and describing the inner mechanisms of the machines in painstaking detail. As he awaited the submission's approval, Louis informed his Woodhouse Lane crew of their next steps: in a few days they would shoot the world's first motion pictures.[5] Legal documents could be challenged, but one thing no one would be able to argue with was the medium itself, played out live on a screen.

On October 8, Thomas Edison finally acted on the conversation he had had with Eadweard Muybridge more than six months earlier. Among the papers he sent his patent agents, Dyer & Seely, on that day was a short stack of preliminary drawings and technical specifications, written in Edison's looping longhand, for a new invention he called the Kinetograph.

"Rush this," Edison urged his lawyers. "I am getting good results. Edison."[6]

The machine was a phonograph retrofitted into a high-speed microscopic camera, which would record a "minimum of 8 exposures per second" on tiny frames each $\frac{1}{32}$nd of an inch wide, which would then be viewable in motion, by one person at a time, using a peepshow box Edison had decided to call the Kinetoscope. His letter entirely appropriated the idea Muybridge had pitched him in February—only with the Kinetoscope as a substitute for the Zoopraxiscope.

The device description Edison sent his lawyers was thin on detail—most likely because Edison, far from "getting good results," hadn't done much experimenting at all. The customer would view the moving pictures through the Kinetoscope's goggles and listen to the synchronized soundtrack using ear tubes, though Edison was not yet able to say how any of it would work. His calculation of the frame rate required for persistence of vision was not achieved through testing but by rough mental arithmetic, scribbled on the edge of one of his sketches.

Any other inventor would have had such a technical specification rejected. But Edison was Edison—and it was not a regular patent he was seeking. Instead, he requested Dyer & Seely submit the Kinetograph and the Kinetoscope to the Patent Office for a "caveat"—a sort of prepatent through which an inventor declared their intention to file a full submission *soon*, laying claim to an innovation they hadn't yet formulated but *intended* to develop in the near future. A caveat did not require a detailed description and was not subjected to thorough examination. The Patent Office simply filed the caveat away in a confidential archive, where it was held valid for one year, renewable for ten dollars per annum. Not only could a caveat be used to establish priority—because the Patent Office would enforce the holder's rights from the date of the caveat filing, not the later date of the full formal patent application—but it also helped established inventors like Edison snuff out rivals: one of the benefits of filing a caveat was that, if another party applied for certification for a similar process or device, the Patent Office would put that application on hold and notify the caveat holder, giving them three months to file a formal application of their own. If accepted, this one would cause the rival application to be rejected for infringement—even though it had been completed and submitted first.

Edison used caveats often. They allowed him to claim entire lines of potential innovation as his own, through carefully worded yet fundamentally hollow filings, renewed year after year on work he had barely begun and, sometimes, had little intention of undertaking at all. Edison's lawyer Frank Dyer estimated his employer had filed "some 120 caveats embracing not less than 1500 inventions" during the course of their time working together[7]—in the fields of electricity, mining, sound recording, and now motion pictures.

Having sketched out a broad direction for each project, and tasked Dyer with drawing up a caveat, Edison usually left it to one of his employees to work out how the new invention would actually *work*—to do, in other words, the legwork of inventing. The early work on the Kinetograph and Kinetoscope had been conducted by Charles Batchelor, Edison's "hands," whose notebook for 1888 includes four pages of preliminary sketches of the devices.[8] Batchelor had prior interest—a decade earlier, he had clipped and pasted into his workbook an article from *La Nature* that described Wordsworth Donisthorpe's unsuccessful Kinesigraph.[9]

Edison made his own drawings of the proposed Kinetoscope and Kinetograph in October 1888, which were witnessed by John Ott, one of his precision mechanics, who may have adapted a phonograph into a Kinetoscope as a proof of concept. Very quickly, however, Edison put W. K. L. Dickson in charge. Dickson was a photographer, a lover of small gadgets of every kind, and he'd done good work on the ore-milling project, even though it was entirely outside his expertise. The first of Dickson's "technical notes" in the Edison archives that deals with motion pictures is logged for June 1888, though it is undated and is likely from later in the year. In it, Dickson already wonders if a "larger Kinetoscope" might be preferable to a smaller viewing box, and makes a note to "try how sensitive" Eastman's paper film might be when used to film at high speeds.[10] Batchelor and Ott had helped Edison brainstorm. With Dickson on board, proper experimenting work began.

Dyer & Seely typed up the caveat application and returned it to Edison for approval on October 12. It was a Friday. Before leaving West Orange for Glenmont, Edison put his signature to the bottom of the application, a distinctive flourish curving from the *T* over the rest of his name: *Thomas a. Edison.*

Two days later, on the morning of Sunday, October 14, thirty-three hundred miles away, Louis Le Prince gathered his family at Roundhay Cottage to film a motion picture. Le Prince's "garden scene," as he came to call it, is the oldest film still in existence and, that we know of, the first ever made.

The sequences, as they survive, are innocuous. Brief snippets of every-day life. Home movies. What better way to demonstrate the novelty of his camera and projector than the taking of real, daily life—of normal people, doing normal things, at home—the kind of sequences no one bothered to commit to a magic lantern or Zoopraxiscope?

We know Adolphe was present, as were Joseph Whitley and his wife, Sarah, and Sarah's friend Annie Hartley. Little is known about Annie, though a letter she wrote in the following weeks would become the best account of that day.

There had been church in the morning, like every week, the people of Roundhay rising and heading to their local chapels in their Sunday best. It was a cheerful morning, Annie remembered: Sarah was "bright and jolly," she wrote, "full of fun and laughing."[11] After the service, the Whitleys returned home for luncheon. As they approached Roundhay, the grass around the stone manor was as green and flat as a cricket lawn; in the autumnal light, the flowers growing against the walls were still blooms of color.

Somewhere in the house was the camera. It was a beautiful machine, the culmination of three years of trials and disasters. It was a large, heavy box of Honduras mahogany, mounted on four squat legs of applewood and iron and polished by Mason to a soft luster, with brass hinges engraved BRAMPTON'S PATENT, after the manufacturer in Birming-ham. Two lenses were sunk inside the front of the machine, almost flush with the wood, with sliding black caps to cover the openings and protect the glass when necessary. They were standard portrait photog-raphy lenses, of the Petzval type, loved by photographers and as good as any lens of their time: sharp and bright in the center, vignetted and occasionally distorted on the outer edges of the image. One was for the taking of images, the other for the operator to use as a viewfinder. The barrels of the lens mounts were built with a narrow opening on the side, to allow for the insertion of Waterhouse stops—metal diaphragms that allowed Louis to control the amount of light that would enter the lens and hit the film. Inside the machine was Louis and Longley's maze of machinery: spools of vulcanite copper, picture belts of wood and metal, a slotted brass shutter, and a flat brass pressure plate to hold each frame of Eastman's film behind the lens for exposure. The speed of filming was controlled by a brass crank on the side of the camera. Adolphe remembered the handle being able to deliver sixteen to twenty frames per second, though tests carried out a century later could not break a rate of eleven.[12] Either was enough for persistence of vision—just.

It was an impressive contraption. The panel at the back could be removed, not just to provide access to the interior, but to permit the fitting of an arc lamp: unlike several of the prototypes, this one could work both as a camera *and* a projector.

The sun was drawing to the west by the time Louis carried the camera outside. He "wanted us all to come out on the front to take a photo with his new machine," Annie remembered.[13] The camera still shook when in use, so Louis had a weight hung from the leg stands to stabilize the machine when cranked into action. He set up facing the house, the sun behind him for maximum exposure.

The first film to be taken was of Adolphe in front of the four stone steps leading to Roundhay Cottage's front door. Now sixteen, he stood tall in his white shirt and black tie, his shoes polished, a melodeon between his hands. As Louis turned the crank, his son began playing, dancing back and forth in light, nimble steps. He smiles a handsome dimpled smile, his face playful and bright.

The sequence was short, perhaps intended to demonstrate how lifelike the moving images could be if synchronized to music.

Next Louis set up the camera on the lawn, by the house's bay windows, and brought the entire family—Joseph, Sarah, Adolphe, and Annie Hartley—to the garden. He seems to have asked them, simply, to *move*. And so they did: Adolphe walking around in long-legged strides; Sarah stepping forward and then back in a straight line, like a child counting steps; Joseph marching with exaggerated resolve, arms pumping back and forth, the tails of his mackintosh whipping behind him. Annie was the most at a loss. The surviving footage opens with her staring at the camera in her long pleated dress and bustle, a top hat with a pale feather shooting up from the brim sitting stiffly on the crown of her head. Her arms hang awkwardly down by her sides. After a short beat, and with everyone around her already moving, she lowers her eyes to the ground and turns away from the camera, walking toward the back of the garden and away from the lens.

The camera whirred, the paper film flashing up and behind the lens, at a rate of at least eleven frames every second. When the roll was exhausted, Louis straightened back up. Not long after he had stopped filming, his mother-in-law, Sarah, suddenly stood still and uneasy, eyes squinting. She reached out for the nearest person—Annie—and made to grip her hand.

"Give me your arm, lass," she said. "I've come over all weak."

And then, Annie wrote, "she collapsed."[14]

MAREY, LE PRINCE, AND DICKSON

October 15–November 29, 1888

■

On Monday, October 29—two weeks after the filming of the Round-hay garden scene—Étienne-Jules Marey strode purposefully off the Quai de Conti and across the stone courtyard of the Institut de France. This was the hallowed heart of Paris, the classical buildings imposing and splendid in the golden-gray light of morning: the École Nationale des Beaux-Arts around the corner, the Louvre across the Seine, Notre Dame de Paris on its island just to the left, the stone arch of the Pont Neuf reaching across the waters.

The institute was the repository of France's knowledge. It was there, in 1839, that Louis Daguerre had unveiled photography, to a joint meeting of the academies of science and the Beaux-Arts. And it was there, forty-nine years later, that Marey was presenting himself to reveal an equally significant innovation.

Marey was a regular at the Academy's meetings, often as a presenter. He was comfortable in the presence of his peers. That day, the physiologist stood in front of the scientists assembled and launched into his address. By the standards of the occasion, it was brief.

"To complete the studies I have kept the Academy informed of throughout our latest meetings," he said, "I have the honor of presenting it today a strip of sensitized paper on which I have obtained a series of photographs, at a rate of twenty images a second." He had built a device that, using paper film, "will allow the collection of successive images of any man or animal in motion, without needing to record in front of a dark background." Marey laid one of his paper strips out on the table in front of him and invited anyone who wished to do so to take a closer look. He explained how he had used an electromagnet to hold each frame behind his lens for "one five-thousandth of a second," capturing a sharp, clear picture. He did not project the images in motion—he had no interest in such an exhibition. Rather, he announced, his new method was "destined to greatly facilitate the study of human and animal locomotion."[1]

The pictures had been taken on Monday, October 15—the day after Le Prince had shot his sequences at Roundhay. Marey had broken chronophotography out of the confines of his laboratory. He no longer needed glass plates nor a uniformly black background; he could take his motion studies anywhere. His recordings were short, he had not explored a new exhibition method, and his paper film gave results more hazy and opaque than Le Prince's. But by a different method, for a different purpose, and almost on the same exact day as his compatriot, Marey had invented his version of a motion picture camera.

Le Prince's other competitors were making progress, too. Edison's caveat petition for "certain Improvements in Photography" had been officially filed on October 17[2]—three days after Le Prince's filming at Roundhay, and two days after Marey's taking of his own pictures at the Parc des Princes. Dyer & Seely had made sure to draft the submission in terms as broad as possible: the Kinetograph's frame rate could be anywhere between eight and twenty-five per second; the emulsion on the cylinder base could be collodion, and possibly any "other photographic film"; the images would be positive photographs but "if it is desired" maybe negatives as well; and "a plate or continuous strip" might also be used as a recording base ("but there are many mechanical difficulties in the way," Edison admitted).

The Patent Office accepted his petition and put it away in its vault that very same day. Benton Jay Hall, the commissioner whose signature had graced the grant of Le Prince's full patent ten months earlier, placed his seal and name on Edison's caveat, and a copy was sent immediately to Dyer & Seely's offices on Wall Street.[3]

W. K. L. Dickson toiled to make the Kinetograph and Kinetoscope a reality. He went back and forth from the machinery shop, on the first floor of the West Orange laboratory, to room 5, the photography studio, on the ground floor, assembling and testing prototypes. He ordered in magic lanterns and studied their workings. He read up on Muybridge's and Marey's achievements in chronophotography and began to call single frames of film "phases," after the physiologists' description of "phases of movement."[4]

The biggest obstacle to Dickson's progress, unexpectedly, was Edison himself. The more Dickson tried to convince Edison that the curved cylinder of the phonograph made no sense as a base for photographs, and that Eastman's film should be used instead, the more Edison insisted on the cylinder. Even worse was that, once the caveat had been accepted by the Patent Office, Dickson found his boss in no rush to take the experimenting any further. He reassigned Dickson to the ore-mining department. When Dickson protested that he wished to continue with the motion picture work, Edison told him to do it "in [his] spare time"—and warned him it "must not interfere with the big work at hand."[5]

Edison did agree to give Dickson an assistant in the photography room, and he sent a machinist, Charles Brown, to help Dickson make the most of his "spare time." Brown, it turned out, had never handled a camera before in his life. Dickson spent the autumn teaching him how to take a photograph.

October turned to November and Dickson had yet to make a single test of images in movement. Instead, either for his benefit or for Brown's, he refreshed himself on the principles of photography. He took still photographs and tried cooking his own emulsions. On November 22 he accepted delivery of a copy of S. D. Humphrey's *American Hand Book of the Daguerreotype*, and the following Wednesday, the day before Thanksgiving, he took the train into New York to buy silver plates from the Scovill Manufacturing Company. From the stockroom at West Orange he collected the requisite chemicals—halogen, iodine, silver halide, mercury.

Daguerreotyping was a nearly fifty-year-old process—even the handbook Dickson had purchased had been published in 1853. Dickson conducted the test anyway.

Edison had already boasted of getting "good results"[6] with eight images per second. Dickson's single-exposure daguerreotype test took three-quarters of a minute.

Louis Le Prince, back in Leeds, was already filming on location.

Shortly after shooting the Roundhay scene, Le Prince had taken his camera even farther out into the field, lugging it up the stairs of number 19 Bridge End in the center of Leeds, where Hicks Brothers, Ironmongers, had its shop and workrooms. He set the camera up at the second-story window, the lens pointing toward Leeds Bridge below, and under a black cloth he opened the back of the device to load a roll of paper stripping film. He emerged, put the shroud away, and began recording.

The footage taken that day ran at least 129 frames, judging from the numbers on the contact sheets. Adolphe recorded the camera running at twenty frames per second, for a scene of at least six and a half seconds; Jim Longley remembered the machine struggling to break faster than seven images every second, at which speed the 129 frames would have run for just under nineteen total seconds. Only the last twenty of these frames have survived. Animated at ten frames per second, they move at approximately the speed of real life, favoring Longley's memory.

What survives shows horse carts moving in both directions across Leeds Bridge, one of them carrying bales of goods, the others landaus and barouches for passengers. A dozen pedestrians make their ways up and down the sidewalks, one man crossing in front of a horse. Someone points as they hold a child's hand. One man rubs the back of his neck before dropping his hand and looking away over the bridge's parapet. Every pedestrian wears a hat, and every one of them is attired in dark, sober Victorian colors.

When these images were thrown on the screen at Woodhouse Lane, Longley judged them "the best pictures"[7] Le Prince had achieved. They were so clear that "the tram horses were seen moving over it," he said, "and all the other traffic, as if you was on the Bridge yourself. I could even see the smoke coming out of a man's pipe who was lounging on the Bridge."[8] (There are no trams visible in the surviving footage, or anyone smoking, which suggests that these images appeared in the section now lost.) A decade later, Mason would also speak of the "very vivid"[9] impression the sequence had made on him when projected.

It was the earliest footage ever taken of an urban environment—of a busy thoroughfare in the center of one of the great cities powering the great industrial leap forward.

It is also the last film taken by Louis Le Prince to survive, even in fragments.

On October 24—either a few days before the Leeds Bridge footage was shot, or a few days after—Sarah Whitley, who had been unwell since her collapse during the filming of the Roundhay garden scene, passed away. She was seventy-two; they buried her in the graveyard at Saint John the Evangelist, a few minutes away from Roundhay Cottage.

Lizzie, who had only recently gone back to America after her summer visit to England, was unable to return to Leeds for her mother's funeral.

Eighteen months after Louis had left New York, his work seemed finally to be drawing to an end—and yet, as it did, Lizzie felt once again the vast distance between herself and her husband, between her life without him in New York and the one he was living in her own home city, with her own family. His race for motion pictures came at a high cost, not only in patience and money—but in all the moments she had missed, and would never capture again.

PART FIVE

MOTION PICTURES

1889–1901

TRANSPARENT, FLEXIBLE, AND UNBREAKABLE

November and December 1888

John Carbutt had lived a full life. The Yorkshireman—born in Sheffield in 1832—had moved to Canada as a twenty-one-year-old and wrangled a job as a photographer for the Grand Trunk Railway, riding the rails from Portland, Maine, to Montreal, Toronto, Ontario, and back. At twenty-six, he quit that job and opened a portrait gallery in recently incorporated Plymouth, Indiana, lasting three years before returning home to Sheffield. But he was not in England long—young John was a restless, enterprising man, and within months he was back on a steamship headed west.

This time Carbutt settled in Chicago. The city was young, younger than Carbutt himself, but it was flourishing—its population booming, its industry thriving, houses and factories sprouting across the clay soil like the wild onions that had given the city its name (*shikaakwa*, in the Algonquin Myaamia language). The railroad had made Illinois the beating heart of America.

Carbutt opened a photography studio on Lake Street, two blocks from the Chicago River, and spent the Civil War years traveling and taking pictures: to Saint Paul and Red Wing, Minnesota; to Niagara Falls; up and down the Mississippi River. Afterward, he took promotional pictures for the Union Pacific Railroad and the Chicago and North Western Railroad and published stereographic prints of the "Great West," which sold successfully, though not as well as the huge landscape prints sold by Carbutt's California rival, Eadweard Muybridge.

By the 1870s Carbutt was wealthy, married, and a father, but he had lost none of his drive. He sold his Chicago gallery, moved to Philadelphia, and started manufacturing photographic equipment. By the end of the decade he was one of the largest producers of dry plates in the United States. When George Eastman rose to preeminence—first with his paper film and, in the summer of 1888, with the Kodak camera, a small box preloaded with a hundred exposures of film—Carbutt was determined to market an innovation of his own, novel enough to push Eastman back on his heels.

He was ready to make an announcement at the Franklin Institute in Philadelphia on November 21, 1888.[1] He had perfected, he declared, a new kind of sheet film, not on paper, or on glass—but on celluloid, the plastic patented by the Hyatt brothers of Newark, New Jersey. A local Newark clergyman, the Reverend Hannibal Goodwin, had just developed a celluloid emulsion, for which he filed a patent in 1887. Carbutt had licensed Goodwin's coating and put the Hyatt brothers' company under contract, and by combining their technologies had achieved his new product: eleven-by-fourteen-inch sheets of celluloid film, which he touted as transparent, flexible, and unbreakable. He showed the professionals assembled at the Franklin Institute a set of photographs taken on celluloid film and revealed he was ready to sell the new product immediately.

Carbutt's announcement rocked the world of photography. It was reported in newspapers and journals across America and reprinted in photography magazines. The reviews came fast, and they were enthusiastic. The celluloid was "as transparent as glass, very tough and flexible, develops easily and its weight is almost unappreciable," wrote the

Photographic Times and American Photographer on December 7.[2] Newspapers promoted it as "a perfect light weight substitute for plates of glass."[3] By January it was being written about in England.[4]

Le Prince's complete specification British patent had been granted three days before Carbutt's talk, on November 18, 1888. The paper strips continued to be his greatest problem—tearing and catching fire, breaking and bending—and so, for Louis, the arrival of celluloid film was a turning point.

He kept a close eye on the trade journals, and he most likely read about Carbutt's celluloid in early 1889, though the sheets were not available for purchase in England until the summer. He had been desperate to get his hands on a better "film vehicle" for a long time. He had even written to Lumière & Fils, in Lyon, and received a sample of their own celluloid, designed for them by the photographer George Balagny. An empty envelope, left behind in Le Prince's papers, bears the distinctive blue label of the Lumière firm, printed "Plaques Souples Balagny: Préparées à Lyon par A. Lumière & Ses Fils." Lizzie remembered this being received as early as 1887,[5] and the film historian Gordon Hendricks found the Balagny celluloid was "mass produced . . . and very popular in France as of May 1888 and before."[6] Paul Spehr, a biographer of W. K. L. Dickson, agreed that celluloid dry plates had been available as early as 1887, from Lumière and Balagny in France as well as through the Vergara Film Company in London, though he noted they were expensive and deeply flawed.[7] Adolphe, writing his own memoir, recalled Louis contacting Lumière & Fils in 1887 to purchase "transparent celluloid in long lengths,"[8] only for Lumière to inform him neither they, nor anyone else, manufactured the product, which cost much to make and had, at that point, no market. Louis then reached out to "Swan & Fry," by which Adolphe likely meant Mawson & Swan of Newcastle and Samuel Fry & Co. of Kingston-upon-Thames, the first two British suppliers licensed to manufacture George Eastman's early dry plates.[9]

Mason remembered the first celluloid coming from the Blair Company,[10] a Boston firm with an English branch in Saint Mary Cray in Kent, and this would have been possible in the summer of 1889. Blair sold sheets of Carbutt's product. When Le Prince eventually got these, they proved impractical. They were stiffer and less flexible than advertised, at least for motion picture work—after all, they had been designed as an alternative to glass plates for still photographers, not as a substitute for paper rolls in roll holders—and they were the wrong size. The sheets had to be cut into strips, which were then awkwardly joined into longer bands. The reels and drums inside the camera and projector had to be rebuilt to fit the size of these "film ribbons," as Le Prince took to calling them.[11] Adolphe wrote that Le Prince's celluloid, once cut, was perforated, pins inside the camera engaging into the holes and moving the film forward; a memory Longley shared, adding that a Maltese cross mechanism, also known as a Geneva drive but which Longley described as a "star wheel," was used in the projector to regulate the film's intermittent movement, "allowing the band to work at the proper time." There were pins on either side of the celluloid reel, which geared into "brass eyelets fixed in the band[,] similar to the eyelets of boots."[12]

Celluloid was still imperfect, but it was an improvement on paper or glass, and in mid-July Louis wrote to Lizzie and told her he was about to "go to Scarborough for two weeks to take pictures of boats, waves, and donkeys etc, on the stands—so as to have something interesting to show either in London or in Paris." The Yorkshire seaside town, perched on limestone cliffs rising up out of the North Sea, was an ideal setting for some summer filming. It had a lovely curved beach, overlooked by medieval Scarborough Castle, on which children built sandcastles and families went for long strolls, their faces shaded from the sun under straw hats.

As a location it would make the perfect contrast to busy Leeds Bridge. But if Louis did make the trip, no footage survives. His plans may have caused a rift between him and his brother-in-law, however. Jack's third exhibition, this one a celebration of Spanish industry, was open at Earl's

Court but, Louis confided in Lizzie, it "has very few visitors, and . . . I settled not to go there." He made the obligatory excuses—the motion picture work was eating up all his time, a "heavy cold" had "put [him] back a great deal." For years Jack had unsuccessfully lobbied Louis to unveil his machines at the fair, and now not only was Louis skipping the exhibition altogether, but he was traveling to the beach instead. Louis's mention to Lizzie of showing pictures "either in London or in Paris" also suggested he had abandoned the idea of giving Jack the opportunity to debut his work. "I have no very settled plan yet," he admitted.[13]

The trials with celluloid were part of a bigger agenda, namely to turn the one-lens camera and projector from a successful prototype, which it was, into a "commercial machine," as Louis described it, which it was not. Though it looked sturdy, the camera was delicate and easily breakable. Rain got into openings and ruined the film. The inner mechanisms were liable to freeze in extremely low temperatures; indeed, filming outdoors in the winter was impossible. The light in the projector was too dim. None of this discredits Le Prince's motion picture devices as the first of their kind. Cameras suffered in the cold and wet well into the twentieth century, though the bravest operators countered it by lighting small oil lamps inside their machine to keep it warm—a bold, even reckless, decision, considering the flammability of celluloid film. And many commercially successful projectors—including the Cinématographe—were criticized in their early years for their lack of brightness.

Louis went about addressing these concerns at Woodhouse Lane. Wilson Hartnell sent one of his engineers, Ernest Kilburn Scott, to install a full electrical system. "I went to see about it," Scott recalled, "and entering the workshop at 160 Woodhouse Lane, saw his assistant, Longley, whom I had known for some years." Scott noticed the "large sheet" hanging at the end of the long room.

"Is that for a magic lantern?" he asked.

"Much better than that," Longley replied. "The pictures actually move and represent life."[14]

A "tall, distinguished looking man" walked over to introduce himself. It was Le Prince. "At first he was somewhat reticent with me," Scott wrote, "but I mentioned that some years before I had been a fellow student with someone of his [unusual] name and this turned out to be his son."[15]

Le Prince walked Scott over to the projector, which "was on a table at one end of the long room," and explained what he needed. He described where the electric light needed to go and what it needed to do, and even let Scott handle the machine himself.

The young electrician arranged for a Robey steam engine—a massive metal beast—to be set up in the yard of Mason & Sons. Connected to it was a direct current dynamo by Crompton & Co. of Chelsmford. Cables were run up the walls, "over the intervening buildings," and into the studio at number 160.[16] Crompton dynamos powered Vienna's opera house and London's King's Cross station, and would soon power a large area of the Paris Exhibition; and Robey were long-established pioneers of steam power. This was close to the best electrical power system available in England. A colleague of Scott's by the name of Walter Gee remembered putting it together "about the middle of 1889." As Gee came in and out of the studio, "Mr. Le Prince worked his projector machine and showed moving pictures on a white sheet hung at the other end of the room," he said, the work unceasing. Finally, "at the time of the first switching on, there was [only] one other person present beside Mr. Le Prince and myself, namely, James W. Longley, who was his assistant. I know nothing of details of construction of the projector machine, but I was very pleased to see it work so well."[17]

The one-lens camera had already proved "a great success,"[18] Mason remembered, but the projector was refined into a smaller, simpler two-lens machine, in the hope two bands of images, focused on the same point, would stabilize the picture and eliminate flicker and blur. At some point this was used in "a successful exhibition to a few friends, including my brother," Mason wrote, another sign Louis was growing sure enough of his devices to hold test screenings for small, friendly audiences. Mason was "enthusiastically driving the dynamo for the powerful arc light fitted up by Mr. Scott" when Le Prince sent someone to the carpentry shop's yard to tell Mason the light was too weak. Without a moment's hesitation Mason disconnected the steam engine's governor—the part that regulated the engine's speed—and disabled its boiler's safety valve, feeding the dynamo with as much power as it could take—"thus, I suppose, risking my life in the cause of the pictures," he admitted. "One does this kind of thing when one is twenty."[19]

The films were "not shown more than two or three times" throughout 1889, however, Mason wrote, "because mainly [sic] from the fact that the electric power was too weak."[20] The electric bulb installed by Scott was bright, but not bright enough to shine through Carbutt's film and carry the images on its beam to the screen.

A way forward presented itself near the end of 1889. George Eastman, perhaps inspired by Carbutt's success, one-upped his rival by releasing a new roll film—not on paper, this time, but on celluloid. It was smaller, more flexible, and more translucent, an all-around improvement on his earlier rolls. It was the brainchild of his newest hire, Henry Reichenbach, a chemist who had spent two years developing it.

Mason remembered that it was "in the early autumn of 1889 that Mr. Le Prince came to me in high spirits to say he had obtained some rolls of sensitized film called celluloid."[21] This has been disputed since, but it is possible. Eastman and Reichenbach had filed for a joint patent in April 1889, and the Eastman Company had broken ground on a new factory in Rochester to manufacture the rolls even earlier than that. The first mention of the project in the press came in *Wilson's Photographic Magazine* in June,[22] and on August 6 the celluloid roll-film was presented at the annual convention of the Photographers' Association in Boston's Mechanics Hall, and soon after it was being actively promoted in the press. It was announced in England as early as August 10, the *Graphic* newspaper informing readers of this "new form of celluloid, which is so flexible that it can be wound on a couple of rollers—panorama fashion—so that a long band of it can be exposed, section by section, to the action of the lens within the camera." This, in a widely read publication, described a film base perfectly suited to Louis's needs. At that point the film was not yet for sale, but the *Graphic* was told it would "very soon . . . be introduced under the parentage of the Eastman Company."[23]

Eastman took his celluloid rolls to the fourth annual convention of British professional and amateur photographers, held in Saint James's Hall, Piccadilly, from August 19 to 24, where it made a sensation. It was "a most important advance," wrote the *Graphic* again, "likely to cause quite a revolution in the method of taking photographic pictures." The new product, the *Boston Globe* reported from London, "obviates every difficulty. [Eastman] has succeeded in producing a strong and perfectly transparent support, of great flexibility and extreme thinness, which can be wound upon rollers, to be exposed, developed and printed like ordinary glass negatives."[24]

The celluloid film went on sale sometime between September 1889 and January 1890. Early in 1890, in a bid to keep up with overwhelming demand, Eastman expanded his manufacturing plants in the United States and even began building a dedicated European factory in Harrow, northwest of London.

Louis could have bought some of the film through one of Eastman's British stockists—Blair was one of them—or he could have acquired an advance sample, as it was standard for manufacturers to send these out to reviewers, established photographers, and local retailers in the hope of drumming up business prior to general sale. In any case Le Prince was beyond himself with excitement—"in high spirits," Mason said. "The incident is clear in my mind," he added, because Le Prince insisted Mason get the rolls ready for testing immediately, and "I had to wait until it was dark" to cut the strips down to size on his lathe, "working with a red lamp at night."

Eastman's film answered most of Le Prince's challenges—it "solved the last difficulty,"[25] Mason said—while posing new ones. The novel emulsion was uneven in thickness and in quality, with dark spots and bubbles in unexpected places, and it sometimes streaked eerily if too close to the electric discharge of the camera shutter. It blistered in the intense heat of Le Prince's arc lamp and occasionally fogged when bathed in the developing chemicals. It was impossible for Le Prince to experiment with the coating, to try and improve it himself: Eastman held patents on the film base, on the coating, on the coating machinery, and on the roll holders. He knew how valuable celluloid film was to his company—more valuable, even, than the portable Kodak camera. "The new film is the 'slickest' product that we ever tried to make," he wrote to a colleague in 1889. "If we can *fully* control it I would not trade it for the telephone. There is more millions in it than anything else."

In any case, making the film was beyond Louis's means. It required long plate glass tables, on which was poured a precisely measured liquid nitrocellulose solution, which was then left to solidify under heaters and fans. This process took several hours, after which photographic emulsion was carefully applied across the celluloid surface, which was finally stripped, cut, and rolled. The equipment was expensive and the process delicate, perhaps deliberately: it put modern photography out of reach of the amateurs who were used to making their own emulsions, and placed its technology securely in the hands of corporations like the Eastman Company, with patents on file and batteries of lawyers on retainer to guard its ownership of a new kind of mass, standardized technology.

Sooner or later, Eastman would improve the celluloid—or one of his rivals would. In the meantime, the rolls Louis had available made it possible for him to fine-tune his "commercial machines" for potential investors and licensees.

In September, Adolphe sailed back to New York. He left with an undertaking: to find a venue in New York suitable to the first public motion picture screening in history. Louis headed to Paris, to take care of unspecified business, leaving Longley and Mason to attempt to reduce the vibration inside the projector. On November 5 Longley mailed him a handwritten note. "Dear Sir:—I have now given the new motion a good testing," it started.[26] "I fixed a piece of rubber to it three inches broad, three inches long, one eighth thick, and it worked beautiful, every way, and almost no noise at all. But I think when made in the proper thing it will be still better; and a good heavy wheel will also make it better still. As it is it is fifty times better than the levers."

The mechanic made no attempt at disguising his excitement. "I am pleased to tell you," he wrote, "that I think it will be perfection."

EDISON AND MAREY

Spring, Summer, and Fall 1889

■

Le Prince's competition, like him, were spurred forward by the new celluloid films. Wordsworth Donisthorpe, now living in London, dusted off his old Kinesigraph patent and actually built the machine, with the help of his friend William Carr Crofts. William Friese-Greene was granted a British patent in June 1889, for a motion picture camera he claimed could take ten celluloid frames every second. In practice the device likely never managed to run faster than four or five frames per second, nor did it ever take pictures at regular intervals, but Friese-Greene—a charming, fashionable man, with the striking good looks of a matinee idol—managed to drum up some interest in the machine: it was briefly written up in the March issue of *Cassell's Family Magazine*, and in the November 5 issue of the *Optical Magic Lantern Journal*, but as he could not demonstrate it practically, he failed to find financial backing. Sinking the entirety of his personal income into perfecting the camera, the young photographer inched closer and closer to bankruptcy.

Ottomar Anschütz was also garnering attention, as he promoted a tabletop version of his Schnellseher, though it would not go on sale for two more years. Louis was aware of Anschütz's work: Lizzie had sent him a clipping of an article about the German, published in November 1889 in *Scientific American*.[1] Louis professed not to be worried: the

Schnellseher was a zoetrope, not a film camera. "The paper you sent me is interesting," he replied,[2] "it is one of <u>many</u> who are trying <u>my</u> problem—but it is only a <u>small</u> part of what I am trying—it does not affect me." He pointed out that the Schnellseher could display only simplistic animations; it had "neither background nor any number of figures moving as in a street."

W. K. L. Dickson kept a close eye on these rivals. The library staff at West Orange scoured every international publication of interest and highlighted any article relevant to work ongoing at the lab, so that by the end of 1889 Dickson was surrounded by other people's ideas: Muybridge's pictures hanging in the library; Marey's announcements detailed in *La Nature* and the reports of the French Academy of Science, to which the laboratory subscribed; and now the lantern slides, mats, and borders of the Schnellseher, which Dickson ordered to enable him to build a replica of Anschütz's device.

And yet Dickson made very little progress himself. When, after several weeks of work, he decided to discard the cylindrical base in favor of a wheeled disk, all he had done was progress from one obsolescent model to the next, from the phonograph to the magic lantern. He filmed white subjects on black backgrounds, and still the images came out indecipherable. In February 1889 Edison had filed a second caveat, intended to preserve and extend the claims made in the first, but he was rarely present to work by Dickson's side. He was spending more and more of his time at a mine in Bechtelsville, Pennsylvania, where he hoped to install his first magnetic ore separators, and was negotiating for the deed to another property in Ogden, in northern New Jersey. By comparison, the Kinetoscope, Edison said repeatedly, was nothing but "a toy."

In August, Edison left America entirely, for over a month, to attend the Exposition Universelle in Paris. He tasked Charles Batchelor and Samuel Insull with cutting the laboratory's operating budget while he was away, shutting down projects and laying off experimenters, so he could funnel most of his income into mining. Dickson, as one of the engineers working on the magnetic ore separator, was kept on, and was allowed to continue work on the motion picture machines—whenever he could find the time.

On August 3, 1889, the day he sailed for Europe, Edison mailed Dyer & Seely a shopping list of new caveats, a "long, rambling"[3] seventy-page document covering a variety of experiments. It was a matter of housekeeping, earmarking all devices and processes left incomplete when Batchelor and Insull shut them down, on the off chance Edison wanted to return to them later. The Kinetoscope and Kinetograph were fifty-first and fifty-second on the list. They had been completely redesigned once more, into hybrids of the phonograph and the Schnellseher. The caveat suggested they would use a glass cylinder as a base—which was unlikely ever to work—and a Leyden jar as a source of light—which was *certain* not to work, a fact Edison, the world's foremost expert on electricity, must well have known.

The design, wrote Dickson biographer Paul Spehr, was "almost desperate."[4]

In Paris, Edison was received like a visiting emperor. "The French public," the correspondent for the New York *Sun* noted dryly, "considers Edison is the sole inventor of the telegraph, telephone, electric light, and even electricity itself, if not of the solar system as well."[5] His picture was in every newspaper, his photograph on sale at every gift shop. Crowds chased his cabs and gathered outside his hotel, chanting his name. Inventors lined up to pitch him their own contraptions or beg for a loan.

French president Sadi Carnot conferred on Edison the medal of the Légion d'Honneur at a reception at the Élysée Palace. An envoy for the king of Italy made Edison and his wife "*Il Conte e la Contessa*" Edison. At the Paris Opera House, the orchestra played "The Star-Spangled

Banner" and the audience turned to Edison and Mina in their private box, applauding and shouting "*Vive Edison!*" The newspaper *Le Figaro* threw its own party in his honor, decorating its dining hall with a portrait of the inventor inscribed with the words "*Sa Majesté Edison.*" Edison rode the elevator to the top of the new Eiffel Tower, the controversial showpiece of the exposition, and attended a private banquet breakfast with Buffalo Bill and his troupe at their camp on the outskirts of Paris. He visited Louis Pasteur's laboratory and Jules Janssen's observatory.

The list of social engagements seemed endless. On the evening of August 19, Edison was at the Hotel Continental, the guest of honor at a dinner in commemoration of Louis Daguerre and his partner Nicéphore Niépce, organized by the Société Française de Photographie. The American inventor took his place at the head table. To his left sat Janssen, arguably the world's foremost astronomer; facing him was the critic Gustave Larroumet, then the director of the Beaux-Arts.

Also seated at the top table was Étienne-Jules Marey.

Elsewhere in the room, leaning over name cards and pulling out chairs, were Pasteur, the photographer Paul Nadar, the chronophotographer Albert Londe, the celluloid manufacturer George Balagny, and the editor of *La Nature*, Gaston Tissandier. Hermann-Josef Mackenstein, Louis's collaborator in Paris, was a member of good standing of the society and also in attendance, as were Antoine Lumière and his sons Auguste and Louis, the leading manufacturers of photographic supplies from Lyon.

At some point during the banquet, which lasted late into the night, Edison finally met Étienne-Jules Marey in person. What the two men spoke about is not recorded, but they seemed to have liked each other. Four days after the dinner, Janssen formally introduced Edison to the Academy of Science, during a meeting at which Marey was also present, and around the same time Edison and Marey visited the World's Fair together.

Marey invited the American to come by his laboratory at the Station Physiologique. There, among the piles of scientific equipment, Marey showed Edison how his instantaneous cameras worked, demonstrated the electric zoetrope he used for exhibition, and elaborated on the advance he had found momentous enough to warrant his talk at the Academy of Sciences the previous fall: his use of paper, now celluloid, strips. Marey was a gracious researcher, admirable in his transparency and willingness to share his progress. He wrote later that he thought Edison had been "inspired, doubtlessly"[6] by what he saw that day at the Station.

Albert Smith, a projectionist who later worked for Edison, wrote that Edison had described this visit to Marey to him. When the doctor demonstrated his motion studies, Edison told Smith, "I knew instantly that Marey had the right idea."[7]

Edison sailed back to America on September 29. On November 2, he drew up a fourth motion picture caveat. For the first time it made no mention of a cylindrical base. Now, Edison wrote, the Kinetoscope, like Marey's camera, would use "a sensitive film in the form of a long band passing from one reel to another."[8]

Edison left it to Dickson to work out the particulars.

I SHALL BE WITH
YOU ALL IN MIND

Christmas 1889

The last known letter sent by Louis in 1889 was a message to his children, written in the week or two before Christmas.[1] His tone was forlorn. He had been suffering from lumbago—"from draughts," Adolphe remembered, "and too close application to his work"[2]—and exhaustion. Longley was frequently ill, with bronchitis and a cough, ailments that ran in his family and were worsened by the filthy Leeds air, and the mood was darkened by Joseph Whitley's own health problems. His wife's death had crushed Joseph's spirit. He forgot things and foundered in melancholy moods. At times he lost awareness of his surroundings. He was losing his wits, grief slicking his mind's slide into dementia.

Le Prince's pen scratched across the paper, his heart reaching out to "all you dear ones," as he called his sons and daughters. "I am sorry I cannot come and see you merry and lively on this coming Xmas—but it's not to be. I am bound to my chain for a while longer, but I shall think of you on those days and want you to be as happy and jolly as you can and surround your dear little Mama with your love and cheerfulness, and not fret over me and my loneliness, for at least I have my mind occupied, and besides, I may see Uncle Jack and your cousins." There is a brief space on the sheet, as if, after this long sentence, Louis had taken a breath. "But I shall be with you all in mind," Louis continued, "and as you will be, I shall be."

"So be merry and jolly, obliging and loving to each other as you can, and the thought of it will be good for me—and we will make up for lost time in January." It was a hopeful suggestion, this—that by the power of thought, his children might transfer their joy to him, brightening his dim room at Roundhay with their celebrations, warming his heart though he was not physically with them. It was the same closeness Louis had longed for in very different circumstances, when he was in a filthy uniform and Paris was under bombing and siege, and it was the closeness motion pictures would one day provide: immersion into someone else's experience, even if you were an ocean away. *And as you will be, I shall be.*

In spite of the difficulties and delays, Le Prince did have cause for encouragement. He may have witnessed Eadweard Muybridge's moving images in person for the first time just a couple of weeks before the writing of his letter, on November 27, when the English photographer, still making stops on his grueling international tour, had lectured at the Leeds Mechanics' Institute before the members and friends of the Leeds Philosophical and Literary Society. Louis was a former member of the society, Muybridge's work was relevant to his own, and the venue was only a third of a mile south of the studio on Woodhouse Lane.

The presentation Muybridge gave that night was much the same as that witnessed by Edison in Orange in February 1887, though by now the photographer had retitled his talk "Animal Locomotion in Its Relation to Design in Art."[3] The audience watched a horse walk, trot, and gallop in two-second time loops, followed by the same movements in other quadrupeds, after which Muybridge, using a brief animation of a monkey, outlined the motor differences in bipeds. The photographer blamed "the equestrian statues of Marcus Aurelius" as well as the works of Albert Dürer and Rosa Bonheur for making us forget what the "cave-dwelling artists" of ancient times had painted correctly, he said, using lantern slides to support his theories.[4] The "white-haired magician, with wand in hand," revealing "silent secrets by the limelight," as the *Pall Mall Gazette* had described Muybridge earlier that year,[5] was still an electrifying speaker, "often droll," and his one-hour lectures habitually left those in attendance hungry for more.

If this was how audiences welcomed Muybridge's brief animations, then one wonders—how rapturous would the reception be for Le Prince's big-screen projections of life as it happened?

Louis hoped to find out soon. In the meantime, he continued to strive for secrecy. He stored his letters of patent with Richard Wilson, "for safe custody,"[6] and worked, Lizzie remembered, as much as possible in "safety and silence."[7]

Louis's promise to his children in that letter—to "make up for lost time in January,"[8] presumably when he hoped to see them—suggested he felt himself, once again, close to the end of the road. But he was overpromising—he would not be in New York in January, or his family in Leeds.

Lately Louis had often felt tired. Guilty, too. He carried a secret, something he hadn't broached with Lizzie. Word had got around that Louis Le Prince was back in Yorkshire, and in November 1888—right after the Roundhay garden scene, right after Sarah Whitley's death, a solicitor's clerk had knocked at the Roundhay door, looking for him. He was delivering a court summons. Le Prince opened the envelope and, scanning the page, recognized the name of George Nelson. The £330 he had owed Nelson in 1882 had now, with interest and costs, accrued to £600—nearly £50,000 in 2021.

In Leeds in 1888, £600 could buy you twenty-one horses, or sixty heads of cattle; it could have paid Mason's or Longley's wages for nearly five years. Unpaid, it could send a man to jail for even longer.

Louis did not tell his wife. The documents related to Nelson would not end up with the other Le Prince notes and letters; today they are to be found with Joseph Whitley's papers, left behind in Yorkshire, passed down through Jack Whitley's son, Arthur. Louis ignored the summons and was ordered, in his absence, to pay a total sum of £607 7s. 4p., as well as court costs. For a while afterward he strove to make dents in the debt. He sent Nelson ten pounds in December 1888 and seven pounds and ten shillings in January 1889, but it was three months before he paid another seven pounds and ten shillings in April, and then the same amount in August. He hadn't made a payment since.

The clock ticked. Louis brought the letter to a close.

And so kiss dear Mama and each other all round for me, and Phoebe and Alma and give my best compliments and regards to our friends Dr. and Mrs. Moore, Mr. and Mrs. McMullen—Mr. and Mrs. Currier, etc.[9]

Your ever loving
Pa.[10]

A TRICK OF
THE LIGHT

1890

◼

This is what we know of Louis Le Prince's life and work in 1890. His final truncated year is a lacuna wrapped around the mystery of his disappearance—eight months and sixteen days of fragmented and missing information, of unknowns and unknowables. Even before September 16, the day that cuts his life short as suddenly as a film reel breaks, Le Prince's 1890 as we know it is like a great director's final unfinished film, a confusion of solitary frames, incomplete scenes, disjointed moments, and inconclusive takes, the intent and coherence behind much of what remains fogged and damaged by time.

Here, then, is an assembly of Le Prince's final months.

Le Prince did not see his children and make up for lost time in January, nor did he ever return to New York City. He was sick with the flu over the New Year, and Longley was mourning the death of his infant daughter from bronchitis.

Louis wrote Lizzie on the fifteenth that he had "still a little to do at the machine," all related to "noise and heavy work . . . weight and shocks."[1] He had not taken a social call in a long time, he wrote, "as

I do not feel much like visiting even if I had time, but have only one object and must get right through."

Around this time Louis also seems to have moved out of Round-hay Cottage. He began heading his letters 37 West Hillary Street, the address right behind Woodhouse Lane. Joseph Whitley was moved to a facility in nearby Ilkley, a historic spa town in which Charles Darwin and Marie Tussaud had also sought treatment. It was a quiet, pleasant village, orderly rows of handsome Victorian stone framed by the dark green moors. Throughout 1890 Le Prince visited his father-in-law there whenever possible, usually on Sundays.

In late February, delighted at Adolphe's ever-deepening interest in chemistry, Louis went down to Briggate to handpick some textbooks. His eldest son was preparing for Columbia College in New York, and on February 28 Louis sent him the volumes he had bought. "My dear Adolphe," the accompanying letter began.[2] "I sent you by this post two books on quantitative analysis—One is rather old and I had the binding repaired; it seemed to me full of useful information . . . and you are now sufficiently advanced to make up and correct what may be old. Bye the bye [sic] begin by correcting in the margin all the errata you will find in this list. The other is Thorp's quantitative analysis which they know nothing of at the Mechanics [Institute], and which I found a few days ago at Beans" (a bookseller's at the top of Briggate). This was a new text, out in its eighth edition in 1889, and not inexpensive. "I think you are now well up in chemical books, and, what with those you may borrow from Dr. Moore and those you might find at the Astor (free library) there is not much fear of your being short for reference whenever needed for the time." He commended his son's decision to specialize his studies in assaying, meaning the analysis and valuation of ore and other precious materials—the kind of work Edison had had Dickson learn on the fly at West Orange a year earlier. Being well trained in "a practical branch" was wise, Louis wrote; "in a country like America it is one of great importance, and will pay best from the beginning soon as you get expert in it without preventing your progress in other branches when you find time to read or experiment in them." He signed off with a promise to find Adolphe even more books—an assayer's handbook, a metallurgy primer, a volume on geology.

On March 19 Louis wrote Lizzie, "It will take me another ten or fourteen days to complete the new machine, every alteration in one part always brings so many in the others. This is absolutely my last trial and I trust it will answer perfectly."[3] Eleven days later, Le Prince was in Paris, demonstrating his projector to the secretary of the Paris National Opera, Ferdinand Mobisson. Mobisson was an administrator, not a creative decision maker, though he was a proud aesthete. He wrote Le Prince a sworn "certificate,"[4] in which he "certif[ied] by this present to have been charged with the study (or examination) by means of the apparatus brought before me, of the system of projection of Animated Pictures for which M. Le Prince, Louis Aimé Augustin of New York, United States, has taken out in France patent rights dated the 11th of January 1888 . . . and to have made a complete study of this system." The Le Prince family later alleged the document was part of a contract for Louis's projections to become part of the National Opera's repertoire later in 1890. This is possible—the certificate, addressed to "whom it may concern" and notarized in front of the mayor of the Ninth Arrondissement, took some inconvenience to draw up and have witnessed, and is written with the formality of an official document. Mobisson's letter made no value judgments; it does not explicitly say Louis projected images for him, whether his "complete study" of Louis's "system" was based on the apparatus or simply Louis's diagrams and paperwork, or whether Mobisson was impressed by it. It is an odd document, aptly described by the French historian Léo Sauvage as "undoubtedly authentic but historically useless."[5] We do not know why Le Prince sought it, or to what purpose he used it.

After an undetermined period of time in France, Louis returned to England. In April he wrote to Lizzie that the projector was almost "perfect," and apologized at the same time for not enclosing "some cash which unfortunately I have not at hand—and it makes me feel very uneasy as I know you do not make much just now."[6] His letters of early 1890 suggest Louis was aware of his wife's growing discouragement, and he made efforts to reassure her the end was in sight. Around this time Louis requested she confirm a venue in which to hold his first public motion picture screening. Lizzie moved into the Jumel Mansion—the historic villa she'd been enchanted by on her first night in New York—sometime in 1890, and records also suggest she quit her post at the Institution for the Deaf sometime in 1889 or 1890. "A few more days and I will be through with the machine all going well so far, but there are so many pieces to adjust it takes an infinity of time," Louis wrote. He promised to send his wife a sketch, he wrote, "to give you an idea."[7]

But progress stalled yet again, and Le Prince's return continued to be delayed. Louis's next letter, on April 18, suggests his previous missive had gone without a reply—"I have not had news for more than a week," it opened,[8] "and hope nothing but occupation has prevented you and that I shall soon have your much prized letters." He promised again to be "reaching the end of the tedious work I was describing in my last, and therefore getting near the trial, the final, and I trust the successful one. What a relief it will be—I shall scarcely believe it is over after all this anxious tugging, waiting, and trying again."[9]

It was not over yet. It was May 24—five weeks later—when he informed Lizzie the projector was at last ready for "final tests."[10] In fairness, these last delays were caused by more than Louis's tinkering. On May 1, Leeds gas workers protesting the city's refusal to pay agreed overtime rates had taken their case to the streets and found widespread support. A thousand tailors joined the gas men in solidarity, as did slipper makers, mill workers, and every other quadrant of Leeds industry. The city fought back by reducing the number of paid hours in a gas worker's shift. The men responded by going on strike. Leeds was still overwhelmingly powered by gas, not electricity, and as the lights began to go out, anxiety gripped the city—and Louis, like many others, found himself working under rationed power.

Nonetheless, "I feel better for a start on Monday," he wrote Lizzie. "All else seems right and ready for the final—next week will settle it."[11] There survives no follow-up correspondence indicating whether this shoot took place on time, or whether it was successful, or whether it was just another in a long line of trials Louis had vainly hoped would be the last. In general, the tone of his letters in 1890 is little changed from his missives of previous years: sometimes hopeful, often frustrated, occasionally exuberant. They suggest his projector was tantalizingly close to being complete, and Longley later asserted that a satisfactory three-lens projector was finished sometime before the autumn of 1890. This projector, Longley recalled, "I considered a perfect one, it being very simple in construction, and gave the picture without blurs."[12]

On June 16, 1890, Ferdinand Mobisson's certificate was stamped "approved by the Préfet de la Seine." It is unclear what this meant, or whether Le Prince was in France for this to be done. On the same day hundreds of gas workers from London and Manchester arrived in Leeds, paid by officials to cross the picket lines and get the city running again. The scabs made their way to the gas plants under police escort, only to be pelted with bricks by the locals. Several days of rioting ensued. By July 1 every light in Leeds was out. The next day the city granted every one of the striking gas workers' demands.

In the fall, according to Lizzie Le Prince, Louis finally made plans to return to New York. She stated he had booked passage for himself and Joseph—and though Joseph did eventually travel with his great-nephew, Arthur Oates, no proof exists of when the tickets were first reserved, or for whom they were originally intended. A former pupil of Lizzie's by the name of Sara Addington wrote that she had visited Louis at Woodhouse Lane in August 1890 and "took upon myself . . . to urge upon him the immediate necessity of his return to the States."[13] Ms. Addington was sailing to New York herself a week later,[14] and "Mr. Le Prince informed me that he had his affairs so arranged that it was possible for him to sail on the same boat (the *Furnessia*) as my self [*sic*] and my brother." In the end, Louis, claiming he could not "have the [motion picture] apparatus packed up in time," elected not to leave Leeds yet.[15]

There is no doubt that Le Prince was in debt. He still owed over £600 to George Nelson's family, having made another small payment in July 1890, just enough to keep the suit against him from escalating. It was a large debt, but at ten pounds a month it would have taken just over five years to pay off—no more onerous than a bank loan or a mortgage, manageable, if absolutely necessary, by the taking of a day job, or the sale of some property. But Le Prince technically lived in New York, and needed only to return there to put himself out of reach of the British debt collectors; perhaps he was paying them the bare minimum required to keep them at bay until his departure. Invoices and receipts in the Le Prince archives show that Louis sometimes paid his bills late: Wilson Hartnell complained on at least one occasion that money was still owed on the arc lamp in the Woodhouse Lane yard, reminding Le Prince it couldn't be returned or repossessed, for it had been built to his peculiar specifications; similarly, Crompton's at least once asked for its dynamo back. At the same time, neither Mason nor Longley ever complained about a payment being skipped or an agreed fee being delayed. "Extremely just, and insisted on paying his account each week," Fred Mason asserted of Le Prince years later.[16] Louis's slowness in paying some of his suppliers may have been motivated not by lack of funds but by his frustration with their work, an emotion he let out regularly in his letters to Lizzie. There was enough cash on hand to board Joseph Whitley in the Ilkley home for several months, and to send him and his chaperone to New York in the fall of 1890; enough for Louis to travel to France repeatedly; enough for Lizzie to lease the Jumel Mansion and enough for all three of Louis's sons to attend Columbia College. Louis was still meeting his costs, and there is no indication that he had come to believe his camera and projector were destined to be failures.

Most important, Louis was still owed a vast sum of money by his brother, Albert, who was legally committed to paying it in full before the summer of 1892. When he traveled across the Channel to France in September 1890 with Richard Wilson and his wife, Louis may simply have intended to pay his brother a social visit before he sailed back to America, as Lizzie and Adolphe believed. But, especially if he was in need of liquidity to keep working or to stave off creditors, Louis had other reasons to want to speak with Albert.

Sixty thousand francs' worth of them, to be exact.

THE JUMEL
MANSION

1890

Even in its dilapidated state, its windows broken and its garden over-run with weeds, the Jumel Mansion was a magnificent house. It sat, behind stern iron gates, atop Harlem Heights, as if from a throne. It was said that from the upstairs windows one could see New Jersey, over Hell Gate to the Bronx, and all of Manhattan, from Spuyten Duyvil to the Battery.

It had first been the Morris Mansion, after Colonel Roger Morris, the monarchist who had had it built in 1765. Morris abandoned it in the fall of 1776, George Washington's ragtag army hot on his heels. Washington turned the house into his field quarters, living there for thirty-seven days, after which the British Army stormed and retook the building. They stayed until the war was over. The young US government then confiscated the mansion and, on July 10, 1790, now-president George Washington returned there with his cabinet and their families for a celebratory dinner. Thomas Jefferson, Alexander Hamilton, Henry Knox, and John Adams joined Washington for the meal—and their first full cabinet meeting.

For the next twenty years, the house passed from hand to hand, until it was bought in 1810 by Stephen and Eliza Jumel, a wealthy, well-gossiped-about local couple. Stephen was a successful wine merchant from France. The money was his; the gossip followed his wife.

Eliza had been born Elizabeth Bowen in a shack on the East Coast, to a penniless, unmarried fourteen-year-old mother. She'd been raised in a brothel on Rhode Island and then, when her mother was jailed for prostitution, sent off to an almshouse, after which, aged only ten, she was indentured out as a domestic servant. Somehow she made her way to New York City. As a young woman, she found work as an actress, treading the boards of Broadway for five years before she met Stephen Jumel. Their wedding outraged the city's upper class, but the newlyweds paid the whispers no heed. They invited them, even, and there was no better taunt than buying the Morris Mansion, the big white house on the hill, from which Eliza could now, literally, look down on those who for so long had looked down on her.

When Stephen's wine business failed in the mid-1810s, it was Eliza who took hold of his affairs while he sunk into a depression. She seized power of attorney over his assets and pursued his debtors and business partners relentlessly. She reinvested the little money they had left and not only saved them from bankruptcy but grew their fortune to a size greater than it had ever been before.

Then Stephen Jumel died in 1832, falling off a wagon and impaling himself on a pitchfork. He left Eliza the entirety of his fortune. The gossips speculated that his death had been no accident, and that his wife had murdered him.

Uncowed, Eliza remarried—within the year. Her new husband was seventy-seven-year-old Aaron Burr, former vice president of the republic, whose political career had ended in infamy the moment he shot and killed Alexander Hamilton in a duel in Weehawken, New Jersey. In the aftermath of the duel Burr had become embroiled in a failed plot to cause the secession of Louisiana and Texas, and he overcame the charges of treason only thanks to a lack of evidence. Perhaps Burr, reviled and badly in debt, saw Eliza as his ticket back to wealth.

He swiftly squandered away much of her money on bad real estate investments. She filed for divorce less than five months after their wedding. In a flourish of spectacular provocation, the divorce attorney Eliza chose to represent her was Alexander Hamilton Jr.

Burr, cut off from Eliza's fortune, died alone in a boardinghouse on Staten Island, just hours after the divorce had been finalized. Eliza outlived him nearly twenty years. She stayed in the house in Harlem Heights, which everyone in New York now referred to as the Jumel Mansion. The seclusion affected her wits. Charles Dickens visited her during his American tour of 1842, and she became an inspiration for one of his new characters, *Great Expectations'* Miss Havisham—a middle-aged woman, formerly wealthy but defrauded by a man, now shut up in the rooms of a decaying mansion following a nervous breakdown.

She died at home, aged ninety, leaving a fortune to a variety of charities and the bulk of her land to a trust for the establishment of a "great Episcopalian church and school."[1] Her descendants fought over her estate for twenty-four years, and it took a trip to the Supreme Court for the will to be settled in 1889. Eliza's son-in-law, to whom the estate was granted, promptly put it up for sale.

The following year an unexpected party made inquiries about leasing the house. Her name, she told the owners, was Elizabeth Le Prince.

Lizzie had felt an affinity with the mansion from the moment she'd seen it that first night in New York, when she and Louis had sat under its willow trees, dreaming about what they might do "if we ever grew rich." There was no better place to mark Louis's return than *that* house.

The owners accepted Lizzie's offer—it turned out the mansion had been difficult to rent out. It was badly in need of upkeep, and people balked when they heard about the ghosts. A Hessian soldier fighting on the British side in 1776 had allegedly tripped down the stairs and impaled himself on his own bayonet, and his spirit was said to linger.

In the past servants had whispered that George Washington's own ghost could be heard in the night, pacing the creaking floorboards after the last gaslight had been snuffed out. Most likely, others said, it was Eliza herself who moved around the rooms after dark.

If Lizzie heard the stories, they didn't bother her. Her memoirs record no hauntings, no apparitions, no mysterious bumps or thuds in the night. All she could see was the house's beauty. Inside there was color everywhere: the parlor all in green, from the chair covers to the curtains, the corner rooms with fireplaces and windowsills painted red. The highlight was the octagon room at the back of the house, the blue wallpaper painted with clouds, light pouring in from four large windows around the fireplace. She could see a motion picture screening there, she thought.[2] The room was long and broad, and the walls were like the sky, transporting you to another place, another state, before the projector ever started rolling. This had been George Washington's war cabinet room, one of the rooms in which America had come into being. It was the kind of room Louis deserved for the day he would add his own chapter to history.

Lizzie moved the entire family into the house and they set about restoring it, "from attic to cellar. It was an arduous task on small means."[3] The work took months, and Mariella, Adolphe, Joseph, Aimée, and Fernand all chipped in: "every inch of the building . . . cleansed, new roofing added, and even its sunken flagstone pathways and carriage drive dug up and relaid," Lizzie listed, "and the remains of a secret entrance from below closed by bricklayers." She set the boys to polishing the oak floors by "rushing flagstones covered in old blankets soaked in beeswax" across them "at a wild pace." When they were done, Lizzie invited Mariella, Aimée, and their friends to dance across the rooms, an old trick she'd learned, their "many light feet" smoothing the boards "to a mirror-like brightness."[4]

It was a happy time. Louis was coming home, the all-consuming work was almost at an end, the family would be together again. The Le Princes prepared for life, finally, to return to normal.

DIJON

◼

T hough there are gaps and contradictions left unclear in the final year of Louis's life, the picture of the last day he was seen is in sharper focus, recorded—firsthand in correspondence, and secondhand in Lizzie and Adolphe's memoirs—by the people who lived it with him.

There was nothing especially striking about September 16, Albert Le Prince said when he walked through the events of the day for Lizzie. Louis had come to Dijon to visit a few days earlier, and the sixteenth was the day he left, on the afternoon express to Paris, after missing the morning train.

Louis had traveled to France sometime in late August or early September, at the invitation of Richard Wilson, his banker friend, and Wilson's wife. The couple planned to tour the cathedrals and vineyards of the country for their fall holiday. They knew Louis would be leaving England in September and "prevailed on my husband to accompany them . . . before sailing to New York,"[1] Lizzie wrote. Louis, who had earlier in the year told his wife he was too preoccupied with experimenting to indulge social calls, accepted—a further sign, Lizzie insisted, that work on the camera and projector was complete.

Fred Mason agreed. In "the spring of 1890," he later declared under oath,[2] "Mr. Le Prince decided to go to New York, where his wife and family were, to show moving pictures there. He ordered from Mr.

Trinder, a maker of port-manteaux in Woodhouse Lane, special cases to hold the apparatus." When the traveling cases arrived, Louis gave Mason and Longley a final list of instructions, and asked them to have the devices ready and packed when he returned: he would be sailing almost immediately. He told Mason he was accepting the Wilsons' invitation so that, while in France, he could also "see about patent business, [and] also bid adieu to his brother, an architect and engineer of Dijon."[3]

Le Prince stayed with the Wilsons until they reached Bourges, a city of picturesque timber houses in central France, where the group visited the famous Gothic cathedral. Richard Wilson remembered Louis being in "high spirits" throughout the trip,[4] and Mason later said he had been shown "several cheerful and optimistic letters" Louis had written from France to his family.[5] These were words no one had used to describe Le Prince in more than three years. He appeared relieved, as if a great weight had been lifted from his shoulders.

On Friday, September 12, Le Prince left his friends, traveling east by rail through Burgundy to Dijon. They agreed, Wilson said, to meet again in Paris on the following Tuesday, the sixteenth, to take the night boat to England, and then stay in London a while, visiting the French Exhibition at Earl's Court before continuing on to Leeds—and, in Louis's case, to America.

Louis alighted in Dijon under a stifling sun. The streets were congested with works: a new tram line was being installed, and copper wires were stretched overhead to prepare for the citywide installation of the telephone.

Albert's home was still at number 40 rue Berbisey, in the house bought for his late wife as a wedding present. It was one of the oldest streets in the city, a narrow strip lined with private homes. Louis stayed with his brother in the town house, where Albert lived with his children: Marie, twenty-one; Marguerite, nineteen; and Ernest, twelve. Albert was busy at work; Marie remembered *Oncle* Louis giving the children English lessons and recommending books for them to read. She, too, remembered Le Prince being lighthearted and joyful. "He looked quite well," she wrote her cousins later,[6] and said "he should be home in a fortnight." She and the children "took long walks with him in the park, and always he spoke of returning to New York."

In her letter, Marie confirmed that Louis left on Tuesday, September 16, "intending to pass by Paris and embark in England." When he did not appear at their agreed rendezvous in Paris, Richard and Mrs. Wilson left for England without him. They may have expected Louis on the morning train—the one he had missed—and perhaps left before the next service arrived, unaware Le Prince had taken that one instead, though there were ways for Louis to inform them in time of his change of plans. Perhaps Le Prince *did* make it to Paris, but the Wilsons had already gone—and something had befallen him there.

By mid-October Lizzie began worrying about her husband's lack of correspondence. Wilson and the Woodhouse Lane crew were also questioning why Louis had yet to return or give any explanation for the delay. Jack Whitley, still in Germany, was contacted, and it appears he was the one to send a relative, Arthur Oates, around to Ilkley to check on Joseph. He also cabled Albert, who seemed stricken to hear Louis had never appeared in Paris. The news, Marie wrote, made him "unquiet and sad."[7]

Longley went to meet Mason at his father's woodworking shop, and the two of them walked next door to 160 Woodhouse Lane. Inside they "found everything quite normal," Mason said, "the machines intact, and tools, drawings, photographs, as well as a quantity of discarded material, lying about." In time, "Mr. Richard Wilson, a friend of the family and manager of Lloyds Bank, Leeds, took charge of all the effects and proceeded to dispose of such parts as could readily be sold."[8] Wilson said he got rid of the "spoilt materials" that could not be put up for sale, and "forwarded to [Louis's] family certain of his possessions and retained some which were either too bulky or too delicate to despatch," including at least one camera, negatives and positives he described as "long series of . . . figures in motion," as well as "a great many drawings of the machinery in the camera and parts thereof."[9]

A local photographer by the name of Charles Pickard bought the heavy four-legged stand Mason had built for the camera. Mason kept for himself "a few relics," though later, as an old man, he said he was "sorry now that I did not secure some exposed films and the drawings, as unfortunately nothing was done to preserve them. That they might have historical importance was not appreciated."[10]

As days turned into weeks, their hopes dwindled. Joseph Whitley signed over control of what was left of Whitley Partners to the firm's manager, Henry Horsman, granting Horsman power of attorney to settle his affairs. The old man bade goodbye to Yorkshire, where he had lived his entire life, and sailed to America without Louis. Lizzie and Mariella began to journey down to Battery Park every day, scanning the faces pouring forth from every arriving steamer. Le Prince's body did not appear at Dijon's morgue, or Paris's. The newspapers, which made hay of violent crimes, sordid mysteries, and *faits divers*, reported no incidents on the train, no unidentified bodies along the tracks. The railway company, which by policy made an investigation of every incident, however minor, had no such case on file for the train in question.

Lizzie received word from Albert and Jack that missing-person files had been opened with Scotland Yard and the Paris police. Albert posted notices in the press, appealing for information. When Lizzie asked if she should come to Europe to help in the search, Albert, through Jack, advised she stay in New York, in case Louis found his way home.

The investigations went nowhere, and the newspaper ads elicited no response. Lizzie contacted the New York City Police Department, and met with an officer she remembered as "Captain Williams"[11]— almost certainly Inspector Alexander "Clubber" Williams, who in 1890 ran the department's First Inspection District, covering the entirety of Manhattan's east side from the Battery to 104th Street. Williams was a corrupt, brutal officer in a corrupt, brutal police department, and had earned his nickname due to a tendency to terrorize citizens rather than investigate their complaints. ("There is more law in the end of a policeman's nightstick than in a decision of the Supreme Court,"[12] he once said, and he proudly claimed to get into at least one physical con-frontation every day.)[13] Williams listened to Lizzie's story and seemed to have decided Louis was a troublesome lowlife. He suggested Lizzie charge her husband with desertion and have his photograph placed in the police department's "rogues' gallery," a book collecting mug shots of wanted criminals. Williams's boss, Head Detective Thomas F. Byrnes, had introduced the gallery as a way to identify and defame suspects. "While [criminals] could use fake names," Byrnes quipped, "they could not grow fake faces."[14]

Lizzie "indignantly"[15] rejected Williams's offer. Perhaps if she accused her husband of a crime other than desertion, Williams suggested, and again Lizzie objected. In that case, Williams replied, the best he could do was have her go through the photographs of "supposed New York citizens found dead abroad,"[16] on the small chance Le Prince was one of them. The pictures were brought and Lizzie thumbed through them. Weeks earlier in the Barge Office, flipping through registries of arrivals, she had longed every day to see her husband's name; now, going through the paper photographs, she must have prayed for the opposite: not to come face-to-face with him, photographed as a corpse.

She reached the end of the album. Louis's photograph was not in it. She left the police station shaken.

"The disappearance of Mr. Le Prince was indeed extraordinary," Frederic Mason recalled decades later. After years of work, Louis had, according to Mason, "achieved undoubted success" with both the camera and projector. His sudden, unexplained vanishing, Mason wrote, was "a tragedy."[17]

Sometime in November, the cold reality of being without a husband must have dawned on Lizzie Le Prince. She was unemployed, having quit teaching in anticipation of Louis's return. She had five children and a senile father to look after; an employee, Phoebe, whom she had stopped being able to afford years earlier; and a lease on a sprawling historic home she no longer had a use for. She could make no money from the camera and projector even if Richard Wilson shipped them over from England: Louis's patents and rights remained his and his alone for seven years, the period required by the law to have him declared dead and his property transferred to his next of kin.

Lizzie sent her brother another telegram. *Should* she come to Europe herself? Was it worth the expense?

Jack replied quickly by Western Union. His message read: "Albert says Gus knows one thousand pounds due him from Boulabert estate some day. Even if you came you could do no more than we are doing."[18]

It's a confusing cable to read, a hundred and thirty years later. Jack had used the present tense—"Gus knows." Did he still hope Louis was alive, two months after September 16? Was he sparing his sister's feelings?

And then there was the money. A thousand pounds, the equivalent of £82,000 (or almost $114,000) in 2021, and only about a third of the amount Albert had agreed to pay for Louis's share of their inheritance just three years earlier. Was it possible Albert had already paid Louis the first two-thirds? It was a very comfortable sum—if he had, why had Louis never mentioned it in his letters? Was it possible the camera and projector had cost so much to develop? Why—though Lizzie did not know this—had Louis not settled his debt with the Nelsons in full, if he'd had that much money at his disposal?

Finally, there was the timeline. The transfer of the deed to the house on rue Bochart de Saron had been very specific: Albert was to pay Louis in full by July 1, 1892. That was now less than two years away, and Albert was promising the remainder "some day." When Lizzie opened the telegram, did those words rankle? Did they stand out?

Christmas crept ever closer as Lizzie and the children awaited more news. If Lizzie ever speculated on her husband's fate, she must have contemplated the obvious. Nineteenth-century cities were dangerous places. The Whitechapel killer, now known as Jack the Ripper, was still strong in the public's mind, as were the deeds of another suspected serial killer, who between 1887 and 1889 had murdered several women and thrown their dismembered body parts into the Thames. In France the newspapers sometimes read like a catalog of horrors, columns stacked with short items each as morbid as anything by Robert Louis Stevenson or Edgar Allan Poe. In the twenty-four hours surrounding Louis's disappearance, in the Dijon press alone, one could read about a tourist who had been set upon in the street and beaten to death by several men; about a taxman in Lyon who, suspecting his wife of adultery, had thrown sulfuric acid in her face, disfiguring her and blinding her in one eye;[19] or about a resident of a small town in the Ardèche, who woke up one morning to find two severed children's feet on the pavement outside his house, a little white bonnet tossed in the mud.[20] In Paris, the bodies of mugging victims were pulled out of the Seine every week.

What if Louis had just been at the wrong place at the wrong time, seized by thieves as he exited the train station in Paris, his valuables ripped from him, a blow to the head cracking his skull, or a knife tearing through his flesh, blood soaking his waistcoat? His body thrown into the river, his pocketbook tossed aside, rendering him unidentifiable? It was the sort of thing that happened every day.

And then, on May 28, 1891, Lizzie's head was turned to another theory. Less than nine months after Louis's disappearance, with his patents still frozen and unusable, she woke up to that morning's edition of the New York *Sun*. The biggest headline on the front page, in bold print over on the far-right column, simply read:

THE KINETOGRAPH.
Edison's Latest and Most Surprising Device.
Pure Motion Recorded and Reproduced

DICKSON DX

■

Edison had done it: he had completed his motion picture device and managed to shoot footage he was ready to show publicly. Unexpectedly, he decided the first Americans to see a photographic moving picture should be the ladies of the Federation of Women's Clubs. In May 1891, after one of the group's council meetings in the Union Hall of Orange, New Jersey,[1] its most notable members were invited to the nearby Glenmont estate for a luncheon hosted by Mrs. Mina Edison. Her famous husband was away on business, but he had left two surprises for Mina to share with her guests. The first was a charming welcome speech, recorded by him beforehand, and played for their delight on his personal phonograph. The second was at the laboratory, a short ride away. It was a small, unassuming pine box, a little like a phonograph, except for the pinhole viewer on the top, which the ladies were invited to examine. Pressing one eye against the small opening in turn, each of them was treated to a brief motion picture of a moustachioed young man, standing in a spotlight in front of a black curtain. He bowed and smiled, then, closing his eyes dramatically, he raised his hat in his right hand, and slowly passed it over to his left.

The machine, they were told, was the Wizard's newest wonder, the Kinetoscope. The man in the picture was a young Scottish photographer and lab assistant by the name of William K. L. Dickson.

*   *   *

The Kinetoscope, as unveiled in the spring of 1891, was a peephole viewer, using a fifty-foot loop of celluloid film on rollers, that could play short black-and-white films. The device was a crossbreed of other people's work—Marey's and Le Prince's long bands of sensitized film, Anschütz's eye-height peephole Schnellseher prototype. The rotating disk shutter appeared inspired by Muybridge, and the perforations along the film followed similar designs by Le Prince, Friese-Greene, and Reynaud.

Dickson, who had overseen the composition of the viewer, had plenty of inspiration at hand. A description of Friese-Greene's camera had appeared in both the *Photographic News* and *Scientific American* in early 1891, and Marey's work had been written about in the latter publication in January. The Kinetoscope worked well, as witnessed by the members of the Federation of Women's Clubs, but the Kinetograph camera didn't. Edison had yet to apply for a full patent on it, and he wouldn't until late August of that year; it's likely the images viewed by Mina's guests in May had actually been taken either on a reproduction of Marey's camera, or as individual stills on glass plates, transferred to pliable film. Dickson insisted the footage of him smiling and raising his hat had been taken on celluloid, but he also claimed to have shown Edison a similar scene in the fall of 1889, this one with synchronized sound—an obvious lie, invented so that Dickson could pretend to have solved moving pictures *before* Edison returned from the Paris World's Fair and his inspection of Marey's laboratory.

Dickson's meaningful contribution was in the final design of the celluloid strips. He corresponded often with George Eastman, requesting changes and improvements to the film as he needed them, effectively guiding Eastman's upgrading of his product. And he eventually settled on an image format—each frame rectangular and 35 mm wide—that would become the standard film exhibition format around the world.

In 1892, with the Kinetograph finally, if imperfectly, completed, Dickson oversaw the erection of a filming stage on the laboratory grounds at West Orange. It was the first studio of its kind in the world and was built to his exact needs and specifications. The building was a blocky, oddly shaped oblong, covered in black tar paper and standing on a revolving platform, so that it could be spun to face the sun at any time of day, the roof hinged like a jaw that could open and close as necessary to let in the optimal amount of sunlight. The walls inside were a dense black, to contrast with the brightly lit film subjects, and a rail ran all around the stage so that the heavy Kinetograph, placed on a table, could be moved as required to set up shots from a variety of angles. The darkroom was on the other end of the studio, down a red-lit tunnel.

The building was complete in January 1893. The Edison staff, struck by how closely it resembled a giant police wagon, called it the Black Maria.

The demonstration for Mina's luncheon guests—details of which were promptly leaked to the press, particularly Edison's favored *Sun*, which always gave him good copy—had unfolded much like Edison's first reveal of the phonograph in the offices of *Scientific American* thirteen years earlier: it was the public unveiling of an unfinished machine. It would be 1894 before the Kinetoscope was ready to be brought to market, and Dickson oversaw those preparations, too. By now, Edison was spending more and more of his time at Ogden with his mine, wasting a fortune and having the time of his life. Ogden was a world away from boardrooms and 65 Fifth Avenue, from the war of the currents Edison wasn't winning and probably wouldn't win. He loved the work crews, the long days, the dusty air. In the winter everything froze; in the summer it was so hot and humid Edison joked the fish in the local pond "swam out into the air."[2] Workers died—five in one swoop in the summer of 1892, crushed under timber when a stock house collapsed—but Edison earned his crews' respect because, one of them said, "he would never send a man anywhere that he would not go himself."[3]

Motion pictures, on the other hand, did not excite him. He had always assessed inventions by their usefulness, and he couldn't see any merit in the entertainment business. The Kinetoscope did "not have any particular commercial value," he told a journalist right after the device was announced. "It will be rather of a sentimental worth."[4] Its sentimentality may have been why Edison thought it appropriate to premiere the device to the members of the Federation of Women's Clubs, rather than to the men of *Scientific American*. It was a reflection of his biases, through and through.

Shortly before the Kinetoscope finally went on the market, Edison wrote to Eadweard Muybridge, with whom he'd kept in loose correspondence. In his letter he mistakenly calls the viewing device the Kinetograph, which was the name of the camera—one of several basic errors about the machines he would make over the years, suggesting he was not as familiar with their construction as the man who allegedly invented them should be. He reiterated his feelings about moving pictures. "I am very doubtful if there is any Commercial in it and fear they will not earn their costs," Edison wrote.[5] When Dyer & Seely told him it would cost $150 to patent the Kinetoscope around the world, and not just in America, Edison told them not to bother. "It isn't worth it," he said.[6] Cost, in this instance, was not his only concern. He knew the applications would not be accepted abroad, where a long list of men—Marey, Reynaud, Anschütz, Friese-Greene, Donisthorpe, and Le Prince among them—already held patents that preempted virtually every design element Dickson had put in Edison's own machines.

The first Kinetoscope parlor opened in April 1894, in a former shoe store in New York, at the corner of Broadway and Twenty-Seventh Street. Inside were ten of the machines, arranged back-to-back in two rows of five. Each was powered by an electric battery and loaded with a different short film. An attendant sold tickets for twenty-five cents, and for the price of admission every customer could choose five of the ten films to view. Each short ran twenty seconds or less, and while it was a bust of Thomas Edison that looked down on every customer who entered the shop, it was Dickson who had directed every film.

All made in the Black Maria—the Kinetograph was too heavy to be moved very far, and too insensitive to take pictures in artificial light— the films included staged boxing bouts and a short demonstration by the bodybuilder Eugen Sandow; circus acrobatics; brief observational scenes of a blacksmith or a barber at work. In time Dickson would film cockfights, cat fights, Broadway dance numbers, and tricks from Buffalo Bill's Wild West show.

Curious New Yorkers lined up outside the Broadway shop, and within months there were Kinetoscope parlors open for business in Chicago, Philadelphia, San Francisco, Atlantic City, and Omaha. Before the end of 1894 there were further outlets in London and Paris.

The Kinetoscope was the last great invention to come out of the West Orange lab in the nineteenth century, as Edison cut costs to the bone and traded his fellowship of experimenters for a new community down the mine. Samuel Insull left for Chicago, and Alfred Tate quit in May 1894. Charles Batchelor retired. The flurry of patent submissions and caveats stopped: Edison applied for only one patent in the three years 1894 to 1896.

Dickson stuck it out the longest. With Edison's inner circle peeling away, he may have felt that Edison himself, the center of power, was laid bare for access. But with no new experiments scheduled and no promotion forthcoming, he found himself effectively a full-time filmmaker, a profession for which he felt no driving passion. Edison appointed a hard-nosed administrator named William Gilmore to take over from Tate, and he and Dickson clashed. Dickson, after his ore-milling breakthroughs and the success of the Kinetoscope, thought of himself as Edison's closest collaborator—the feeling, on Edison's part, was not mutual—and he resented Gilmore, an outsider he referred to as his "arch enemy," being appointed his "successor."[7]

When, at the end of 1894, Dickson was separately approached by two businessmen, the Kinetoscope distributor Otway Latham and a Syracuse engineer named Henry Marvin, each of whom asked Dickson to join them in building a machine to rival the Kinetoscope, Dickson listened to their offers. To Latham, he complained that he was the true inventor of the Kinetograph and Kinetoscope and resented Edison's stealing his credit.[8] With Marvin, he pulled out a stack of cards and drew a series of Xs on them, flipping through them like a book and suggesting a similar sort of system, using Eastman's celluloid film and a hand crank in a design somewhere between a Zoopraxiscope and a Kinetoscope. Marvin, along with a fellow engineer by the name of Herman Casler, refined the concept and applied for a patent on a motion picture device he called the Mutoscope. Dickson agreed to consult on the paperwork, pledging to help Marvin and Casler steer clear of any mechanisms that might infringe on Edison's own patents, as long as the Syracuse men kept his involvement a secret.[9] Latham, meanwhile, hired Dickson's former assistant Eugene Lauste to work for him instead, and Lauste engineered a projector he called the Eidoloscope, a model most notable for its use of a mechanical part that became known as the Latham loop, which steadied the celluloid film as it moved through the machine.

Dickson was present with Lauste and Latham when they made their first film, a boxing match they filmed on the roof of Madison Square Garden, the brightest location they could think of. They premiered it in a hall on Broadway, but the projection was a failure, the image too dark to be clearly visible. Lauste returned to the drawing board.

Soon Gilmore caught wind of the double-dealing. He called Dickson into his office on April 2, 1895. Dickson protested that Edison "knew what I was doing" and saw no problem with it—so Gilmore, calling his bluff, stood up out of his chair and told him they would go confirm this with Edison, who happened to be down from Ogden. Dickson knew this meant humiliation. As Gilmore explained the situation to Edison, in the same library office where the Wizard had met Eadweard Muybridge and first considered the topic of motion pictures, Dickson lost his temper. He gave Edison an ultimatum: it was Gilmore or him, he said, there was no going back to working together.

Edison told Dickson to clear his desk.

After seven years, Dickson's time working for a man he described as "his favorite scientific hero"[10] was over. He was embarrassed and deeply hurt. Later he would insist, to save his pride, that he had "resigned."[11] Edison never forgot the day either, but for different reasons. For years to come, whenever Dickson came up in lab correspondence, Edison would underline his name and refer to him as "DX"—double cross.

Dickson packed his things and left.

CINEMA

1895–1901

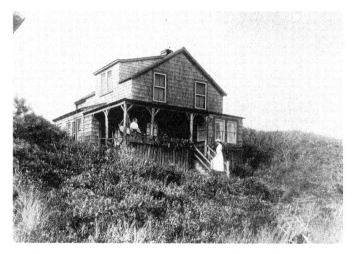

The Le Princes' summer home at Point O' Woods, Fire Island,
date unknown. (Private Collection. Courtesy of Laurie Snyder)

Three days after Christmas 1895, the Lumière brothers premiered their newest invention in the basement of the Grand Café, on the Boulevard des Capucines, a fifteen-minute walk south of the rue Bochart de Saron. The basement, billed grandly as the Salon Indien, was a small, pokey space, often rented out by photographers and artists as a gallery. Auguste and Louis Lumière stretched a white screen at one end of the room and arranged five rows of metallic chairs to face it. At the back of the room, on a sturdy four-legged easel, was their camera-and-projector, a portable box of wood and metal with brass lenses. The brothers' father, Antoine, was outside, propping a wooden sign up on the sidewalk under the red awning of the Grand Café. Antoine, who had been a sign painter in his youth, had taken particular care with this one. He'd drawn an arrow, pointing down to the basement, and above it the name of the invention on display: *Cinématographe*.

Their first screening, in the afternoon, was private, held for the press (none of whom deigned to show up) and a handful of friends: the manufacturer of cameras and magic lanterns Léon Gaumont, the illusionist Georges Méliès, the directors of the Folies Bergère and the Musée Grévin. The excitable Méliès, who owned the Théâtre Robert-Houdin, was intrigued as he strolled down the boulevard and hopped down the steps, the crisp sunshine fading to black as he entered the obscure basement. Méliès had heard whispers of this new machine, which had already been seen by select businessmen. Word was it reproduced animated pictures in a quality never seen before, better still than the dancing paintings of Charles-Émile Reynaud's Théâtre Optique, which had been raking in money at the Musée Grévin for three years without showing any signs of tiring the public.

Méliès took his seat. Antoine Lumière spoke briefly, introducing the invention and apologizing playfully for its long, off-putting name. The lights dimmed. "We found ourselves in the presence of a small screen," Méliès remembered,[1] "and after several seconds, a still photograph showing the Place Bellecour in Lyon appeared on the screen." He rolled his eyes and scoffed. *A magic lantern show?* He leaned into the ear of the man sitting next to him. "So, it's for projections they bothered us," Méliès whispered with a shrug. "I've been doing them for ten years."

"I had hardly finished my sentence," Méliès said, "when a horse-drawn cart *moved* toward us, followed by other vehicles and then pedestrians—in a word—street life! We stared flabbergasted at this sight, stupefied and surprised beyond all expression. At the end of the show there was complete chaos."[2] The man from the Musée Grévin rushed to Auguste and Louis, congratulated them, offered them 20,000 francs for the rights to the device. The director of the Folies Bergère shouted over him—*he* would pay *50,000* francs!

Méliès couldn't get close to the young brothers, but their father, Antoine, was standing by on his own. The magician walked up to him and offered 10,000 francs—less than the others, but all he had. He'd have paid "a fortune in gold" if he had it, he said. The elder Lumière turned him down, just as his sons were turning down the others. Antoine smiled, his hair and moustache as white as fresh snow. "Young man, you'll thank me," he told Méliès. "My sons' invention is not for sale. It would ruin you." It was an enjoyable "curiosity," to be sure, but "it has no commercial future." He wouldn't budge—no matter how forcefully Méliès disagreed.

The evening screening, the first paying showing, seemed to prove Antoine right. Only thirty-five people followed the hand-painted sign down into the basement, paying a franc each. It was not even enough money to cover the room rental. As no journalists had come to the preview, none of the next day's papers mentioned the event even happening.

Except for one. A man for the progressive daily *Le Radical*, the offices of which were just a few streets away from the Grand Café, had wandered in. His reaction was published on New Year's Eve. The Cinématographe, he wrote,[3] was a "marvel," "one of the most peculiar inventions of our time." Watching the images thrown onto the screen had been like living a dozen experiences, "with all the illusion of real life," without ever changing place: he'd been watching a blacksmith, flames rising from the hearth, a column of white steam hissing when the horseshoe was dunked in water, and then suddenly he was among pedestrians and the traffic of Lyon, only then to be transported to the sea, "a sea so real, full of waves, so colourful, so restless."[4] This invention, he knew, would change the world. "We can now record and play back life," he wrote. "We will be able to see our families again, long after they are gone."[5]

Word of mouth spread. In the first week of the New Year, 1896, a line of people gathered at Antoine's wooden sign before the first showing of the day, and soon snaked four hundred yards down the Boulevard des Capucines. It never seemed to get any shorter. By mid-January, the gate receipts to the little basement under the café amounted to 2,500 francs—a day.

Every day.

In New York City, W. K. L. Dickson and his new partners—Henry Marvin, Herman Casler, and their financial backer Elias Koopman—incorporated their own motion picture company, which they named American Mutoscope. Their peepshow Mutoscope competed with Edison's Kinetoscopes, both machines coin operated for a nickel a view. The movie parlors accordingly became known as "nickelodeons." The runaway success of the Cinématographe motivated Dickson to design his own projector, the Biograph.

Thomas Edison, too, had taken notice of the Cinématographe, which was about to debut in New York. Without Dickson, Edison was unable to design a projector of his own, leading him to buy the rights to an experimental device called the Vitascope, invented by Thomas Armat and Charles Francis Jenkins, and to promote it as his own instead. The Vitascope, advertised as "Edison's Greatest Marvel," premiered at Koster and Bial's Music Hall in April 1896, with Edison sitting in a box, accepting the applause of the crowd—and Armat sweating in the projection booth. Within three months it was outdone by the Cinématographe anyway, as well as by Dickson's Biograph, which used a wider film format for higher-quality big-screen projections. Edison withdrew the Vitascope in November and released a Projecting Kinetoscope. In doing so, he caught up, finally, not just to the Lumière brothers' version of moving images, but to Le Prince's original conception of the theatrical experience, obsessively sketched out in his notebooks years earlier. But the Projecting Kinetoscope was a failure. Edison didn't understand photography as his rivals did, and it left him, uncharacteristically, behind the curve.

In the summer of 1896, Lizzie Le Prince sailed to Europe with Mariella, for the first time in nearly a decade, on a mission to track down the policemen who had investigated Louis's disappearance. In a year's time Louis would be declared legally dead and his patent rights would revert to his wife; the journey seems to have been one last attempt to follow in his final footsteps. Lizzie and Mariella stayed briefly in England, traveling over to France to see Albert, as well as Jack, who now lived full time in Brittany. They looked for signs of Louis, for evidence that might lead back to Edison, but the trails that had been cold for years were invisible now. Jim Longley was away from Leeds, being treated for ill health.[6] Le Prince's landlady at West Hillary Street had suffered a paralytic stroke and was taking no visitors. In Paris it was the same. Monsieur Dougan, the inspector who had handled Louis's case, could not be found—Lizzie was told he had retired. She met with Albert and "went carefully over every detail of my husband's visit to him, and his departure in good health and spirits from the Dijon station," but identified no new clues.[7] Albert reassured her again "that every hospital, asylum, morgue etc. had been inquired of between Dijon and Leeds."

Back in New York, Lizzie watched bitterly as her husband's invention, as she saw it, took the world by storm under different names, lining everyone's pockets but her own family's. She'd held on to the Jumel Mansion until 1894, when she was finally forced to give it up and move back to smaller accommodation on West 170th Street. She had returned to work, starting her own school, and Mariella and Aimée were employed as teachers, too, their incomes just enough to cover tuition for the three boys—Adolphe, Joseph, and Fernand Léon—all attending Columbia College uptown.

Lizzie was certain Thomas Edison had something to do with her husband's disappearance. Everyone knew he stole credit that wasn't his, and Louis had vanished eight months before Edison had suddenly unveiled "his" Kinetoscope, so similar to Louis's invention. Adolphe, too, was certain his father had been "eliminated."[8] It was said, after all, that Edison sometimes worked with Allan Pinkerton's National

Detective Agency, whose squads infiltrated unions and violently broke up labor movements, whose armed watchmen could be relied on to do whatever it took to protect the financial interests of their clients. The first convict to die by electricity, William Kemmler, had been executed in August 1890, just weeks before Louis's disappearance—and the press had revealed since that, in an effort to smear George Westinghouse, whose alternative current was used in the death chamber, Edison had paid expert witnesses to campaign for the use of electrocution, had sanctioned disturbing experiments on stray dogs at the West Orange laboratory, and had even helped design the electric chair.

Who was to say what lengths the Wizard would have gone to for "his" last great invention?

Lizzie's only comfort was a large, rambling summer house her sons had built for the family out in Point O' Woods, on the tip of Fire Island, on land recently bought by the Chautauqua Institution. Only there, in the warm sand and yellowing grass, the waves crashing gently onto the beach, were they away from the motion pictures, from the Kinetoscopes and Cinématographes and Biographs and Vitascopes, the Eidoloscopes and Phantascopes and Kineopticons.

Only there could Lizzie resign herself to never being able to hold Thomas Edison accountable.

That all changed when Edison—of all people—inadvertently threw out the rope with which she might hang him.

ADOLPHE

1897–1901

Edison, like Lizzie, resented the heap of motion picture shows raking in cash in every theater and fairground in America, and for much the same reason: the motion pictures, he felt, were *his* invention. His first caveat of the fall of 1888 preceded the Lumières and everyone who came after them. He instructed Frank Dyer, his patent lawyer, to initiate lawsuits against every movie company operating in New York, on the basis that Edison Manufacturing owned not only the rights to the Kinetoscope and Kinetograph themselves, but to the very medium of motion pictures on celluloid.

The first few companies threatened by Dyer chose to wind up their businesses rather than face expensive litigation. Those that did fight were strung out until they were on the verge of bankruptcy and then surrendered. Emboldened, Edison and Dyer decided to go after their biggest domestic rival: American Mutoscope.

Henry Marvin was ready and waiting for them. Barrel-chested and over six feet tall, Marvin had one thing in common with Frank Dyer: he saw patent lawsuits as street fights. "We did what people do" in court, he explained. "We fought the best we knew how. We belittled the possessions of our enemies, and we magnified our own possessions."[1]

Marvin had one ace up his sleeve, another bit of insider information provided by Dickson. As early as 1892, Edison had tried to turn his motion picture caveats into full patents, but the Patent Office refused him, on the basis that the Kinetoscope and Kinetograph were two different devices, which could not be patented under the same application—so Edison divided them up, and the Kinetoscope patent had been approved in March 1893. The application for the camera continued to be rejected throughout 1892 because, as the patent examiner William H. Blodgett wrote Edison, its design infringed on multiple patents—the earliest being the patent "to Le Prince, 376,247, 10 January 1888."[2]

At the time, Frank Dyer's counsel to Edison was pragmatic. If they couldn't get the application around the patents by Le Prince and others, he advised, then "let it soak."[3] The Patent Office would threaten the pending submission with dismissal every year, but Dyer would find ways to keep it alive, and they would push to have it finalized only if, and when, it was necessary. The application soaked past 1895, the last year it should have remained eligible for consideration—and then, in August 1897, just as Edison decided to sue every motion picture competitor on the East Coast, the Patent Office suddenly granted his submission, dated retroactively to late 1888. The examiners did not explain why it was no longer considered in infringement of others. Less than a month later, the seven years since Louis Le Prince's disappearance elapsed. He was officially declared dead—and his patent rights fell to his widow, to exploit as she saw fit.

Henry Marvin's plan was simple: it would be difficult, now that Edison had his patent secured, for American Mutoscope to argue its own licenses, approved earlier but dated later, did not infringe him. The only motion picture patent left that had been submitted, approved, and dated before Edison's original caveat was Louis Le Prince's. If it could be proved in court that Le Prince preceded Edison in the fundamental underlying concept of motion pictures, Edison would be preempted from suing others for infringing *him*, because what was infringed was not his in the first place.

A lawyer was sent uptown to seek out Lizzie Le Prince. This was how, in December 1898, Adolphe found himself testifying in the preliminary hearings to Equity 6928, between Edison Manufacturing and American Mutoscope.

The Le Prince family would have an opportunity to hold Thomas Edison accountable after all.

Adolphe, by then twenty-six years old, prepared diligently. He sailed to England, tracked down Fred Mason and Jim Longley and Richard Wilson and a dozen others, and had them swear to what they remembered under oath in front of the US consul. He returned to Woodhouse Lane, and to Roundhay, where his father had staged his motion pictures all those years earlier. He visited his grandmother's grave. He recovered drawings, notebooks, filmstrips, and the one-lens camera, and brought them back to America with him.

His father had only recently been declared legally dead. Lizzie had had to travel downtown to the municipal building next to City Hall Park and accept that her husband, at least in the eyes of the law, was never coming back. She sat with the court recorder and testified to everything she knew. That, to the best of her knowledge, "the said Louis Aimé Augustin Le Prince in the month of September 1890 went to Dijon in France to see his brother Albert Le Prince, who was then and is now residing there; that on the sixteenth day of September 1890, the said Albert Le Prince saw the said Louis Aimé Augustin Le Prince take a railroad train at the railroad station in Dijon aforesaid" but "never arrived at Paris or Leeds."[4] That she and his family had made "many and diligent efforts to find him," that she had "employed skilful detectives to search for him, but that all of such efforts have been unsuccessful, and nothing has been heard or seen of the said Louis Aimé Augustin Le Prince since the said sixteenth day of September 1890, at the railroad station at Dijon aforesaid." She swore "that the relations existing between the said Louis Aimé Augustin Le Prince and his wife and children were most cordial and affectionate in character," the prudish officiality chafing with implication demanding to be refuted.

Louis had prepared no will or testament. Lizzie estimated the value of the physical property in his name at less than $1,000, and the notary recorded that, too. Then she had to affix her signature to the document in five different places. The last word in each mark, *Prince*, is an anxious squiggle. The notary handed her a copy on her way out. The words on the top of the first page, heavy with the impressed weight of the type, were so plain and final they could no longer be ignored—"<u>Louis Aimé Augustin Le Prince</u>, deceased."

Adolphe knew his mother held Edison responsible. She had considered suing the famous inventor herself, but she knew Edison would win, defeating her by attrition, driving up costs until she could no longer go on. Lawyer after lawyer had told her as much, warned her, she recalled, that there was "not a chance in a hundred thousand"[5] a court would find in her favor. She had thought of asking for the help of Clarence Seward, Louis and Jack's former patent lawyer, only to find out Seward was now one of Edison's attorneys. The revelation left her feeling betrayed, "submerged by a wave of loneliness and despair," she wrote. "There seemed to be no honour or justice anywhere."[6]

The overture from American Mutoscope was a godsend. Mutoscope would pay all the necessary bills and legal fees; it would have advisers on hand to prepare testimony. Every newspaper would be covering the proceedings. The Le Princes would present themselves in court, evidence in hand, and even the front page of the *New York Times* would be forced to give Louis Le Prince his due.

And so, on December 7, 1898, in a wood-paneled room in Lower Manhattan, Adolphe took his seat in front of the lawyers.

They questioned Adolphe over two days.[7] The hearing started well enough. One of the lawyers for Mutoscope introduced Le Prince's US patent—which predated any held by Edison—into evidence.

"Did you see or assist in making or using this apparatus?" he asked Adolphe.

"Yes," Adolphe replied. "I saw the shutter and camera apparatus in Paris. I saw my father using it and assisted him in taking pictures."

"Had your father, before his disappearance, pursued his work beyond the making of the sixteen-lens camera, aforementioned?"

"He had." Adolphe, though nervous, was honest to a fault. Yes, his father had built a multiple-lens camera, and yes, he had been in Paris with him when he'd made it and tested it. Yes, he had some prints showing Hermann-Josef Mackenstein walking out of the factory and around the corner—he presented them into evidence. He tried to clearly explain the process of preparing the film for projection. You could tell which pictures had been taken with a one-lens camera because of the frequency rate, Adolphe told the men in suits—see how Mackenstein, here, moves around the frame from picture to picture? It's because the shots taken from each of the sixteen lenses are from a slightly different point of view, and so the subject is seen from a slightly different angle, which cannot work when projected at high speed.

Parker Page, the lead attorney for American Mutoscope, asked whether Adolphe had "any specimens of the work done by the one-lens camera" he might show into the record. Adolphe said he had. He directed the lawyers' and their clerks' attentions to a large sheet of card, onto which he had pasted the square gray images. Grandpa Joseph and Grandmama, marching in Roundhay Garden, and Annie Hartley, and himself, too, much younger and smiling.

"When were these photographs taken, if you know?" Page asked.

About October 1888, Adolphe replied. The lawyer for Mr. Edison made to protest that there was no way to prove when the photographs had been taken.

Adolphe interjected. "I can fix the date exactly," he said, "by the fact that my grandmother died on the 24th of October 1888."

A brief silence fell over the room. It was an answer Mr. Edison's lawyer had not been expecting.

He had brought along a photograph of her grave—if it might help allay any doubts.

*   *   *

It was to be Adolphe's last victory of the day. As the hearings progressed, his case fell apart. Adolphe had assumed American Mutoscope was interested in the truth, but he realized now that neither side cared about the case he had hoped to make—that his father was *the* first to make motion pictures, that *he* alone had invented the technology and, arguably, should be the one reaping the benefits Edison was claiming for himself. Indeed, if Adolphe could prove that claim, both Edison and Mutoscope would come out losers—suddenly liable to pay royalties and damages to the estate of a man who had hitherto been no threat to them.

Edison's lawyers tried to discredit Adolphe; those for American Mutoscope steered him close to their own purposes. They ignored Le Prince's European patents—those that explicitly mentioned a single-lens camera—as irrelevant to their jurisdiction, and dismissed the sworn declarations of eyewitnesses Adolphe had collected in England. They even told him there was no need to present the one-lens camera as evidence. They'd built a three-lens camera of their own, to the exact specifications of Louis's 1888 US patent, and would use it to project pictures.

Edison's own expert witness, a respected university professor, put an end to that. What could a facsimile camera, built in 1898, prove about the legal viability of a missing camera, allegedly built ten years earlier? In a filing he speculated Mutoscope had built a new camera because Le Prince's originals were "useless," "constructed on the wrong principles," "defective in [their] capacity to operate."[8] One of Edison's battery of attorneys, a man by the name of Edmonds, went even further. He suggested Adolphe, by claiming he had the one-lens camera and then failing to produce it, had committed fraud against the court. "A doubt is cast upon the entire story by the failure to produce these models or parts of apparatus, which are apparently in the hands of the witness Le Prince," Edmonds asserted. Adolphe, it should not be forgotten, "is friendly to the defendants and [his] interest is to glorify as far as possible the work of his father. . . . The failure to produce apparatus in support of a prior claim is absolutely destructive of the defence unless the construction of the apparatus is conclusively proved and the failure to produce it adequately explained."[9]

Lizzie was aghast. Louis's "foreign patents were not used," she wrote years later, even though "the foreign patents of others were quoted. The lawyers on both sides had access to the machinery left by Le Prince, and to [his] photographs, documents, and sketches . . . but they did not profit us, and were set aside unquoted, and in some instances their very existence was denied."[10]

"Edison's whole case up to 1897 rests on his caveats filed October 17, 1888," Adolphe wrote afterward.[11] The case should have been "a question of the effective dates of the English and French patents of Le Prince as against this caveat of Edison." His father's patents had come first—and wasn't that the entire case, to decide who had come first?

Adolphe was never called back to testify in the preliminary hearings, and Frank Dyer brought full suit against American Mutoscope in 1901, accusing Dickson's new employer of four counts of infringement of Edison's Kinetoscope patent. During proceedings, Edison and his lawyers filed laboratory notebooks, almost certainly backdated, into evidence, and lied about the dates of several of their breakthroughs. On July 15 of the same year, Judge Hoyt H. Wheeler of the US Circuit Court, Southern Division, handed down his verdict, finding in favor of the complainant. The ruling effectively confirmed Edison's position that he had invented the entire medium of motion pictures, including every motion picture device that had ever existed, and any that would ever exist in future. Judge Wheeler, whose full decision made clear how little he understood the technical problems being argued, ratified a patent filed by Edison after multiple motion picture devices had been publicly exhibited by others, retroactively dated to 1888 by a Patent Office that had rejected previous incarnations until 1893. Edison's argument, wrote the historian Martin Sopocy a century later, was "questionable"[12]; Wheeler's decision was a "farce."[13]

American Mutoscope immediately appealed the decision. Its lawyers did not call Adolphe Le Prince to testify at all this time, though they couldn't even if they had wanted to. For his entire adult life, Adolphe had tried to find his father. Failing that, he'd tried to protect his legacy. After receiving word of Wheeler's decision, he retreated to Point O' Woods for the summer, to the house he and his brothers had built as a refuge for his mother. The rest of the family joined him at the house for the month of August, escaping the heat of the city. On the afternoon of Tuesday, August 20, he picked up his hunting gun and told his mother he was going shooting for ducks, as he often did. He walked out into the sand dunes, turned the gun so that the butt rested near his feet, and shot himself through the forehead.[14]

THE FATHERS OF
THE MOVIES

1902–2020

◼

On March 10, 1902, six months after Adolphe Le Prince's body was put into the ground, the US Circuit Court of Appeals reversed Judge Wheeler's decision and dismissed Thomas Edison's complaint. A new judge, William J. Wallace, condemned Edison's use of patents as a means to subvert the law, and reminded him that animated photographs "had been accomplished long before Mr. Edison entered the field."[1] He cited Le Prince's patent—along with Marey's and Muybridge's—in support of his judgment, adding: "It is obvious that Mr. Edison was not a pioneer, in the large sense of the term, or in the more limited sense in which he would have been if he had also invented the film. He was not the inventor of the film. He was not the first inventor of apparatus capable of producing suitable negatives, taken from practically a single point of view, in single-line sequence, upon a film like his, and embodying the same general means of rotating drums and shutters for bringing the sensitized surface across the lens, and exposing successive portions of it in rapid succession. . . . The predecessors of Edison invented apparatus, during a period of transition from plates to flexible paper film, and from paper film to celluloid film, which was capable of producing negatives suitable for reproduction in exhibiting machines. No new principle was to be discovered, or essentially new form of machine invented."[2] Wallace dismantled Dyer's patent application and the unexplained decision to have it granted in 1897, and accused Edison of deliberately broadening the scope of his patent to cover processes he knew he hadn't invented. He stopped just short of accusing Edison of fraud.

The decision could not be appealed. Edison had lost.

Or he would have lost, if he hadn't been Thomas Edison, the Wizard of Menlo Park. He told Dyer to revise the patent and resubmit it to the Patent Office. Two years later, in 1904, he sued Mutoscope again, this time for infringing the reissued patent, which, dated September 30, 1902, was excised of the more egregious claims in the first patent—thereby, Edison argued, nullifying Judge Wallace's decision.

"It is doubtful that a man less powerful than Edison could have obtained a rehearing," wrote historian Martin Sopocy, but Edison, using "his personal power and influence," did, "in defiance of all right or reason and by whatever means necessary."[3] Edison got his new trial. He lost. He appealed. He won—sort of. This final judgment found American Mutoscope and Biograph, as it was now called, not to have infringed on the Kinetoscope—but declared that every other camera in the United States had. All filmmakers in America not working for Thomas Edison or W. K. L. Dickson suddenly found themselves outlaws.

On the strength of this decision, Edison and the Mutoscope and Biograph, after five years in court, decided to join forces. In 1908, they formed the Motion Pictures Patents Company—colloquially known as the Edison Trust—comprising Edison Studios, American Mutoscope and Biograph, Vitagraph, Selig Polyscope, Lubin Manufacturing, Kalem Company, and Essanay, as well as the two biggest foreign companies (Georges Méliès's Star Films, and Pathé). Eastman Kodak had already agreed not to sell any celluloid film to producers outside the group. Now able to enforce their claims over ten meaningful camera and projector patents, the trust went about putting everybody else out of business.

The trust's European competition suffered the most. Charles-Émile Reynaud lost everything and, in an attack of desperation, smashed his

Théâtre Optique to pieces and threw his animated films into the Seine; he died penniless in a nearby hospice. Although a member of the trust, Georges Méliès was driven to sign a contract with the larger Pathé Frères company and quickly fell into debt. When the world war came, his studio was seized and converted into a hospital for the wounded; hundreds of his films were melted down for silver, and the celluloid reconstituted for use in the making of soldiers' boot heels. Méliès himself disappeared into obscurity and spent several years selling toys and candy from a small shop in Paris's Gare Montparnasse. William Friese-Greene was forgotten and died of heart failure at a meeting of cinema representatives in 1921. W. K. L. Dickson left the Mutoscope and Biograph and returned to England, and he, too, died an unknown. He spent the last years of his life corresponding with independent film historians, pleading for his role in the invention of cinema to be recorded and remembered.

Many American independent producers refused to yield to Thomas Edison. Instead they fled as far away from the trust's lawyers as they could, to a small, sun-drenched town on the California coast. The skies were blue twelve months out of the year, the labor was cheap, the locations were spectacular—and, most important, the local Ninth Circuit Court of Appeals was notoriously lax about enforcing patent claims. The town, founded by the real estate developer Hobart Whitley (no relation), was surrounded by ranch lands and orange groves. Its name was Hollywood.

Edison's final victory in court left Lizzie Le Prince with nowhere to flee. Point O' Wood was no longer a refuge. Adolphe's death haunted her, for the remaining twenty-five years of her life, as much as or more than Louis's disappearance. She did not believe he killed himself. "My grandmother thought they had shot him," Lizzie's granddaughter Julie told Le Prince's biographer, Christopher Rawlence, in the early 1980s. "They didn't like how he'd spoken up for his father's camera at the trial. He knew too much."[4]

"They," to Lizzie, was Thomas Edison, and whoever had helped him steal her husband's work—and had now contributed to taking away her son. Six months after Adolphe's death, one of the newspapers had described Edison's loss in the court of appeals as a form of "poetic justice."

Writing years later, Lizzie bitterly admitted she "failed to see either poetry or justice" in any of it.[5]

Point O' Woods was shipwreck territory, as dangerous and haunted as any spot on the New York coastline. A stone lighthouse stood across the rocks from the houses, scanning the horizon.

Late on the night of Thursday, March 5, 1903, Bart Hulso, of the US Life-Saving Service, stepped out of the lighthouse and headed down Great South Beach for his midnight patrol. The men of the Life-Saving Service were known as "surfmen." Their unofficial motto was "You have to go out, but you don't have to come back."

Hulso walked up and down the beach, eyes trained on the dark ocean, looking for any hint of a wreck. If he saw one, he'd blow his whistle and his crewmates, sleeping back at the station, would run out with breeches, buoys, and cables and save as many people as they could. That night, fortunately, was quiet. The hotels were closed for the season. Most of the summer residents were gone, too.

About fifteen minutes into his patrol, when he was a mile or so from the lighthouse, Hulso was startled to hear a voice, carried along by the breeze in the dark. He stopped and listened. The voice seemed to be coming from a sand ridge nearby. Huslo stepped toward the dune, more confused than alarmed. The words spoken by the voice became intelligible as he approached.

"There are evil spirits abroad on the beach!" it shouted. "Hurry along!"[6]

Hulso tried to locate the source. Suddenly a black figure rose up on top of the dune. In its hand was a double-barreled shotgun.

"Halt!" the black figure cried, pointing the gun at Hulso's head. "I've got you at last; you are one of the evil spirits which infest this beach region at night; you get!"

Hulso fell back. There was something terrifying about the man standing over him—Hulso would later describe him as "demented," his voice "sepulchral." Hulso scrambled to his feet and ran the entire mile back to the life-saving station.

He threw the door open, waking his mates. He had been "attacked by a wild man with a gun," he said. His six colleagues grabbed their flashlights and followed Hulso out into the cold, salty air.

The black figure with the gun did not back away from the surfmen as they approached. "Hurry along!" he repeated, frantic. "Evil spirits are out on the beach!" He bid them return where they had come from. The hand clutched around the firearm made Hulso uneasy. Slowly, cautiously, the surfmen fanned out, surrounding the man in a wide horseshoe, while calmly asking him to put the gun down. The man refused to listen, but his tone grew mournful. One of the men, by the name of Charles Baker, managed to exchange some calm words with him. The others closed in and tackled him to the ground.

Now that he was close enough, Hulso recognized the stranger. He was one of the summer people, from the city, and couldn't be more than twenty-five years old—powerfully built, with dark, deep-set eyes under thick black eyebrows and a thin moustache on his upper lip. He'd stayed on the island through the winter that year, overseeing the construction of an extension to his family's house, spending his nights alone in the dark, unheated home. His name was Fernand Léon, one of the surfmen said. Le Prince.

The name was familiar. Someone else with that name had put his shotgun to his head and ended his life eighteen months earlier, not far from the very spot they were standing on.

*   *   *

In the small sailboat taking him across the water to Long Island the next morning, Fernand was entirely calm. He had brought his dog, and he held it in his lap. And then, halfway across the bay, he started screaming again, jumping to his feet and warning Baker, who accompanied him, that "the spirits were surely after them." He tried to dive overboard, and Baker barely managed to restrain him. Finally, Fernand quieted down, but his dog started barking—at what, none of the men could tell.[7]

Fernand had been a star rower and football player at Columbia, popular, studying architecture. After Adolphe's death he'd dropped out and never returned. He was admitted to Middletown State Homeopathic Hospital and registered as a "mentally insane patient."[8]

He was twenty-six. He had never before lived at an address different from his mother's. It is not known whether the double-barreled shotgun they had wrestled away from Fernand that night, the standard weapon for duck hunting, was the same one Adolphe had used to kill himself.

Fernand would live out the rest of his life as a resident of the institution.

Joseph, the last of the Le Prince boys, had fled after Adolphe's death. He packed his bags and went to Cuba, volunteering for a position as assistant to Dr. William Crawford Gorgas, who was working with another military physician, Walter Reed, to research the causes of yellow fever. Reed and Gorgas proved mosquitoes played a key role in the spread of the disease and began implementing a series of trial sanitation programs aimed at controlling its dissemination.

Joseph's training as an engineer was instrumental. He rose from assistant to sanitary engineer, and then to general inspector. Under his guidance, swamps were drained, hundreds of buildings fumigated, and thousands of mosquito nets installed in private homes. In 1903, he followed Gorgas to Panama, where they designed systems to safeguard workers constructing the canal from disease and Joseph became known as "the Health Officer of the Strip." The American Society of Tropical Medicine and Hygiene (ASTMH) records Le Prince as "the first person to control malaria by killing mosquitoes in [private] dwellings."[9] He was also on the first boat to sail through the completed canal.

In Havana, the tall, lanky twenty-seven-year-old Le Prince had met Julia Mercedes Lluria, five feet tall and sixteen years old. They were married and had several children, living in colonial comfort in a large home on the Pacific end of the Panama Canal Zone, along with two Jamaican servants they called "Jake" and "Sarah."

It was in Panama that Joseph's children saw their first film. Dr. Gorgas's housekeeper, Tranquelena, took them to the picture house along with a gaggle of other children, "to see a jungle movie."[10] It felt like an event—the party traveled into town in an ornate Victoria carriage—and it remained one of the children's happiest memories.

Joseph did not go with them.

The history of early motion pictures, which had started with Louis Le Prince in besieged Paris in 1870, was bookended by another war. In 1914 the world set itself on fire, and by the time the fighting was over four years later, France's film industry lay in ruins. Its two largest production companies, Pathé and Gaumont, were nearly wiped out. The American economy, on the other hand, was thriving. Hollywood films moved into the vacuum left by European companies. Films became longer and nickelodeons disappeared. Exhibitors built picture palaces instead and began renting feature films directly from their producers, changing their offerings week to week or month to month, to create repeat business.

Joseph enlisted in the US Army in 1914 but was not sent to the front. In the 1920s he moved his family to Memphis, Tennessee, and arranged for his mother, elderly and alone, to come live with them. She lived there until her death on November 4, 1925. She was seventy-nine.

Five years later Mariella sailed to England, her first time back since 1896. She was heading to her hometown of Leeds, to meet E. Kilburn Scott, Wilson Hartnell's former electrician. Scott, after a long and tireless campaign, had raised funds for a plaque to be mounted on the face of

160 Woodhouse Lane, commemorating it as one of the birthplaces of cinema. The debate over who had invented motion pictures had flared up in the late 1920s, with France and the United States both keen to claim the right for their respective national heroes. The decline of the French film industry, and the parallel rise of Hollywood studios, caused tensions, and the argument over the birth of cinema was the beginning of a discourse that cast France as the cradle of artistic filmmaking and America as a commercial factory, churning out *flicks*. Le Prince—born French, naturalized American, working in England—was no patriotic historian's idea of a suitable champion. Kilburn Scott's plaque, paid for by private subscription, was the only monument to his work.

Mariella stayed at Roundhay and walked in the garden where her father had shot the earliest surviving motion picture. She sat on the steps where Adolphe had once played the melodeon, hopping and grinning. Everyone else was gone—her parents, her grandparents, two of her brothers, even Uncle Jack, who had died in France shortly before Lizzie. She had never met Jim Longley, but he was gone, too, dead of pneumonia in 1905 at the age of forty-four.

Writing before her death, Lizzie had thought back to Louis's limitless hopes for motion pictures, the "scope and value" he knew they would have. "I remember some almost solemn thoughts he had on the effects his invention was destined to bring about; and the changes that would follow its adoption by many nations," she recorded. "He believed that moving pictures would prove more potent than diplomacy in bringing nations into closer touch, and that as a peace propaganda it was without a rival. What mother who has watched a realistic reproduction by camera of a battlefield in action would see her son become food for cannon in an unnecessary war?"

Standing outside Woodhouse Lane in front of local dignitaries and newsreel cameras, Mariella was reminded of her father's predictions. "I often heard him say that films would one day talk and have colour," she said. "He also said that the film would change politics. And government. . . . I remember my father, when I was a very small child, always talking about this idea."[12] She considered herself the first child ever to have seen a motion picture. That night in the Institution for the Deaf counted—she was sure of it.

Thomas Edison died at Glenmont the following year, in October 1931. His last breath was allegedly captured in a test tube for his friend Henry Ford. Three days after he passed, incandescent lights were dimmed or turned off simultaneously across the United States, from the Statue of Liberty to Hollywood. He is still widely held to be the inventor of motion pictures.

Mariella died in New York City in February 1953 at the age of eighty-three. Many of her father's more hopeful forecasts had failed to come to pass. There were movies everywhere and the Second World War had still happened; a war in Korea was happening even then. The television and movie screens of the twentieth century were used to disseminate images of horror just as often as they could prevent them.

But other things Louis predicted *had* come true. Nineteen fifty-three was the year of Marilyn Monroe, of *Niagara*, *Gentlemen Prefer Blondes*, and *How to Marry a Millionaire*; of Ozu's *Tokyo Story* and Clouzot's *The Wages of Fear* and Fellini's *I Vitelloni*. Movies had color, and sound, and music. They transcended borders and languages, and were being made on every inhabited continent on earth. They connected people, sitting together in a room in the dark, watching life unfold on a screen—just as Louis had said, just as he had imagined when he sketched an outline of a theater in one of his notebooks. Just as he, Adolphe, Mason, and Longley had done, standing side by side a lifetime ago, in the long, drafty workshop at Woodhouse Lane.

CODA:
THE DROWNED MAN

October 1890

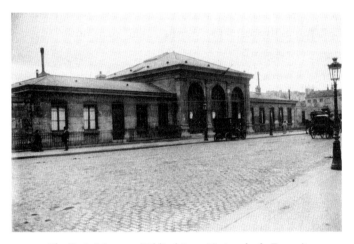

The Paris Morgue. (Bibliothèque Nationale de France)

On the morning of Friday, October 10, 1890, twenty-four days after Louis Le Prince's disappearance somewhere between Dijon and Paris, Dr. Paul Brouardel, *médecin inspecteur* of the Paris Morgue, came in from the crisp, sunny cold into the dim hallways of his workplace.

The Paris Morgue, which Brouardel ran with pride and dedication, was tucked behind Notre Dame de Paris, a squat, U-shaped sliver of a building at the mouth of the Pont Saint-Louis. Outside, street vendors were already flogging their wares despite the early hour, loudly selling gingerbread, toys, "oranges, cookies, and coconut slices"[1] to the visitors queuing to go inside—through the morgue's arched doors and into its large, airy *salle d'exposition*—to gawk at the dead.

The cadavers were displayed on marble slabs behind a long glass window, ostensibly so the public could help identify them. Admission was free and the doors were open seven days a week from dawn to dusk. The crowd was diverse, adults and children, bourgeois and working class. On the busiest days, up to forty thousand people visited the *salle publique*, their interest stoked by the morning's lurid front pages. Alphonse Devergie, Brouardel's predecessor as medical inspector, had once explained plainly that "if the Morgue could be considered a theatre of crime, then the newspaper was its program."[2] The morgue's audience came in droves, wrote Émile Zola, "so as not to miss . . . these performances of death."[3]

Brouardel's work took place deeper inside the building's dark, cold rooms—where dieners washed the corpses and clerks filed away their belongings, where policemen and magistrates came to study the bodies as evidence, and where Brouardel himself spent much of his waking hours investigating them, dissecting them, trying to understand how they had ended up there.

Brouardel was fifty-three and one of France's most distinguished physicians. He had almost single-handedly pioneered the craft of forensic medicine in the country. He'd chaired the Faculty of Medicine and served as dean of the School of Medicine. Louis Pasteur was among his close professional friends, as was Étienne-Jules Marey, whom Brouardel had known since they'd met as graduates thirty years earlier. During the war of 1870–71, after medical school, Brouardel had volunteered to work in the ambulance service of the Gardes Mobiles, and may have crossed paths, if not exchanged words, with Louis Le Prince.

That Friday morning, as on every morning, Brouardel got to work with his assistants, Drs. Descourts and Vibert. As supervising *médecin inspecteur*, Brouardel examined every corpse that came into the morgue and prepared a summary for the prosecutor's office of the circumstances in which the body was found, as well as an assessment of the likely cause of death. If foul play was suspected, an autopsy would be ordered. If a body went six months without being identified or claimed, its clothing and personal effects were sent to a chemical company to be turned into fertilizer, and the cadaver itself would be disposed of or dissected for the purposes of medical research.

Two corpses had been brought in that day. They arrived one after the other in the midmorning. There was Virginie Basset, a forty-three-year-old maid, who had been walking down the street near the Palais Royal when she collapsed and died suddenly.

And then there was the drowned man.

The drowned man gave Brouardel difficulty. In the morgue log, there are more blank boxes on his report for him than for any other arrival that day or the day before. The dead man, tag number 756 for the year 1890, looked to be in midlife; Brouardel and the clerk judged him to be aged somewhere between forty-five and fifty-five. He'd died by "submersion" (drowning) and had been brought in by the policemen of Grenelle, a little neighborhood in the Fifteenth Arrondissement just south of the river, notorious for its École Militaire and barracks—and for the surrounding bordellos, wine merchants, and brasseries, which thrived on the reliable custom of the young soldiers. It is likely the corpse had been found in the Seine, which formed the northern boundary of the district.

The clerk took an inventory of the subject's appearance and belongings. "Wears a full grey beard," he recorded into the register. "Trousers of *drap de fantaisie* [a term for trendy, eye-catching clothing made of a variety of lesser fabrics stitched, quilted, or weaved together, and often manufactured industrially], cotton shirt monogrammed J.H. Flannel vest. Coat and vest of black serge. Elasticated boots, white underpants, white socks, white handkerchief with red stripes monogrammed A.H." His pockets were otherwise empty. Meanwhile Brouardel studied the man's features. The beard was medium length and almost white, with darker patches around the upper lip and chin. His hair was thin and gray and there was clear trauma on the face. His nose was bent to the right, the ridge bruised and raw, as if it had been broken. There were small scratches—or were they discolorations?—on the forehead, the right cheek, and on the orbital bone under the left eye. His ears were tumefied and blackened at the lobes. There was none of the bloat and softening of the flesh common to many drowning victims. Brouardel had seen bodies so waterlogged their skin had come off in translucent gray slices, like slivers of ginger. This man, on the other hand, could not have been in the water long.

The corpse was placed into one of the compartments on the upper levels of the "fridge." Over the next days, the drowned man was most likely shown in the *salle publique*, either fully dressed or naked on one of the twelve black slabs, his clothes displayed on a wicker mannequin by his side. No one recognized him. No one claimed him.

This was unusual—in 1888, an average year, only 100 of 660 adult dead from the morgue had failed to be identified. There would usually be an identifying mark on the deceased person's body, or he or she would match a listing in the missing-persons book. Sensationalist newspapers printed detailed information on every crime and assault, with extensive descriptions of victims and perpetrators alike. Failing everything, the viewing gallery was often a success: it was thought the public contributed to the identification of roughly 10 percent of corpses annually.

This was not one of them. A photograph was taken of the drowned man on his sheet metal bed and attached to his morgue record. On November 4, twenty-five days after his arrival at the morgue, the dead man was given a pauper's burial and laid to rest in the winter ground.[4]

The weather turned colder. It was 15 degrees below zero Celsius on November 28, the coldest November day Paris had seen in over a hundred years. Almost no snow fell that winter. There was only ice and biting wind, dismal day after tenebrous, dismal day. In January the Seine was frozen solid for two weeks. Crowds collected on the bridges to watch the electric lights, many of them Edison's, gleam on the frost below.

The soil covering the pauper's grave hardened and froze. Brouardel never found out if the drowned man had a family.

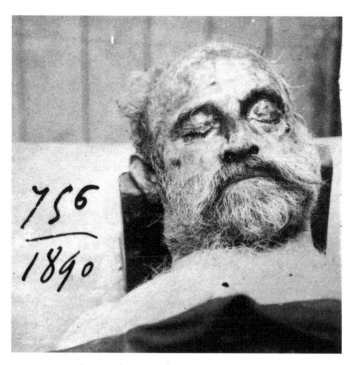

Drowned man in the Paris Morgue. 1890.
(Archives de la Préfecture de police de Paris)

A hundred and three years after he was wheeled into the morgue's autopsy room, a crew of documentary filmmakers, working on a television program about Louis Le Prince, scoured the morgue's archives and stumbled upon the drowned man's picture, stapled to Brouardel's log. They wondered—could this be their man?

There was no way to know for sure. The physical resemblance was sufficiently uncanny, however, for the photograph to become famous among those who still remembered history's first filmmaker. Over the following years it was disseminated across the Internet, shared on message boards, debated by amateur sleuths. It was the nearest thing to a smoking gun—substantial evidence solving the mystery of Le Prince's disappearance—they were ever likely to get. In their longing for an answer, many of these devotees, who had spent years trying to restore Le Prince's legacy, ignored the gaps in this new theory. Le Prince had boarded the train in Dijon on September 16—why had he only appeared at the morgue on October 9, a full twenty-three days later, twenty-three days during which he was not seen or heard from anywhere—during which he did not write or cable his family once? If he'd been killed on the sixteenth, or soon after, and then dumped in the river, why had his body not decomposed, softened and discolored by the water? Why had he been found in Grenelle, across Paris from both the train station and Le Prince's usual accommodation?

Draps de fantaisie were not Le Prince's usual style, and the monograms on the dead man's belongings—J.H. and A.H.—did not match his initials. The drowned man's height is not noted in Brouardel's log, and the medical examiner, if faced with a corpse of Le Prince's unusual height, likely would have made a record of this distinguishing feature. The full beard didn't make sense either. Le Prince had worn a Hulihee his whole adult life, the chin bare and framed by moustache and thick muttonchops. To grow the beard worn by the drowned man he would have had to shave his cheeks and let his facial hair grow out; in any case, the dead man's salt-and-pepper moustache was darker than the white whiskers sported by Le Prince in the last pictures taken of him alive. Where would he have been for twenty-three days? Why change his clothes? Why change his facial hair?

If Le Prince had been killed, why would his murderers have gone to the trouble of transforming his appearance? And if he had committed suicide, who had beaten him?

*   *   *

For a small group of people the world over, solving Le Prince's vanishing act is an obsession. Jacques Pfend, a French historian from Louis's hometown of Metz, has devoted his life to it, collecting boxes and boxes of evidence, collating hundreds of pages of exhaustive marginalia and anecdotal information in the hope some of it might add up to a theory. Irfan Shah, a researcher from Leeds, has combed Le Prince's life himself—written chapters about him in local history books; participated in documentaries; produced and released a sprawling podcast series. David Wilkinson, also from Leeds, produced a documentary film to cement Le Prince's *Roundhay Garden Scene* as history's first motion picture. Before that, Christopher Rawlence, an English television director, had released a book and documentary of his own. Each of them continues to be frustrated by the insolubility of Louis's disappearance. It's hard enough to solve any century-old mystery. It's almost impossible when there is so little to go on in the first place.

But we long for answers. There is romance in the story of an underdog inventor disappearing, as if by magic, from a Victorian train, as there is romance in the sensational theory that Thomas Edison, one of the world's most famous men, had him assassinated—and as there is romance, of a tragic kind, in the photograph of the drowned man, the tantalizing possibility of an answer, buried deep in an old archive; the necessary final frame in a great motion picture, wrapping the story up with a neat bow: Rosebud is the sled, Norman Bates dresses up as his mother, Louis Le Prince was found and fished out of the water.

The truth is without romance. The smoking gun we crave does not exist, it's true, but that doesn't mean the evidence isn't there.

On September 16, 1890, Louis Le Prince did not board the train from Dijon to Paris. We take it for granted that he did because the last person known to have seen him alive, his brother Albert, wrote that he did.

At the time of Louis's final visit, Albert, fifty years old, owed his younger brother an enormous sum of money. Legal and financial documents strongly suggest he did not have it. His wife, Gabrielle, the wealthy half of the union, had died just three years earlier, and her assets, including the house Albert continued to live in, were frozen in trust for their three children, to be divided among them when they came of age. Gabrielle had been sick, and two weeks before she passed, in the cold days before Christmas 1886, Albert had petitioned her family for an inheritance and a "gift" of his own on her death. Neither seems to have been granted. In May 1887, five months after Gabrielle's death, Albert and Louis's mother, Elizabeth Boulabert Le Prince, also died, and Albert accepted—or lobbied for—the opportunity to buy his brother's share in the building she owned on rue Bochart de Saron in Paris. He needed the asset; he needed to be able to rent it out unencumbered, or sell it outright for cash. He was a widower, a father of three, and broke, living in a house that now, technically, belonged to his teenage children.

France was in a period of economic downturn. Albert's main assets when he had married Gabrielle were shares in railway companies, shares now worth a fraction of their original price, as those businesses had shrunk or been swallowed up by larger competitors. He does not seem to have been an architect of even regional notoriety, and few distinctive buildings in or around Dijon were designed by him. One indication of Albert's financial difficulties was given in 1892, two years after Louis's disappearance, when his eldest daughter, Marie, was married. Marie's dowry, in cash and assets that had been held for her since her mother's death, amounted to more than 65,000 francs, to which she added her share of the house and one-sixth of a claim to another property in Dijon, also inherited from her mother. A cousin on her mother's side gifted her another 100,000 francs. Albert, meanwhile, was able to give his daughter just 7,000 francs—and only as a partial advance on the inheritance he planned to leave her when he died.

When Louis traveled south to Dijon in September 1890, he, too, needed money. And he needed it urgently—to premiere his invention, to file patents internationally, to settle his accounts in Leeds and return to America, to feed his family. As the later telegram from Jack Whitley to

Lizzie Le Prince showed, at least part of the money was still outstanding. But Albert had none to give.

No direct account in Albert's hand exists of Louis's stay. Marie, then seventeen, wrote to her cousin Mariella that Louis had arrived on Monday the fourteenth (actually a Sunday) and stayed "three days," though she also wrote he had "departed on Friday morning, 16th of September" (actually the earlier Tuesday). Lizzie Le Prince wrote that Albert told her Louis had left on the *afternoon* train, having missed the morning express. Were these all errors on Marie's part? Or had Albert told his children Louis had left in the morning, to explain why he was no longer in Dijon, and told Lizzie and Richard Wilson he had left in the afternoon, to explain why he did not arrive in Paris on the expected train?

Marie said her father had, "unfortunately," ended up being "very busy" during Louis's visit "and could not speak to him as much as he wished to do"—even though Louis had traveled a great distance to see him and, if he returned to New York as planned, would not see him again for a long time. The evidence suggests Albert's claims that he was too busy at work to spend time with his brother—claims repeated by his daughter—were not entirely honest: two of the three full days Louis spent in Dijon were over the weekend. For some reason, Albert had avoided Louis's company.

Marie wrote her letter on November 10, by which time the family had failed to hear from Louis in over a month and had begun to grow concerned. For that entire time—five weeks, an interminable and calamitous amount of time to waste in a missing-persons case—no one even suspected Louis had disappeared. The only reason they didn't was because Albert assured them he had boarded the train to Paris, and that nothing was amiss.

In the final months of 1890, according to Lizzie Le Prince, Albert coordinated the search for his older brother. Lizzie was in New York, cash poor and with children to look after; Jack Whitley was traveling between London and Germany, frantically trying to pull together one final exhibition at Earl's Court. Albert reassured them both that he was turning over every stone. Through Whitley—for whatever reason, Albert does not seem to have communicated directly with his sister-in-law at all during this time—Albert informed Lizzie that he had opened a missing-persons investigation with the Bureau de Recherches Pour Familles of the Paris police, with a Detective Dougan placed in charge of the inquiry.

Opening a case in Paris assumed Paris—not Dijon—was where Louis had come to harm. No records of any such investigation exist today, but much of the Paris police archives has been lost over the years. No department called the Bureau de Recherches Pour Familles seems to have ever existed, however. In 1896, when Lizzie finally managed to visit Europe herself, she was told in Paris that the only Detective Dougan with which the force was familiar had retired years earlier, possibly even before 1890, and could not be contacted. If Dougan did run an investigation, neither Lizzie nor anyone else in Le Prince's circle was ever contacted by him directly. The only document related to the Paris police still left in the Le Prince papers, kept at the University of Leeds, is a letter the Police Prefecture sent Lizzie in 1900, returning a photograph of Le Prince and informing her their search for her husband had "concluded unsuccessfully."[5] The photograph in question hadn't even been sent to them by Albert—Lizzie had dropped it off herself on her visit to France in 1896.[6]

Through Whitley, Albert also told Lizzie he had taken advertisements in Dijon and Paris newspapers, calling for information that might lead to solving Louis's disappearance. Digitized copies of every major paper from both cities are available to view online today. Not a single notice of the kind can be found in any of them, in any issue between September 16, 1890 and January 1, 1891. None can be found because none were ever placed.

When Lizzie cabled to ask if she should come to France to look for her husband, it was Albert—again, through Jack—who insisted it was best she stay away. Remain in New York, he said. *Watch incoming steamers and passenger lists.* If Louis did finally arrive in America, it was suggested, they didn't want to miss him. Why they would have missed him is anyone's guess. Louis, had he arrived in America, would simply have proceeded to the Jumel Mansion—which he knew Lizzie had rented out—or to the Institution for the Deaf, or to any number of places where he and his family were known. But Lizzie was heartbroken and overwhelmed and could ill afford the trip to Europe anyway, and she followed Albert's advice.

Research has found the primary form of homicide-scene staging consists of the perpetrator's manipulation of physical and verbal evidence to misdirect any investigation as soon as it is begun.[7] Albert Le Prince owed his brother a large sum of money, at a time when he was struggling himself. He failed to adequately report Louis missing when he disappeared, and he actively lied about the efforts made to find him. And then he convinced Louis's wife not to come looking for him herself.

At some point in the late 1890s, Albert likely paid Lizzie and her children the money he still owed Louis. Albert and Louis's uncle Pierre had never moved out of the building on rue Bochart de Saron, which probably thwarted any hopes Albert might have had of making a fair rental income from the property. But Pierre died in 1898, and around the same time Lizzie was able to build the house at Point O' Woods, while simultaneously putting Joseph and Fernand through Columbia College and sending Adolphe to England to gather evidence for the Mutoscope trial. Perhaps Albert had finally paid her. Perhaps he was relieved to find Lizzie so obsessed with, and distracted by, Thomas Edison.

Albert was never investigated or suspected in Louis Le Prince's disappearance, even though he was a textbook prime suspect, a close family member tainted by every indicator of suspicion: a motive to commit the crime, the means to commit the crime, the opportunity to commit the crime. He was never a suspect because he never reported a crime to the French Police in the first place, and so the authorities were not aware there was one to investigate. He was never a suspect because he told Lizzie Le Prince her husband had boarded the express to Paris in Dijon. And Lizzie—who had known Albert for over twenty years—believed him.

Albert died in 1914, in the house on rue Berbisey. Seventy-four years old, and his children were still his landlords. His death notice described him as an architect and a civil engineer, but the accounts he left behind show humble savings and few possessions. The house on rue Bochart de Saron, which he still owned, was his only substantial asset.

He also left behind one final strand of misinformation—one last red herring to confuse any remaining bloodhounds.

In the 1930s, the French film historian Georges Potonniée became the first scholar to publicly hypothesize that Louis Le Prince had not disappeared or been killed but committed suicide, "having taken all necessary steps not to be found." In a lecture to the Société Française de Photographie, Potonniée, claiming inside knowledge, said Louis had been depressed, humiliated, "on the brink of ruin." Suicide had seemed the only honorable way out.

Though not strictly impossible, it was a theory contradicted by every contemporary account, and by Le Prince's own personal history and correspondence. But Potonniée had a source—one he trusted above all else. He never revealed the name, but on the typed draft of his speech, in the margins, is a handwritten note, twice underlined as "confidential," that identifies the source as "a great nephew of Augustin Le Prince." This great-nephew had received this information firsthand decades earlier from his grandfather, who had assured him of its veracity without any shadow of a doubt. The grandfather, Potonniée noted, "was Augustin Le Prince's brother, an architect in Dijon," Albert Le Prince.[8]

As she tried to piece together the final reel of her husband's life, Lizzie Le Prince accused his rivals—but never those closest to him. The identity of his killer, like the role he might have gone on to have in shaping cinema history, will never be known with certainty.

ACKNOWLEDGMENTS

This book would not exist without the faith and enthusiasm of my agent, Jenny Hewson, at Lutyens & Rubinstein. Jenny believed in the book I wanted to write at a time when I was at a crossroads, and for this I will be eternally grateful.

My editors, Walter Donohue at Faber & Faber and Emily Graff at Simon & Schuster, worked tirelessly to make this book what it is. Their notes and feedback were invaluable, and their patience even more so. Many people put great care and grace into bringing a book into the world—it takes a village with too many inhabitants to exhaustively name. I am particularly indebted to Brittany Adames, Elise Ringo, Sherry Wasserman, Jackie Seow, Lashanda Anakwah, and Douglas Johnson at Simon & Schuster, and Francesca Davies at Lutyens & Rubinstein.

I am indebted to the Society of Authors for supporting the writing of this book with an Authors' Foundation grant, without which I would not have been able to conduct so much of the necessary research across two continents and several countries. The receipt of the grant also helped my confidence in the book tremendously. I am particularly thankful to Paula Johnson, the society's head of prizes and awards, and to Sarah Baxter.

No one can attempt to solve a 130-year-old mystery on their own. A very short list of the people without whom I could not have given it a crack:

In France: Maureen Soulard helped me with research on multiple occasions I was unable to do so myself, and was kindly introduced to me by Sophie Berlin at Flammarion. Sophie Boudarel tracked down original documents dealing with Albert Le Prince, his work, and his family. I was also assisted by Ben Iken Chérifa and Didier Houlbert at the archives of the Service National du Chemin de Fer (SNCF) in Le Mans; Sébastien Langlois at the Bibliothèque Municipale in Dijon; and Christine Minjollet at the Musée de la Légion d'Honneur in Paris.

In the United Kingdom: Mary Jane Hill-Strathy and D'arcy Darlimaz made inquiries at archives and collections I was unable to visit myself. Helen Rappaport was generous with her knowledge of Louis Daguerre. I am grateful for help from Jacqueline Cox, at the Oxford University Archives; archives manager Neil Parkinson, of the Royal College of Art; Karen Mee and Alexandra Anderson, of the Special Collections department at the University of Leeds Library; Alison Depledge, Sue Pad, and Danielle Triggs, of the West Yorkshire Archives; Chris Day, of the National Archives in London; and Dr. David Buck, of the Yorkshire Archeological and Historical Society. The National Media Museum in Bradford is an British institution, and my particular thanks go to associate curator of film Toni Booth and to my friend and fellow author Kendra Bean, collections assistant, for their access to the museum's collections, which include the surviving frames of *Roundhay Garden Scene* and *Traffic Crossing Leeds Bridge*, as well as Le Prince's cameras, film drying spools, and other documentation and artifacts. Their generosity and expertise were indispensable. Judith Curtis took time to provide me with information and documentation regarding her ancestor James Longley. Miles Thompson extended the same kindness in relation to his own great-great-grandfather William Mason. Le Prince's many collaborators, particularly the ingenious men of the Woodhouse Lane crew, deserve their place in cinema history, and I am grateful to Judith and Miles for giving me the opportunity to preserve their memory as human beings, and not just names in the background.

In the United States: Elizabeth McCall and Daniel Lynn Grenier turned stones I was unable to turn over in person. Tim Lindholm, of the Daguerreian Society, shed light on the alleged daguerreotype of the

Le Prince family. Bill Reiter, at Cinema Antiques, gave me his expert opinion on Le Prince's surviving devices. Wendy Annibell, of the Suffolk County Historical Society Library and Archives, shed light on Adolphe Le Prince's fate in the dunes of Point O' Woods. Maureen Harrison, of the Morris-Jumel Mansion, told me about the house's history and the Le Prince family's place within it. Tina Sansome found and sent me documents on the life of Joseph Le Prince held at the Memphis Public Library. Professor Vanessa Schwartz, currently director of the Visual Studies Research Institute at the University of Southern California, took time to answer my questions about the Paris Morgue at the turn of the century. Paul Israel, the director and general editor of the Thomas Edison Papers at Rutgers University, was not only extremely helpful, but went above and beyond for me—a total stranger—in accommodating my access to documents that had not yet been publicly digitized. I was also assisted by archivist Jon Schmitz, at the Chautauqua Institution; Jocelyn Will, at the Columbia University Archives; Valerie Shoffner and Leonard DeGraaf, at the Thomas Edison National Historical Park; and Kelly McAnnaney, at the National Archives at New York City.

Copies of Louis Le Prince's patents were kindly procured to me by Bob Beebe at the National Archives at Kansas City and Wilhelm Korinek at the Osterreichischen Patentamt in Vienna. Maryse Smyczynski at the Institut Nationale de la Propriété Industrielle helped me track down Le Prince's French patent. Sandy Muhl at the Universitätsarchiv Leipzig helped shed light on Le Prince's university years in Germany.

Thank you to Jurgen Fischer, Nadia Fischer, Gary Forrester, Becky Forrester, and Jack Weatherley for their support, and to Joel Gomez for the artwork of Louis Le Prince, which was my phone background for two years. Thank you to Uzoamaka Nduka, for looking after many of my adult responsibilities during the hectic final rush of writing this book. Thank you to David Hull, whose friendship ensures this book will sell at least one copy.

Laurie Snyder, a descendant of the Le Prince family, was open and generous in every way, sharing family papers and unpublished memoirs.

Laurie was always available to answer my queries, read sections of several drafts of the book, and petitioned on my behalf, although unsuccessfully, for records of Fernand Le Prince's time at Middletown Hospital, which could be requested only by family. A relative of Laurie's, Gwen Graves Maxwell, kindly permitted the reproduction of Louis Le Prince's watercolor portrait of a young Lizzie Whitley. I am deeply grateful to both Laurie and Gwen for their trust.

Thank you as usual to Owen Pelechytik, for always being around, and to Kelty Pelechytik, for making all things possible.

Almost no movies are made or projected on film anymore, and the news is dominated by announcements of cinema's imminent death. But as I write this, the world has been in a pandemic for nearly two years, during which moving pictures have provided much of the entertainment and connectivity people rely on to endure—as Louis Le Prince, who was also once cut off from his loved ones, in his case during a military siege, believed they would. I am profoundly indebted to the writers and researchers of the birth of motion pictures, who, to a fault, were generous and helpful to this newcomer: Jacques Pfend, Irfan Shah, Stephen Herbert, Marta Braun, and Michael Harvey. It is my privilege, in writing this book, to become part of the same tradition.

NOTES

PROLOGUE

1 *Roundhay Garden Scene*, remastered footage, Science Museum Group Collection, as well as glass copy negative of *Roundhay Garden Scene*, National Science and Media Museum, Bradford, object number 2019-259, and "Two Frames from *Roundhay Garden Scene*, same collection, object number 2015-5014.

2 Declaration of Frederic Mason, 21 April 1931, reproduced in Fielding, 81–83, and Lizzie Le Prince, 116.

3 Ibid.

4 Le Prince's terms for the parts of his machines, as well as how he referred to the respective scenes he filmed, are taken from his patents, correspondence, and are consistent in the accounts of his family and collaborators.

THE TRAIN

1 Marie Emma Adèle Le Prince to Marie Gabriella Le Prince, 10 November 1890.

2 Ibid.

3 Victor Hugo, *En Voyage, Tome II. Oeuvres Complètes de Victor Hugo* (Librairie Ollendorff, 1910), 262. (Translated from the French by the author.)

4 Lizzie Le Prince, 42.

MARKING TIME

1 Louis Le Prince to Lizzie Le Prince, 19 March 1890, quoted in Adolphe Le Prince, 37.

2 Louis Le Prince to Lizzie Le Prince, 11 April 1890, quoted in Adolphe Le Prince, 37.

3 Louis Le Prince to Lizzie Le Prince, 18 April 1890.

4 Lizzie Le Prince describes Oates as "a relative" who "volunteered" to take Louis's place on the already-booked journey. Oates's description matches records of an Arthur Oates, born April 1857 in Dewsbury, just south of Leeds proper. Oates spent his adult life in Southowram, a Yorkshire village south of Halifax, working

as a stone quarrier. He had four children with May Ann (née Nicholl) and his date of death is unknown, though census records show he was still alive as late as 1901.

5 Lizzie Le Prince, 50.

6 Ibid., 51.

7 Ibid.

8 José Manuel Fajardo, "Marseille: Visions d'écrivains," *Le Monde*, 6 May 2010, https://www.lemonde.fr/voyage/article/2010/05/06/visions-d-ecrivains_1347393 _3546.html.

9 Lizzie Le Prince, 51.

10 Ibid.

11 *Topeka Daily Capital*, 2 February 1890, p. 11.

12 There is some uncertainty whether Le Prince's application for US citizenship was ever finalized. Lizzie writes that he became one, and this perspective is honored here as this tracks her own thought process, but the most "common" feeling "is that he put his papers in but the process was never completed," according to Le Prince researcher Irfan Shah. Irfan Shah email to the author, 5 September 2019.

13 Passenger Lists of Vessels Arriving at New York, New York, 1820–1897. Microfilm Publication M237. NAI: 6256867. Year: 1890. Arrival: New York, New York, USA. Line 20, List Number 1673. Records of the U.S. Customs Service, Record Group 36. National Archives at Washington, DC.

EDISON'S NEWEST WONDER

1 "The Kinetograph," *The Sun* (New York), 28 May 1891, p. 1.

2 Ibid., 1–2.

3 Lizzie Le Prince, 46.

4 "Edison's Newest Wonder," *Evening World* (New York), 28 May 1891, p. 1.

5 "Work of the Wizard," *Pittsburg Dispatch*, 29 May 1891, p. 4.

6 "The Kinetograph a Big Success," *Philadelphia Inquirer*, 29 May 1891, p. 4.

7 Lizzie Le Prince, 48.

8 Sworn declaration by Henry M. Woolf, 4 April 1899, New York.

9 Sworn declaration by Mary Elizabeth Borer, 9 March 1899, New York.

10 "The Kinetograph," *Salt Lake Herald*, 29 May 1891, p. 1.

11 Lizzie Le Prince, 33.

12 See *Evening World* (New York), 26 May 1891; *New York Tribune*, 27 May 1891; *The Sun* (New York), 27 May 1891; and others.

13 On this point at least Lizzie seems mistaken: Church Street and Broadway run parallel and do not intersect. Church Street branches off into Sixth Avenue at its northern end, just below Canal Street.

14 Newspapers and census records of the day suggest this may be Alfred Pickard, quarry owner and stone merchant of Shipley, near Bradford in Yorkshire. See notices in the *Bradford Observer*, 31 August 1882.

15 Lizzie Le Prince, 68.
16 Ibid., 19

LETTERS OF INTRODUCTION

1 Edmond About, *Salon de 1866* (Hachette, 1867), 305–6.
2 Maxime Du Camp, *Les beaux-arts à l'exposition universelle et aux salons de 1863, 1864, 1865, 1866 et 1867* (Jules Renouard, 1867).
3 Fehrer, 752.
4 Different sources give the opening of the Julian's atelier as 1866, 1867, or 1868. The Académie Julian officially opened in 1868, but classes at the atelier were likely already running in an ad hoc fashion before then. Classes were originally mixed, before the genders were separated in the mid-1870s. The first concrete firsthand accounts of women students at the Académie date from 1873—Elizabeth Jane Gardner, admitted that year, claimed to have been Julian's first female pupil—but Julian himself, in an 1893 interview with *The Sketch*, says women were welcome at the Passage des Panoramas from day one. The earliest secondhand accounts on the subject suggest Lizzie Le Prince met Louis in Paris in 1869, shortly before they were married.
5 Fehrer, 752.
6 Ibid.
7 Rodin, 29.
8 Ibid., 100.
9 Lowe and Whitley, 19.
10 Ibid.
11 Lizzie Le Prince, 12.
12 Rodin, 71.
13 Lizzie Le Prince, 7.
14 Ibid.
15 Ibid.

GOD'S OWN COUNTRY

1 Fraser, xii.
2 J. G. Kohl, quoted ibid., 200.
3 Ibid., 73.
4 Simon Bradley, "Archeology of the Voice: Exploring Oral History, Locative Media, Audio Walks, and Sound Art as Sitespecific Displacement Activities" (doctoral thesis, University of Huddersfield, 2016), 31.
5 *Report on the Sanitary State of Leeds*, 1874, quoted by C. J. Morgan, "Demographic Change, 1771–1911," in Fraser, 56.
6 Lizzie Le Prince, 3. There is some evidence Joseph Whitley sired another son, a year before or after Jack's birth, who was named after his father, but the records are conflicting, and Whitley is a common name in the north of England. If Joseph did have a third child, he did not seem to survive into adulthood or

to stay with the family long, which may add another explanation to Joseph's taking to Louis as a sort of adopted son.

7 Joseph Whitley to Lizzie Le Prince, 10 October 1886.

8 Both Lizzie and Adolphe Le Prince claim Louis also acted as a representative at the fair for several other Leeds firms, and though it is possible, no hard evidence can be found; he is not listed as a representative for any other exhibitors.

SILVER AND SALT

1 Lizzie Le Prince, 1.

2 During the Paris Commune of 1871 a fire destroyed the palace of Salm, where the Légion d'Honneur's records and museum were kept. Louis Abraham Le Prince's papers were among those burned in the blaze, so that he does not appear on the French government's current official database. The Musée de la Légion d'Honneur et des Ordres de Chevalerie confirmed to the author that Le Prince was awarded the distinction while captain of the Seventh Regiment of Artillery, by a decree dated 10 December 1849. (Correspondence with the author, 25 April 2019.)

3 As he was then unequivocally considered, particularly in France. That legacy has since been challenged and it is now generally accepted Daguerre was one of several pioneers of the new medium.

4 Philippe Burty, "Exposition de la Société française de photographie," in *Gazette des Beaux-Arts*, 2 (May 1859): 221.

5 Lizzie Le Prince, 2.

6 "In around 1845," write biographers Roger Watson and Helen Rappaport, "Daguerre finally returned to photography, now using the vastly improved version of his original process, but he did so for pleasure, making a few portraits of family members and friends at Bry-sur-Marne." This timeline aligns with the Le Prince claim the photograph was authored by Daguerre. Watson and Rappaport, 170.

7 Louis Jacques Mandé Daguerre, "Daguerréotype," 1838, reproduced in the Daguerreotype Archive at http://www.daguerreotypearchive.org/texts/M8380001 _DAGUERRE_BROADSIDE_FR_1838.pdf.

8 Lizzie Le Prince, 2.

9 Watson and Rappaport, 178.

10 Charles Baudelaire, "Le public moderne et la photographie," *Études Photographiques* [en ligne], accessed 24 September 2020 at http://journals.openedition .org/etudesphotographiques/185.

WAR

1 *Leeds Mercury*, 20 July 1870, p. 2.

2 *Leeds Mercury*, 22 July 1870, p. 2.

3 Horne, loc. 921.

4 The concept of *Schwerpunkt*, and its many various meanings, is referred to in Clausewitz's influential *On War*, published posthumously in 1832.

5 Badsey, 4.

6 *Leeds Mercury*, 8 August 1870, p. 2.

7 Draper, ch. 3.

8 Gluckstein, 68.

9 Adolphe Le Prince, 2.

10 Ibid.

11 Ibid.

12 *Le Temps*, 17 August 1870, p. 4.

13 See the *Liverpool Daily Post*, 24 August 1870, p. 9; *Cardiff Times*, 29 August 1870, p. 2; *Staffordshire Advertiser*, 27 August 1870, p. 6.

14 Archives Nationales de Pierrefitte, correspondence with the author, 4 September 2018. Le Prince, identified as an officer of that battalion, also has his name affixed to an open letter to the government, published in *Le Temps* of 22 October 1870, denying rumors of schisms along ideological lines in the National Guard and pledging to be firm with any insurrectionists.

15 *Le Gaulois*, 2 September 1870, p. 1.

16 *Le Gaulois*, 5 September 1870, p. 1.

17 6 September 1870 front pages of the newspapers in question.

BURIED ALIVE

1 Jean-Christophe Rouxel, "Jean François Edouard Hugueteau de Challié," in *Biographies et Histoires de la Marine Française*, at http://ecole.nav.traditions .free.fr/officiers_hugueteau_jean.htm. Last updated 7 January 2018.

2 Horne, loc. 1610.

3 Victor Hugo, "Aux Allemands," *Oeuvres Complètes de Victor Hugo: Actes et Paroles III: Depuis L'Exile* (Paris: J. Hetzel & A. Quantin, Société d'éditions littéraires et artistiques, 1884), 51.

4 Quoted in Horne, loc. 2039.

5 Adolphe Le Prince, 3.

6 Ibid.

7 Horne, loc. 4268.

8 Nass, 13.

9 Spang, 753.

10 Lizzie Le Prince, 97.

WASHED ASHORE AT THE LIZARD

1 Lizzie Le Prince, 5.

2 Not the North Sea.

3 Only one of the original envelopes from *Le Jacquard* allegedly survives today. Addressed to a recipient in Dover, it was auctioned off in 2013 by a dealer, David Feldman S. A. of Geneva, who started the bidding at 18,000 euros.

4 Lizzie Le Prince mentions another letter picked up on the Hebrides, on the other side of Scotland, and posted from there to Yorkshire, but none of the balloons officially registered as having departed Paris during the siege are known to have landed in that area.

5 Lizzie Le Prince, 15.

6 Ibid., 9.

PARENTHESIS: OCCIDENT IN MOTION

1 Ambarin Afsar, "Eadweard Muybridge," *Better Photography*, 13 Feb 2015, http://www.betterphotography.in/perspectives/great-masters/eadweard-muybridge/25646/.

2 George Rust, *National Live Stock Journal* 4 (1873): 410.

3 "Photograph Studies," *Daily Alta California*, 7 April 1873, p. 1.

4 Rebecca Solnit, "The Annihilation of Time and Space," *New England Review* (1990–) 24, no. 1 (Winter 2003): 5–19.

5 Ibid.

ARTISTS

1 Adolphe Le Prince, pt. 2, p. 4.

2 Lizzie Le Prince, 9.

3 *The Standard* (London), 14 May 1875, p. 3.

4 *Reports of the United States Commissioners to the Paris Universal Exposition, 1878*, vol. 3 (Washington, DC: US Government Printing Office, 1880), 131. Le Prince is also listed in the *Official Catalogue of the British Section* for the fair, vol. 1, p. 87.

5 Adolphe Le Prince, pt. 2, p. 4.

6 Ibid.

7 Ibid.

8 Ibid.

9 Ibid.

THE SPARK

1 Lizzie Le Prince, 11.

2 Ibid., 12.

3 If original glass negatives were unavailable, photographers could also work from transparent paper reproductions.

4 Lizzie Le Prince, 11.

5 Ibid.
6 Ibid.
7 Wordsworth Donisthorpe, "Apparatus for Taking and Exhibiting Photographs," British patent 4,344, dated 9 November 1876.
8 Lizzie Le Prince, 2.

THE NEW WORLD

1 Lincrusta's full original patent name was "Linoleum Muralis." See https://lincrusta.com/our-history/, accessed 14 January 2021.
2 Lizzie Le Prince, 28.
3 Ibid.
4 Ibid.
5 Ibid.
6 Ibid.
7 Ibid.
8 Ibid., 102.
9 Ibid.
10 An old photograph belonging to the Le Prince family gives this address as between 168th and 169th Streets and Broadway, likely an error. Censuses and official records give the Le Prince address as "corner of 171st Street and Kingsbridge Road," one of several names routinely used for Saint Nicholas Avenue at the time, and not to be confused with Kingsbridge Road in the Bronx.
11 Lizzie Le Prince, 18.
12 Ibid.
13 Ibid.

PARENTHESIS: WKL

1 William Kennedy Laurie Dickson to Thomas Alva Edison, 17 February 1879, Edison Papers Digital Edition, http://edison.rutgers.edu/digital/document/D7913K.
2 Correspondence between the author and Jacky Emerson (archive service delivery officer, Cambridge Assessment Group Archives), Rebekah Johnson (archives assistant, Cambridge Assessment Group Archives), and Jacqueline Cox (Cambridge University Archives). 13 May 2019, 15 May 2019, 20 May 2019.
3 Raymond Sayer to Thomas Alva Edison, 28 March 1883, Edison Papers Digital Edition, http://edison.rutgers.edu/digital/document/D8313I.
4 Charles Lawrence Bristol to Thomas Alva Edison, 24 September 1883, Edison Papers Digital Edition, http://edison.rutgers.edu/digital/document/D8330ZAY.
5 William Kennedy Laurie Dickson. "A Brief History of the Kinetograph, the Kinetoscope, and the Kineto-Phonograph," *Journal of the SMPE* 21, December 1933.

6 Dickson and Dickson, 54.

7 Smith, xiv.

8 Dickson and Dickson, 54.

9 Smith, xiv.

10 William Kennedy Laurie Dickson to Thomas Alva Edison, 17 February 1879, Edison Papers Digital Edition, http://edison.rutgers.edu/digital/document/D7913K.

11 Smith, xiii.

12 In 1898 the *Ladies' Home Journal* and *Youth's Companion* both printed versions of Edison asserting that "ninety-eight per cent of genius is hard work," a quote he workshopped over the years until it became the "one percent inspiration, ninety-nine percent perspiration" aphorism known today. See "The Anecdotal Side of Edison," *Ladies' Home Journal*, April 1898, p. 8, and "Current Topics," *Youth's Companion* 72, no. 16 (21 April 1898): 194.

13 Edison, in fact, was a teetotaler much of his adult life.

14 Morris, 368.

15 Stross, 111–12.

16 Ibid., 81.

LOUISIANA CENTENNIAL

1 At least one photograph of this era shows them with a pet.

2 Lizzie Le Prince, quoted in *Proceedings of the 11th Convention of American Instructors of the Deaf, Held at Berkeley, Cal., July 15–22, 1886,* (California State Office, 1887), 197–205.

3 Ibid.

4 Ibid.

5 Lizzie Le Prince, 21.

6 "Fanwood: Off for the New Orleans Exposition," *Deaf-Mutes' Journal,* 25 December 1884, p. 4.

7 Ibid.

8 *Standard Union* (Brooklyn), 20 February 1927, p. 2.

9 *Saint Charles Herald,* 7 February 1885, p. 1.

10 Lizzie Le Prince, 22.

11 Le Prince's work on moving pictures, as described in his correspondence, the memoirs of his widow and son, and the sworn testimony of collaborators and witnesses, began soon after he returned from New Orleans. Lizzie Le Prince alleges Louis's first "working models" of a camera and projector were made in 1885 (Lizzie Le Prince, 19)—these almost certainly did not work, or were adapted from magic lanterns or other preexisting devices—and it was in 1885 that the board granted Le Prince the use of the kiln room at the institution, which gradually became his workshop for motion picture work in New York. Adolphe Le Prince remembers his father's "work," however intensive or successful, beginning in "January 1885," which would have been in the middle of the New Orleans fair. (Adolphe Le Prince, 11)

A GUN THAT KILLS NOTHING

1 "A Startling Tragedy," *Los Angeles Herald*, 22 October 1874, p. 4.
2 "The Higher Law: Muybridge Acquitted of the Charge of Murder," *San Francisco Chronicle*, 7 February 1875, p. 8.
3 *Scientific American*, 5 June 1880.
4 *Illustrated London News*, 18 March 1882.
5 Silverman, 341.
6 *La Nature*, 28 December 1878.
7 Though he read Marey's book *La Machine Animale*, and kept a copy of it in his library.
8 Coe, 20.
9 Étienne-Jules Marey to his mother, Marie-Joséphine Bernard Marey, 3 February 1882.

SHADOWS WALKING ON THE WALLS

1 The actual name of the Union ship is USS *Merrimack*, but this chapter retains the spelling used in Poilpot's own documents and advertising.
2 Adolphe Le Prince, pt. 2, p. 5.
3 Christopher Rawlence suggests Le Prince also took photographic studies of models in Union and Confederate uniforms for the painters to work from (141).
4 "Popular in Its Second Year," *New York Times*, 15 May 1887, p. 3; and David A. Mindell, *Iron Coffin: War, Technology, and Experience aboard the USS Monitor* (Johns Hopkins University Press, 2012).
5 "Watching the Battle Again," *New York Times*, 1 August 1886, p. 3.
6 *New York Tribune*, 12 December 1886, p. 3.
7 "City and Suburban News," *New York Times*, 12 December 1886, p. 7.
8 Quoted in E. K. Scott, *Technological History*, 76.
9 Lizzie Le Prince, 20.
10 Joseph Whitley to Lizzie Le Prince, 10 October 1886.
11 Ibid.
12 Ibid.
13 Louis Le Prince to Richard Wilson, 2 November 1886.
14 Lizzie Le Prince, 24.
15 Declaration by Joseph Banks, undated. Reproduced in Lizzie Le Prince, 26.
16 Sworn declaration by William Kuhn, notarized by John T. Duff, 28 February 1899.
17 Lizzie Le Prince, 25.
18 E. K. Scott, 76, and Pfend, 9.
19 *Proceedings of the Meeting of the Convention of American Instructors of the Deaf*, 1887, p. 199.
20 Lizzie Le Prince, 23.
21 *Santa Cruz Sentinel*, 15 July 1886, p. 3.

22 Elmer Clarence Sandmeyer, *The Anti-Chinese Movement in California* (University of Illinois Press, 1991), 43–44.

23 Rawlence, 156.

24 Lizzie Le Prince, 24.

25 Ibid.

THE WIZARD'S TOWER

1 *New York Times*, 5 September 1882, pp. 1, 8.

2 Spehr, 24.

3 Antonia Dickson and William Kennedy Laurie Dickson, *The Life and Inventions of Thomas Alva Edison* (T. Y. Crowell, 1894), 236.

4 Spehr, 27.

5 "Stories from the 'Sun,'" *New York Herald*, 2 June 1918, p. 32.

6 Tate, 223.

7 Samuel Insull, quoted in Dyer and Martin, 109.

8 Oser, 8.

9 The Lincrusta Walton covering is still in the reception hall at Glenmont, which is managed by the Thomas Edison National Historical Park. For the history of the installation and finish, see *Thomas Edison Historic Furnishings Report*, vol. 1, p. 39; *Thomas Edison Historic Structure Report*, vol. 1, pp. 273–74; as well as author's email correspondence with Valerie Shoffner, museum technician at Thomas Edison National Historical Park, 28 August 2019.

10 Stross, 153.

11 Ibid., 164.

12 The blame for Tesla's being let go by Edison may, if A. O. Tate is to be trusted, be laid at the door of Charles Batchelor. According to Tate, Batchelor was the man in charge of approving Tesla's raise from $18 to $25 a week, and vetoed it, saying, "The woods are full of men like him. I can get any number of them I want for eighteen dollars a week" (Tate, 149).

13 Stross, 165–66.

14 *Miami Metropolis*, 23 June 1911.

15 Morris, 11.

16 Sherburne Blake Eaton to Thomas Alva Edison, 9 May 1884, Edison Papers Digital Edition, http://edison.rutgers.edu/digital/document/D8427ZAY.

17 Ibid.

LIFE ON GLASS

1 *La Nature*, January 1885, p. 119.

2 *Yorkshire Evening Post*, 12 December 1930, p. 13.

3 "Method of and Apparatus for Producing Animated Pictures of Natural Scenery and Life," US Patent 376,247, filed 2 November 1886, issued 10 January 1888.

4 "Two metallic ribbons punched with holes" (line 6), "endless metallic ribbons accurately punched with small round holes" (lines 79–81), ibid.

5 Louis Le Prince Collection, University of Leeds, MS/DEP/2015/1.

6 "Postponing Bartholdi's Statue until There Is Liberty for Colored as Well," *Cleveland Gazette*, 27 November 1886, p. 1.

7 Adolphe Le Prince, 11.

8 Lowe and Whitley, 32.

9 Ibid.

10 Ibid.

11 Ibid., 58.

12 Lizzie Le Prince, 69, and Adolphe Le Prince, 12.

13 William Guthrie to Lizzie Le Prince, 23 March 1899.

14 John Robinson Whitley to Lizzie Le Prince, 9 February 1899.

15 Ibid.

16 Lowe and Whitley, 56.

17 Adolphe Le Prince, pt. 2, p. 9.

18 U.S. Patent 376,247, p. 3.

19 Ibid.

20 Adolphe Le Prince, pt. 2, p. 11.

21 Ibid., 11–12.

22 Ibid., 12.

23 Adolphe Le Prince, p. 8.

24 Rossell, 29.

25 To describe that workflow simply: Ducos's camera worked with wet process glass plates, the most sensitive in his day, which needed to be prepared immediately before and processed immediately after exposure, so that his multilens camera would have necessitated up to forty-eight people to "turn the cranks, change plates, spread collodion on the glasses, and immediately after exposure, develop, fix, and wash the negatives," changing plates "about every 18–30 seconds." Even then the emulsions were not fast enough, nor would Ducos have been able to make films longer than those 18 to 30 seconds without a break or edit in the action. Walter Stainton, "The Prophet Louis Ducos Du Hauron and His Marvelous Moving Picture Machine," *Cinema Journal* 6 (1966–1967): 46–51.

26 Ibid.

27 *Photographic Times*, May 1860 (quoted in Herbert, 26).

28 Adolphe Le Prince, 8.

29 Tate, 194.

30 Lizzie Le Prince, 33.

31 *New York Times*, 8 November 1886, p. 2.

32 Rawlence, 148.

THOMAS A. EDISON CAN GO TO HELL

1 "Method of and Apparatus for Producing Animated Pictures of Natural Scenery and Life," US Patent 376,247, file and wrapper.

2 H. A. West to H. S. Mackaye, 1919.

3 Rawlence, 167.

4 Louis Le Prince to Lizzie Le Prince, 30 March 1887.

5 Lizzie Le Prince, 33.

6 "Improvement in Photographic Cameras," US Patent 78408A, granted to Simon Wing on 26 May 1868.

7 Edmund Maher, *Scientific American*, 28 April 1849 (quoted in Post, 24).

8 *Scientific American*, 3 January 1857 (quoted in Post, 24).

9 *Scientific American*, 21 April 1849 (quoted in Post, 39).

10 Samuel F. B. Morse, *Samuel F. B. Morse: His Letters and Journals*, vol. 2 (1914), 283.

11 Repeated, for instance, in Matthew M. Welch, "Warning! Patent Agent Privilege Ends Abruptly," *Journal of the Patent & Trademark Office Society*, 20 May 2019, https://www.jptos.org/news/599/97.html.

12 Lizzie Le Prince, 49.

13 The projector as it then existed would have made a terrible toy for the market—even a perfected version of it would have been too heavy and complicated, without even mentioning the fact that Louis had, as yet, not been able to shoot anything that was good enough to sell as content for the machine to project.

14 John Whitley to Lizzie Le Prince, 9 February 1899, Le Prince papers.

15 Lizzie Le Prince, 34.

16 Stross, 157.

17 Rawlence, 158.

18 Lizzie Le Prince, 34.

19 Ibid.

20 Ibid., 33.

KEEPING CLEAR OF THE SHARKS

1 Registres d'état civil, Etat civil de la Côte-d'Or, 1887, archives de Côte-d'Or, digital document number FRAD021EC 239/415, images created from register 2 E 239/370, Vue 24.

2 Marriage contract, Albert Le Prince and Gabrielle Chevrot, 19 September 1868, archives départementales de la Côte d'Or, Dijon, identifier Mariages, 1868, 2 E 232/311.

3 Compte de Tutelle Presenté par Louis Auguste Albert Le Prince à Marie Emma Adèle Le Prince, archives départementales de la Côte d'Or, Dijon, archives notariées, Maitre Caussin, identifier 4 E 5/584.

4 Lizzie Le Prince, 33.

THE STARTING POINT OF ALL MOTION

1 Louis Le Prince to Lizzie Le Prince, 6 May 1887.
2 "Reynold & Branson Limited," *Historic Camera*, accessed on 9 January 2020 at http://historiccamera.com/cgi-bin/librarium2/pm.cgi?action=app _display&app=datasheet&app_id=2517.
3 Henry James, *The Letters of Henry James* (Floating Press, 2016), 134.
4 Lizzie Le Prince, 39.
5 Ibid.
6 "The American Exhibition," *The Times* (London), 10 May 1887, p. 10.
7 "Opening of the American Exhibition," *Lloyd's Weekly Newspaper*, 15 May 1887, p. 1.
8 Louis Le Prince to Lizzie Le Prince, 18 May 1887.
9 Ibid.
10 Quoted in Lizzie Le Prince, 9.
11 Louis Le Prince to Lizzie Le Prince, 18 May 1887.
12 Louis Le Prince to Lizzie Le Prince, 27 May 1887.
13 Acte de décès d'Elizabeth Boulabert Le Prince, May 1887.
14 Acte de Notoriété Après le Décès d'Elisabeth Marie Antoinette Boulabert, veuve de Louis Abraham Ambroise Le Prince, survenu en son domicile 6 rue Bochart-de-Saron, le 28 mai 1887, 22 June 1887, Archives Nationales de France, reference code MC/ET/LXXII/1097.
15 Vente par M. et Mme. Louis Aimé Augustin Le Prince à M. Louis Auguste Albert Le Prince, 15 July 1887, Archives Nationales de France, reference code MC /ET/LXXII/1098; and Obligation par Louis Aimé Augustin Le Prince, artiste peintre, au profit de Pierre Louis Ferdinand Demaison, propriétaire. 26 August 1887, Archives Nationales de France, reference code MC/ET/LXXII/1099.
16 Pfend, 124.
17 Lizzie Le Prince, 49.
18 Warner, 47.
19 The specific timeline of this decision is unclear. Christopher Rawlence claims the entire Le Prince family vacations in England, though he also writes that Le Prince's mother was alive that summer (she died in May). Jacques Pfend believes Lizzie and Adolphe traveled to Europe in late summer or early fall to help Louis with the legal ramifications of his mother's death, and that Adolphe stayed with his father when his mother returned to America. There is no definitive primary proof either way, though Pfend's timeline is supported by the better circumstantial evidence.

A MAN WALKS AROUND A CORNER

1 "Method of and Apparatus for Producing Animated Pictures of Natural Scenery and Life," US Patent 376,247, file & wrapper.
2 Ibid.

3 A. Le Prince, per Munn & Co., to Commissioner of Patents, US Patent Office, 15 June 1887.

4 Lizzie Le Prince, 18.

5 Louis Le Prince to Lizzie Le Prince, 18 August 1887.

6 Adolphe Le Prince, pt. 2, p. 5.

7 In the early twentieth century Mackenstein would patent a shutter and camera he sold as L'indéréglable—the "Foolproof"—and it enhanced his reputation in photographic circles even further.

8 Louis Le Prince to Lizzie Le Prince, 18 August 1887.

9 Silent films of the Charlie Chaplin era were played at sixteen to twenty frames per second. The standard frame rate for synchronized-sound motion pictures in the twentieth century was 24 fps, adapted to 29.97 fps in the age of video. At the time of writing, a section of the filmmaking community, including most notably Peter Jackson and Ang Lee, is arguing for the superiority of high frame rate movies, ranging from 48 fps (Jackson's *The Hobbit*) to as high as 120 fps (Lee's *Gemini Man*).

10 Louis Le Prince to Lizzie Le Prince, 18 August 1887.

11 Myrent, 192.

12 Christopher Bertram, "Jean Jacques Rousseau," *The Stanford Encyclopedia of Philosophy* (Fall 2018 edition), accessed 17 January 2020, https://plato.stanford .edu/archives/fall2018/entries/rousseau/.

"INVESTIGATORS" AT WOODHOUSE LANE

1 US Patent Office archives, serial no. 217809.

2 Louis Le Prince to Lizzie Le Prince, 2 December 1887, quoted in Adolphe Le Prince, 20.

3 Joseph Whitley, diary, courtesy of Arthur Whitley. Also quoted in Lizzie Le Prince, 101.

4 Louis Le Prince to Lizzie Le Prince, 23 December 1887, quoted in Adolphe Le Prince, 20.

5 Ibid.

6 J. H. Horsman to Lizzie Le Prince, 1911.

7 Lizzie Le Prince, 79.

8 Family information provided to the author by Miles Thompson, great-great-grandson of William Mason.

9 Frederic Mason, letter to the editor of the *Yorkshire Evening Post*, January 1923, quoted in Lizzie Le Prince, 117.

10 Frederic Mason, declaration of 21 April 1931.

11 Frederic Mason, letter to the editor of the *Yorkshire Evening Post*, 27 June 1930, p. 4.

12 Frederic Mason, letter to the editor of the *Yorkshire Evening Post*, 29 December 1930, p. 4.

13 Declaration of Arthur Wood, 25 November 1930, quoted in E. K. Scott.

14 Frederic Mason, declaration of 21 April 1931.

15 This date is according to E. Kilburn Scott, who in a letter to the New York *Sunday Tribune* dated 11 February 1920 recalled his first visit happening "somewhere about 1887 or 1888."

16 According to the sworn declarations of other Hartnell engineers, namely Walter Gee and J. T. Baron.

17 Sworn declaration of John William Vine, 19 September 1898.

18 E. K. Scott, letter to the editor of the New York *Sunday Tribune*, 11 February 1920.

19 Frederic Mason, declaration of 21 April 1931.

20 Ibid.

21 Sworn declaration by William Mason Jr., 19 September 1898.

22 E. K. Scott, "The Pioneer Work of Le Prince in Kinematography," lecture to the Royal Photographic Society of London, 8 May 1923, published in the *Journal of the Society of Motion Picture Engineers* xvii, no. 1 (July 1931): 46–66.

23 Adolphe Le Prince, pt. 2, p. 9.

24 Ibid., 15.

25 Declaration of Walter Gee, 1930, quoted in E. K. Scott.

26 Declaration of Arthur Wood, quoted in E. K. Scott.

27 Louis Le Prince to Lizzie Le Prince, 2 February 1888, quoted in Adolphe Le Prince, pt. 2, p. 25.

28 Thomas Edison to Theodore Puskas, 13 November 1878, Edison archives.

29 Louis Le Prince to Lizzie Le Prince, 23 December 1887.

30 Louis Le Prince to Lizzie Le Prince, 22 January 1888.

31 Louis Le Prince to Lizzie Le Prince, 2 February 1888.

THE MUYBRIDGE LECTURE

1 *The Nation*, 19 January 1888, 53–54.

2 *Boston Transcript*, circulated in the *Quad-City Times* (Davenport, IA), 4 January 1887, p. 2.

3 Marta Braun, "Animal Locomotion," in *Eadweard Muybridge: The Kingston Museum Bequest*, ed. Stephen Herbert (The Projection Box, 2004), 29–31.

4 Ibid.

5 W. K. L. Dickson may also have been in the audience. Dickson, as well as working as an experimenter at the West Orange laboratory, was Edison's photographer, and he would have jumped at the opportunity to see Muybridge's work in person—especially if it meant a social evening shared with his boss. See Hendricks, *Edison Motion Picture Myth*, 11.

6 As described in Herbert, *Muybridge*, 116.

7 "Animal Locomotion," Orange *Chronicle*, 3 March 1888, p. 3.

8 "Technical Note, Thomas Alva Edison, February 27th, 1888," Edison Papers Digital Edition, accessed January 25, 2020, http://edison.rutgers.edu/digital/document/PT032AAV2.

9 Ball, 363.

10 *The World* (New York), 3 June 1888, p. 16.

11 Muybridge, 4.

12 *The World* (New York), 3 June 1888, p. 16.

13 Ibid.; *Electrical Review*, 9 June 1888, Gordon Hendricks Collection; *Photographic Times*, 22 June 1888, Gordon Hendricks Collection.

14 *The World* (New York), 3 June 1888, p. 16.

15 Hendricks, *Edison Motion Picture Myth*, 12; Spehr, 76; Solnit, 229; Musser, *Emergence of Cinema*, 62.

HAGGARD MILES OF HALF-BURIED HOUSES

1 *New York Herald*, 14 March 1888.

2 Louis Le Prince to Lizzie Le Prince, 18 March 1888.

3 Ibid.

4 Lizzie Le Prince, 19.

5 Ibid., 21.

6 Ibid., 32.

7 Ibid., 34.

8 Adolphe Le Prince, 11.

9 Lizzie Le Prince, 97.

10 Ibid., 23.

11 As he called film reels—see "Improvements for Producing Animated Photographic Pictures," *British Journal of Photography*, 14 December 1888, p. 794.

A SEWING MACHINE, MULTIPLIED BY THREE

1 Adolphe Le Prince, pt. 2, p. 6.

2 Lizzie Le Prince, 35.

3 Referred to as such in Le Prince's patent applications, as well as Adolphe Le Prince's recollections.

4 Adolphe Le Prince, pt. 2, p. 12.

5 Louis Le Prince to Lizzie Le Prince, 2 February 1888.

6 Adolphe Le Prince, pt. 2, p. 7.

7 Ibid., 8.

8 His letter of January 22 enclosed a check of an unknown sum, for "house repairs."

9 Adolphe Le Prince, pt. 2, p. 8.

10 Louis Le Prince to Thompson & Boult, 20 January 1888.

11 Louis Le Prince to Lizzie Le Prince, 19 March 1890.

12 Louis Le Prince to Thompson & Boult, 4 October 1888.

13 Louis Le Prince to Thompson & Boult, 20 January 1888.

14 Sworn declaration of Edgar Rhodes, 29 September 1898.

15 Ibid.

16 Louis Le Prince to Lizzie Le Prince, 18 March 1888.

17 Though he was not necessarily the first person to use the word "bug" to refer to a glitch or imperfection in a system or machine, Edison certainly was one of the earliest and most enthusiastic adopters of the word. He referred to a false break in his duplex telegraph as a "bug" as early as 1873, and described his struggle with "bugs" in his experiment notebooks as well as in conversation. See "Did You Know? Edison Coined the Term 'Bug,'" by Alexander B. Magoun and Paul Israel, *IEEE Spectrum*, 1 August 2013. Edison is frequently quoted using the word, e.g., in Dyer and Martin, 56; Shaw, loc. 428; Morris, 412; or Josephson, loc. 3616.

A YORKSHIRE SUMMER

1 Lizzie Le Prince, 98.
2 Ibid., 79.
3 Ibid., 97.
4 Ibid.
5 London *Daily News*, quoted in Lowe and Whitley, 174.
6 Lizzie Le Prince, 50.
7 Ibid., 98.
8 Ibid.

ROUNDHAY GARDEN SCENE

1 Louis Le Prince to Thompson & Boult, 22 September 1888, quoted in Adolphe Le Prince, 28.
2 Louis Le Prince to Thompson & Boult, 4 October 1888.
3 Draft of letter to Thompson & Boult dated 4 October 1888, by Louis Le Prince, reproduced in Lizzie Le Prince, 30.
4 "Improvements in the Method of and Apparatus for Producing Animated Photographic Pictures," UK Patent 423, filed 10 January 1888, issued 16 November 1888.
5 Longley, Mason, and others later referred to an earlier scene shot by Le Prince, of a "blacksmith" in an "apron" walking and occupied at several tasks. This was most likely the footage taken of Mackenstein in Paris, which was shot on the multiple-lens camera using glass plates.
6 Thomas Alva Edison to Dyer & Seely, 8 October 1888.
7 Dyer and Martin, 191.
8 "Technical Note, Charles Batchelor, Thomas Alva Edison, 1888," Edison Papers Digital Edition, accessed February 3, 2020, http://edison.rutgers.edu/digital/document/NSUN11.
9 Baldwin, 211. A letter from Donisthorpe describing his work and headed "Talking Photographs: Apparatus Called Kinesigraph (Band Illuminated by Electric Spark) Combined with Phonograph" appeared in *La Nature* on 24 January 1878.

10 "Technical Note, William Kennedy Laurie Dickson, June 1888," Edison Papers Digital Edition, accessed February 3, 2020, http://edison.rutgers.edu/digital/document/NB005046.

11 Annie Hartley to Lizzie Le Prince, 18 November 1888.

12 Letter from J. P. Ward, Photography & Cinematography Collection, National Science Museum (UK) to Christopher Rawlence, 15 January 1981.

13 Annie Hartley to Lizzie Le Prince, 18 November 1888.

14 Ibid.

MAREY, LE PRINCE, AND DICKSON

1 Étienne-Jules Marey, "Décomposition des phases d'un mouvement au moyen d'images photographiques successives, recueillies sur une bande de papier sensible qui se déroule," extrait des *Comptes rendus des séances de l'Académie des Sciences*, vol. CVII, session of 29 October 1888, translated by the author.

2 "Patent Caveat, Thomas Alva Edison, October 15th, 1888," Edison Papers Digital Edition, accessed February 3, 2020, http://edison.rutgers.edu/digital/document/QM001348.

3 "Patent Caveat, Thomas Alva Edison, October 15th, 1888," Edison Papers Digital Edition, accessed February 3, 2020, http://edison.rutgers.edu/digital/document/PT031AAA.

4 Spehr, 89.

5 W. K. L. Dickson testimony, equity no. 28,605, Edison archives, legal box 173.

6 Thomas Edison to Dyer & Seely, 8 October 1888.

7 Sworn declaration by James William Longley, 19 September 1898.

8 Ibid.

9 Sworn declaration by William Mason Jr., 19 September 1898.

TRANSPARENT, FLEXIBLE, AND UNBREAKABLE

1 "Franklin Institute," *Philadelphia Inquirer*, 22 November 1888, p. 3.

2 Gordon Hendricks collection, National Museum of American History.

3 *The Mississippian*, 30 January 1889, p. 1.

4 *The Graphic Weekly*, 26 January 1889, p. 21.

5 Lizzie Le Prince, 36.

6 Hendricks, *Edison Motion Picture Myth*, 170.

7 Spehr, 136–37.

8 Adolphe Le Prince, pt. 2, p. 13.

9 David Simkin, "Samuel Fry—Brighton Photographer," *Sussex PhotoHistory*, accessed 2 February 2020, https://www.photohistory-sussex.co.uk/BTNFrySamuel.htm.

10 Lizzie Le Prince, 37.

11 "Improvements for Producing Animated Photographic Pictures," *British Journal of Photography*, 14 December 1888, p. 794.

12 Fielding, 79.

13 Louis Le Prince to Lizzie Le Prince, 15 July 1889.

14 Fielding, 80.

15 E. K. Scott to the editor of the Sunday New York *Tribune*, 11 February 1920.

16 Ibid.

17 Declaration of Walter Gee, 1931, quoted in Scott.

18 Frederic Mason, letter to the editor of the *Yorkshire Evening Post*, January 1923, (quoted in Lizzie Le Prince, 117). In a letter to Adolphe Le Prince, Mason also stated a three-lens projector had been built and proved "perfect," an assessment Longley agreed with.

19 Frederic Mason, letter to the *Yorkshire Post*, January 1923 (quoted in Lizzie Le Prince, 117).

20 Ibid.

21 E. K. Scott, letter to the editor of the Sunday New York *Tribune*, 11 February 1920.

22 Hendricks, *Edison Motion Picture Myth*, 38.

23 *The Graphic*, 10 August 1889, p. 21.

24 *Boston Globe*, 30 September 1889, p. 3.

25 Declaration of Frederic Mason, 21 April 1931.

26 James Longley to Louis Le Prince, 5 November 1889 (quoted in Adolphe Le Prince, 33).

EDISON AND MAREY

1 *Scientific American* 56, no. 20 (16 November 1889): 1.

2 Louis Le Prince to Lizzie Le Prince, 25 December 1889.

3 Spehr, 131.

4 Ibid., 132.

5 "Edison Is Enjoying Himself—New York *Sun* Cable from London," *Chicago Tribune*, 13 September 1889, p. 9. Issues of the *Sun* dated August 1–October 31, 1889 are not in the Library of Congress's digital collection, but the cable was reprinted widely across the United States.

6 Braun, 190.

7 Smith & Koury, 80.

8 Patent caveat application for Kinetograph camera and Kinetoscope viewer, 2 November 1889.

I SHALL BE WITH YOU ALL IN MIND

1 Louis Le Prince to his family in New York, December 1889 (quoted in part in Adolphe Le Prince, 34).

2 Adolphe Le Prince, 95.

3 *Yorkshire Evening Press*, 29 November 1889, p. 2.

4 "The Science of Animal Locomotion," *Yorkshire Post and Leeds Intelligencer*, 29 November 1889, p. 6.

5   "The Menagerie of Muybridge the Magician; or, the Silent Secrets Revealed by the Limelight," *Pall Mall Gazette*, 23 March 1889, p. 6.
6   Sworn testimony of Richard Wilson, 20 October 1898.
7   Lizzie Le Prince, 35.
8   Louis Le Prince to family, December 1889 (quoted ibid.).
9   Mr. Currier was Enoch Henry Currier, professor of articulation, lip-reading, and aural development at the New York Institution for the Deaf and, starting in 1893, the school's principal, succeeding Isaac Peet. A brief biography of Currier appeared on his death in Edwin Allan Hodgson, "Enoch Henry Currier," *American Annals of the Deaf* 62, no. 5 (1917): 404–12.
10 Louis Le Prince to family, December 1889.

A TRICK OF THE LIGHT

1   Louis Le Prince to Lizzie Le Prince, 15 January 1890.
2   Louis Le Prince to Adolphe Le Prince, 28 February 1890.
3   Louis Le Prince to Lizzie Le Prince, 19 March 1890.
4   Fernand Mobisson, certificate of examination, 30 March 1890 (quoted in Lizzie Le Prince, 99).
5   Sauvage, 162.
6   Louis Le Prince to Lizzie Le Prince, 11 April 1890.
7   Ibid.
8   Louis Le Prince to Lizzie Le Prince, 18 April 1890.
9   Ibid.
10 Louis Le Prince to Lizzie Le Prince, 24 May 1890.
11 Ibid.
12 Sworn declaration of James W. Longley, 25 March 1899.
13 Sara Addington to Adolphe Le Prince, undated, reproduced in Lizzie Le Prince, 75–76. I have not been able to trace the original letter.
14 Her name, as well as that of her brother J. W. Gisburn, appear on the passenger lists for the SS *Furnessia* when it landed in New York on September 2. "Passenger Lists of Vessels Arriving at New York, New York, 1820–1897," National Archives at Washington, DC.
15 Sara Addington to Adolphe Le Prince, reproduced in Lizzie Le Prince, 75–76.
16 Rawlence, 251.

THE JUMEL MANSION

1   *The Sun* (New York), 19 March 1890, p. 8.
2   Lizzie Le Prince, 41.
3   Ibid.
4   In her memoirs Lizzie claims, wrongly, that this was done in 1889, not 1890. Correspondence between the author and Maureen Harrison, assistant curator, Morris-Jumel Mansion, 11 August 2018.

DIJON

1 Lizzie Le Prince, 42.
2 Sworn declaration of Frederic Mason, 21 April 1931.
3 Ibid.
4 Rawlence, 47.
5 Lizzie Le Prince, 118.
6 Marie Emma Adèle Le Prince to Marie Gabriella Le Prince, 10 November 1890.
7 Ibid.
8 Sworn declaration of Frederic Mason, 21 April 1931.
9 Sworn declaration of Richard Wilson, 20 October 1898.
10 Sworn declaration of Frederic Mason, 21 April 1931.
11 Lizzie Le Prince, 43.
12 Asbury, 237.
13 Lincoln Steffens, *The Autobiography of Lincoln Steffens* (Harcourt, Brace, 1931), 206.
14 Byrnes, 18.
15 Lizzie Le Prince, 41.
16 Ibid., 43.
17 Frederic Mason, letter to the editor of the *Yorkshire Evening Post* (quoted in Lizzie Le Prince, 118).
18 Telegram in the possession of Billy Huettel, descendant of Louis and Lizzie Le Prince, read to Christopher Rawlence. See Rawlence, 272.
19 *Le Progrès de la Côte-d'Or*, 16 September 1890, p. 2.
20 *Le Progrès de la Côte-d'Or*, 17 September 1890, p. 3.

DICKSON DX

1 *The Sun* (New York), 21 May 1891, p. 2. See also Karen J. Blair, "General Federation of Women's Clubs," in *The Reader's Companion to US Women's History*, ed. Wilma Mankiller et al. (Houghton Mifflin, 1998), 242.
2 Spehr, 189–93.
3 DeGraaf, 156.
4 *Chicago Evening Post*, 12 May 1891.
5 Stross, 199.
6 Ibid., 197.
7 Ibid., 311.
8 Patent Interference 18,461, December 1897.
9 Spehr, 351–54.
10 Dickson and Dickson, 54.
11 Bibliothèque du Film, Cinémathèque Française, Fonds Will Day, Dickson to Day, undated document. "Extra notes for Mr. W. K. L. Dickson in conjunction with his book," c. 1933.

CINEMA

1 Georges Méliès to Georges Sadoul, in *Histoire Générale du Cinéma*, quoted in Glenn Myrent, "When Movies Began and No One Came," *New York Times*, 29 December 1985, and Sadoul, *L'Invention du Cinéma*, 271–72.

2 Georges Méliès to Georges Sadoul, *Histoire Générale du Cinéma*.

3 *Le Radical*, 31 December 1895, p. 3.

4 The views described by the journalist are uncannily similar to many Le Prince took, or planned on taking: the blacksmith (Mackenstein), the city traffic (Leeds Bridge), the seaside.

5 *Le Radical*, 31 December 1895, p. 3.

6 Lizzie Le Prince, 43.

7 Ibid., 54.

8 Adolphe Le Prince, pt. 2, p. 15.

ADOLPHE

1 Musser, 379.

2 William H. Blodgett, examiner, Patent Office, to Dyer & Seely, 2 January 1892.

3 Dyer & Seely to Thomas Alva Edison, 1 December 1892, Edison papers.

4 Petition of Sarah Elizabeth Le Prince "in the matter of the application for letters of administration on the goods, chattels and credits which were of Louis Aimé Augustin Le Prince, deceased," Surrogate's Court of the County of New York, sworn to and signed by Sarah Elizabeth Le Prince, 29 November 1898.

5 Lizzie Le Prince, 61.

6 Ibid., 47.

7 The quotes in the paragraphs that follow are taken from the transcripts of preliminary hearings for Equity 6928, US Court for the Southern District of New York, held at the US National Archives at New York.

8 Prof. Morton to Dyer, Edmonds, and Dyer, 28 June 1899, Equity 6928. Morton asserts, wrongly, that Le Prince's intentions as to the use of a single-lens camera were "left wholly to conjecture" and that Le Prince's described version of that camera was "useless," "constructed on the wrong principles," and "defective in its capacity to operate." An exact replica of the camera, built in the twenty-first century using the same materials, by craftsmen in Leeds, was shown to work exactly as described by Le Prince in his patent applications. (See Wilkinson, *The First Film*.)

9 Equity 6928, brief for appellant, 28 October 1901, Edison Archives.

10 Lizzie Le Prince, 61.

11 Quoted ibid., 88.

12 Sopocy, 11.

13 Sopocy, 14.

14 "Suicide at the Seaside," *Brooklyn Daily Eagle*, 21 August 1901, p. 3. Also *Suffolk County News*, 23 August 1901.

THE FATHERS OF THE MOVIES

1 Decision of the US Circuit Court of Appeals, Second Circuit, in Equity 6928, 10 March 1902.
2 Ibid.
3 Sopocy, 17.
4 Rawlence, 274.
5 Lizzie Le Prince, 66.
6 "Point O' Woods Surfmen Encounter a Lunatic," *Brooklyn Daily Eagle*, 6 March 1903, p. 6.
7 Ibid.
8 New York State Census, 1915, and draft registration card, serial number 4342, 12 September 1918.
9 Description for the Joseph Augustin Le Prince Medal in recognition of outstanding work in the field of malariology, first awarded in 1951 (to Joseph himself), from the ASTMH website at http://www.astmh.org/awards-fellowships-medals/awards-and-honors/joseph-augustin-leprince-medal.
10 Le Prince Graves, 2.
11 Lizzie Le Prince, 97.
12 From newsreel interviews given by Mariella Le Prince, 1930.

CODA: THE DROWNED MAN

1 Vanessa Ruth Schwartz, "Cinematic Spectatorship before the Apparatus: The Public Taste for Reality in Fin-de-Siècle Paris," in *Viewing Positions*, 88–93.
2 Ibid.
3 Zola, Emile Zola, *Thérèse Raquin*, ch. 13.
4 Registers of the Paris Morgue, Archives de la Préfecture de Police de Paris. Additional sources for this chapter include: Arthur Good, "La Morgue de Paris et Les Nouveaux Appareils Frigorifiques," *La Nature*, no. 711 (15 January 1887); *La Nature,* Quinzième Année—1887, Dunod, 1886; Michael Waters, "Death as Entertainment at the Paris Morgue," *Atlas Obscura*, 11 January 2018, https://www.atlasobscura.com/articles/paris-morgue-public-viewing.
5 Letter from the Prefecture de Police to Elizabeth Le Prince, archive file MS/DEP/2015/2/13, Louis Le Prince collection, Leeds University Library.
6 Lizzie Le Prince, 44.
7 Yifat Bitton and Hava Dayan, "'The Perfect Murder': An Exploratory Study of Staged Murder Scenes and Concealed Femicide," *British Journal of Criminology* 59, no. 5 (September 2019): 1054–75, https://doi.org/10.1093/bjc/azz015.
8 *Bulletin de l'Association Française des Ingénieurs et Techniciens du Cinéma*, no. 29, 1969, p. 14. See also Sauvage, 163–64, and Pfend and Aulas.

SELECTED
BIBLIOGRAPHY

B iographical information in this book was taken from firsthand
accounts or censuses of the period. Detail for specific moments in the
narrative—including the weather, visual descriptors, and so on—were
taken from firsthand accounts and contemporary newspaper records.
Unless noted otherwise, correspondence to and/or from any member
of the Le Prince family is held in the Louis Le Prince Collection (collection MS/DEP/2015), in the Special Collections of Leeds University
Library, donated by the Le Prince family and the Leeds Philosophical
and Literary Society. The sworn declarations collected by Adolphe Le
Prince after his father's disappearance are held by the Le Prince family
and reproduced in Lizzie Le Prince's unpublished memoir. Travel dates
and itineraries were corroborated using passenger and immigration lists
in the United States and the United Kingdom. Milestones in the lives
of many cinema pioneers—including Le Prince and Edison, but also
Muybridge, Marey, the Lumière brothers, Méliès, and others—can be
traced in the newspapers of the day, as can developments and public opinion around events discussed in the book, such as the Franco-
Prussian War, the Great Blizzard of 1888, or economic struggles and labor
unrest in Britain in the 1880s. Patent announcements, and reports on
the inventors' respective progress in their work, appear in the pages of
trade publications of the time, most notably *Scientific American* in the

United States and *La Nature* in Europe. The other main repositories of information are outlined in the earlier author's note.

The bibliography that follows is organized by main topic of concern, though many of the works referenced overlap subjects.

■ On the life, work, and disappearance of Louis Le Prince, and the life and work of his family:

Anonymous. *Diary of the Siege of Paris, Taken from Galigniani's Messenger.* Simpkin & Marshall, 1871.
Anonymous. *John R. Whitley: A Sketch of His Life and Work.* Dryden Press, J. Davy & Sons, 1912.
Badsey, Stephen. *The Franco-Prussian War, 1870–1871.* Osprey Publishing, 2014.
Burchell, S. C. *Imperial Masquerade: The Paris of Napoleon III.* Atheneum, 1971.
Cladel, Judith. *Rodin: The Man and His Art, with Leaves from His Notebook.* Century Company, 1917.
Dembowski, Irénée. "La Naissance du Cinéma: Cent Sept Ans et un Crime . . ." *Alliage*, no. 22 (1995).
Desbiolles, Maryline. *Avec Rodin.* Fayard, 2017.
Desprez, Adrien. *Histoire de la Guerre de 1870–71 et du Siège de Paris.* Librairie Générale Illustrée, 1873.
Dobyns, J. R. "Exhibits of Deaf Mutes, Made at the World's Industrial and Cotton Centennial Exposition at New Orleans, in the Deaf-Mute Department and in the State Departments." *American Annals of the Deaf and Dumb* 30, no. 4 (October 1885).
Dorsch, Michael. *French Sculpture Following the Franco-Prussian War, 1870–80.* Routledge, 2017.
Elderkin, John. *A Brief History of the Lotos Club.* Lotos Club, 1895.
Esmail, Jennifer. *Reading Victorian Deafness.* Ohio University Press, 2013.
Fay, Edward Allen, ed. *Histories of American Schools for the Deaf, 1817–1893.* Volta Bureau, 1893.
Fehrer, Catherine. "Women at the Académie Julian." *Burlington Magazine* 136, no. 1100 (November 1994).
Hargrove, June. *The Life and Work of Albert Ernest Carrier-Belleuse.* Garland Publishing, 1977.
Hole, James. *The Homes of the Working Classes.* Longmans, Green, 1866.
Horne, Alastair. *The Fall of Paris: The Siege and the Commune, 1870–71.* Penguin Books (e-book edition), 2007.
Howells, Richard. "Louis Le Prince: The Body of Evidence." *Screen, Oxford Journals* (2006).
Le Prince, Adolphe W. "Missing Pages in the History of Moving Pictures." Unpublished. c. 1899–1900. In two parts, numbered separately in the manuscript, the

latter indicated in the source notes as "pt. 2." Private collection, courtesy of Laurie Snyder.

Le Prince, Sarah Elizabeth [Lizzie]. "Missing Chapters in the History of Moving Pictures: The Life Story of Augustin Le Prince, Inventor of Moving Pictures, with Letters and Affidavits." Unpublished, undated (early 1920s). Private collection, courtesy of Laurie Snyder.

Le Prince Graves, Julia Helen Elizabeth. Untitled Memoir. Unpublished, c. 1993–1994. Private collection, courtesy of Gwen Graves Maxwell.

Liste de ballons sortis de Paris pendant le siège—1871. Poster. E. Pichot, imprimeur, 1874. https://www.loc.gov/item/2002716373/.

Lowe, Charles, and John Robinson Whitley. *Four National Exhibitions in London and Their Organiser.* T. F. Urwin, 1892.

Maas, Jeremy. *This Brilliant Year: Queen Victoria's Jubilee, 1877.* Royal Academy of Arts, 1977.

Manet, Édouard. *Corréspondence du Siège de Paris et de la Commune, 1870–1871.* L'Échoppe, 2014.

Merrimac and Monitor Panorama Company. *A Comprehensive Sketch of the Merrimac and Monitor Naval Battle, Giving an Accurate Account of the Most Important Naval Engagement in the Annals of War.* New York: The Merrimac and Monitor Panorama Company, 1886.

McCullough, David. *1776.* Simon & Schuster, 2005.

———. *The Path Between the Seas: The Creation of the Panama Canal, 1870–1914.* Simon & Schuster, 1977.

Moreno, Barry. *Castle Garden and Battery Park.* Arcadia Publishing, 2007.

Moses, L. G. *Wild West Shows and the Images of American Indians, 1883–1933.* University of New Mexico Press, 1999.

Nass, Lucien. *Le Siège de Paris et la Commune.* Librairie Plon, 1914.

Oppenheimer, Margaret. *The Remarkable Rise of Eliza Jumel.* Chicago Review Press, 2016.

Pfend, Jacques, and Jean-Jacques Aulas. "Louis Aimé Augustin Leprince, Inventeur et Artiste, Précurseur du Cinéma." *1895: Mille huit cent quatre-vingt-quinze* no. 32 (2000; published online 28 November 2007).

Pfend, Jacques. "The Facts! Concerning the Life and Death of Louis Aimé Augustin Le Prince, Pioneer of the Moving Picture, and His Family." Unpublished manuscript (ISBN 9782954244198), 2014.

Puhl, Michel. "Louis Le Prince, un des pionniers du cinéma, a disparu en 1890 dans le train Dijon-Paris." *Le Bien Public,* 16 January 2000.

Rawlence, Christopher. *The Missing Reel.* Fontana, 1991.

Rodin, Auguste. *Rodin on Art and Artists: Conversations with Paul Gsell.* Dover Publications, 1983.

Rydell, Robert W., and Rob Kroes. *Buffalo Bill in Bologna: The Americanization of the World, 1869–1922.* University of Chicago Press, 2005.

Saly-Monzingo, Camilla, ed. *The Morris-Jumel Mansion.* Riverdale Avenue Books, 2016.

Sarcey, Francisque. *Le Siège de Paris: Impressions et Souvenirs.* D. C. Heath, 1904.

Scarle, Alfred, and Charles Albert Braim. *History of the Lodge of Fidelity no. 285.* Beck & Inchbold, printers, 1894. Courtesy of Leeds University Library, Special Collections.

Scott, E. Kilburn. *Memorial to Louis Aimé Augustin Le Prince: "Father" of Kinematography.* Leeds, circa 1924.

Shah, Irfan. "Louis Le Prince." *Leeds: Cradle of Innovation*, edited by Rachel Unsworth and Steven Burt, 2018.

————. *The Shadow Traps.* Podcast. 2019–2021. https://feeds.buzzsprout .com/275917.rss

Sibbert, Robert Lowry. *The Siege of Paris.* Meyers Printing and Publishing House, 1892.

Simpson, Pamela H. *Cheap, Quick, and Easy: Imitative Architectural Materials, 1870–1930.* University of Tennessee Press, 1999.

Simpson, Pamela H. "Linoleum and Lincrusta: The Democratic Coverings for Floors and Walls." *Perspectives in Vernacular Architecture* 7 (1997): 281–92.

Spang, Rebecca L. "'And They Ate the Zoo': Relating Gastronomic Exoticism in the Siege of Paris." *MLN* 107, no. 4 (1992): 752–73.

"The First Cinema Camera," an interview with Mariella Le Prince. *The Sphere* 27 (December 1930): 28.

Tinterow, Gary, Michael Pantazzi, and Vincent Pomarède. *Corot.* Metropolitan Museum of Art, 1996.

Wawro, Geoffrey. *The Franco-Prussian War: The German Conquest of France in 1870–1871.* Cambridge University Press, 2003.

Wilkinson, David, dir. *The First Film.* Documentary produced by Guerilla Docs. 2015.

Wilson, Richard George. *Gentlemen Merchants: The Merchant Community in Leeds, 1700–1830.* Manchester University Press, 1971.

Wray, Suzanne. "A Fad That Faded." *Panorama: International Panorama Council Journal* 2 (2018), 55–59.

The Fonds d'Archives Militaires in Vincennes, France, preserves the military record of Abraham Le Prince. The Library and Museum of Freemasonry retains registers of contributions for nineteenth-century lodges; Le Prince and Richard Wilson appear in their *Leeds Philanthropic Lodge, Register of Contributions, 1751–1921.* The Whitley Partners bankruptcy was announced in the *London Gazette*, 21 September 1875, p. 4590, and 15 October 1875, p. 4871. Many of Le Prince's family members and collaborators also shared recollections in newspaper interviews and letters to the editor, particularly around the time of the unveiling of Le Prince's memorial plaque in Leeds in 1930. Examples include, but are not limited to:

Daily Mirror, 9 December 1930
Kinematograph Weekly, 25 September 1930

Leeds Mercury, 2 July 1930, 12 December 1930, 13 December 1930
Lancashire Evening Post, 8 December 1930
Liverpool Echo, 8 December 1930
The Sphere, 27 December 1930.
Yorkshire Post, 9 December 1930, 12 December 1930, 13 December 1930
Yorkshire Evening Post, 27 June 1930, 11 December 1930, 12 December 1930, 16 December 1930, 7 January 1931

▨ On the motion picture work of Thomas Edison and W. K. L. Dickson:

Baldwin, Neil. *Edison: Inventing the Century.* University of Chicago Press, 2001.
Bradley, Robert L. Jr. *Edison to Enron: Energy Markets and Political Strategies.* John Wiley & Sons, 2011.
Edison Oser, Marion. "The Wizard of Menlo Park, by His Daughter Marion Edison Oser." Unpublished typescript, 1956. Thomas Edison Papers, identifier: X018A5Z.
DeGraaf, Leonard. *Edison and the Rise of Innovation.* Sterling Signature, 2013.
Dickson, W. K. L., and Antonia Dickson. *History of the Kinetograph, Kinetoscope, and Kineto-Phonograph.* Albert Bunn, 1895 (facsimile edition by the Museum of Modern Art, 2000).
Dyer, Frank Lewis, and Thomas Commerford Martin. *Edison: His Life and Inventions.* Harper & Brothers, 1910 (public domain edition on Kindle).
Essig, Mark. *Edison and the Electric Chair: A Story of Light and Death.* Walker, 2003.
Gray, Charlotte. *Reluctant Genius: The Passionate Life and Inventive Genius of Alexander Graham Bell.* HarperCollins, 2010.
Hames, Margaret Julia. " 'I Have No Pride': William Kennedy Laurie Dickson in His Own Words—An Autobiography." *Proceedings of the 68th New York State Communication Association* vol. 2010, art. 6, pp. 88–112.
Hendricks, Gordon. *Origins of the American Film.* Arno Press, 1972.
———. *The Edison Motion Picture Myth.* University of California Press, 1961.
Herron, Kristin S. *The House at Glenmont: Historic Furnishings Report, Edison National Historic Site, West Orange, New Jersey*, vol. 1. National Park Service, 1998.
Hughbanks, Leroy. *Talking Wax, or the Story of the Phonograph.* Hobson Book Press, 1945.
Israel, Paul. *Edison: A Life of Invention.* John Wiley & Sons, 1998.
Jonnes, Jill. *Empires of Light: Edison, Tesla, Westinghouse, and the Race to Electrify the World.* Random House, 2003.
Josephson, Matthew. *Edison: A Biography.* Plunkett Lake Press, 2018.
Morris, Edmund. *Edison.* Random House, 2019.
Munson, Richard. *Tesla: Inventor of the Modern.* W. W. Norton, 2018.
Shaw, Quincy. *Edison.* New World City LLC, 2016 (Kindle edition).
Smith, Albert E., and Phil A. Koury. *Two Reels and a Crank.* Garland, 1985.
Smith, Alvy Ray. *William Kennedy Laurie Dickson: A Genealogical Investigation of a Cinema Pioneer.* Vol. 2.22. Ars Longa, 2015.

Spehr, Paul. *The Man Who Made Movies: W. K. L. Dickson.* John Libbey, 2008.

Stross, Randall. *The Wizard of Menlo Park: How Thomas Alva Edison Invented the Modern World.* Crown, 2007.

Tate, Alfred O. *Edison's Open Door: The Life Story of Thomas A. Edison, a Great Individualist.* E. P. Dutton, 1938.

Tesla, Nikola, "The Discovery of the Tesla Coil and Transformer," *Electrical Experimenter,* May 1919. Reproduced in the collected edition of Tesla's essays for the publication, published as *My Inventions: The Autobiography of Nikola Tesla,* Hart Brothers, 1983.

Wasik, John F. *The Merchant of Power: Sam Insull, Thomas Edison, and the Creation of the Modern Metropolis.* Palgrave Macmillan, 2006.

Yocum, Barbara A. *The House at Glenmont: Historic Structure Report, Edison National Historic Site,* vol. 1. National Park Service, 1998.

Edison's movements are dated as much as possible from contemporary newspaper records (e.g., *Cincinnati Enquirer,* 26 February 1885, p. 4 for his arrival in New Orleans for the Louisiana Centennial, and regular reporting of his activities in the New York *Sun,* New York *World,* New York *Evening World,* and New York *Tribune*).

■ On the motion picture work of Eadweard Muybridge, Étienne-Jules Marey, Charles-Émile Reynaud, the Lumière brothers, and others:

Ackerman, Carl W. *George Eastman: Founder of Kodak and the Photography Business.* Beard Books, 2000.

Association Les Amis d'Émile Reynaud, www.emilereynaud.fr.

Auzel, Dominique. *Émile Reynaud et l'image s'anima.* Editions du May, 2000.

Ball, Edward. *The Inventor and the Tycoon: The Murderer Eadweard Muybridge, the Entrepreneur Leland Stanford, and the Birth of Moving Pictures.* Anchor, 2013.

Braun, Marta. *Picturing Time: The Work of Etienne-Jules Marey.* University of Chicago Press, 1992.

Brayer, Elizabeth. *George Eastman: A Biography.* University of Rochester Press, 2006.

Chardère, Bernard. *Le Roman des Lumière.* Gallimard, 1995.

Clegg, Brian. *The Man Who Stopped Time: Eadweard Muybridge—Pioneer Photographer, Father of the Motion Picture, Murderer.* Sutton, 2007.

Coe, Brian. *Muybridge & The Chronophotographers.* Museum of the Moving Image, 1992.

Ezra, Elizabeth. *Georges Méliès.* Manchester University Press, 2000.

Faucheux, Michel. *Auguste et Louis Lumière.* Biographies Folio, Éditions Gallimard, 2011.

Hendricks, Gordon. *Eadweard Muybridge: The Father of the Motion Picture.* Grossman, 1975.

Herbert, Stephen. *Industry, Liberty, and a Vision: Wordsworth Donisthorpe's Kinesigraph.* The Projection Box, 1998.

Lonjon, Bernard. *Émile Reynaud: Le véritable inventeur du cinéma.* Editions du Roure, 2007.

Marey, Étienne-Jules. *La Machine Animale.* F. Alcan, 1886.

Méliès, Georges, *La Vie et l'Oeuvre d'un Pionnier du Cinéma.* Edited and presented by Jean-Pierre Sirois-Trahan. La Petite Collection des Éditions du Sonneur, 2012.

Muybridge, Eadweard. *The Science of Animal Locomotion (Zoopraxography).* E. Muybridge, 1891.

Muybridge, Eadweard, and J. D. B. Stillman. *The Horse in Motion.* James R. Osgood, 1882.

Myrent, Glenn. "Émile Reynaud: First Motion Picture Cartoonist." *Film History,* vol. 3 (1989): 191–202.

Palmquist, Peter E., and Thomas R Kailbourn. *Pioneer Photographers from the Mississippi to the Continental Divide: A Biographical Dictionary, 1839–1865.* Stanford University Press, 2005.

Pinel, Vincent. *Louis Lumière: Inventeur et Cinéaste.* Éditions Nathan, 1994.

Ranganathan, S. R. "Hyatt (John Wesley), 1837–1920." *Current Science 6,* no. 5 (1937): 236.

Robinson, David. *Georges Méliès: Father of Film Fantasy.* British Film Institute, 1993.

Sadoul, Georges. *Georges Méliès.* Seghers, 1970.

Sauvage, Léo. *L'Affaire Lumière.* Lherminier, 1985.

Silverman, Mark E. "Profiles in Cardiology: Etienne-Jules Marey: 19th Century Cardiovascular Physiologist and Inventor of Cinematography." *Clinical Cardiology,* no. 19 (1996): 339–41.

Solnit, Rebecca. *River of Shadows: Eadweard Muybridge and the Technological Wild West.* Penguin Books, 2003.

Muybridge's work for Leland Stanford was particularly reported upon in the California press. See, for instance, for the first chapter in which Muybridge appears here: "Occident's Picture" (*San Francisco Examiner,* 7 April 1873, p. 3.); "Taking Occident's Picture" (*San Francisco Chronicle,* 8 April 1873, p. 3); or "A Photographic Triumph" (*Stockton Daily Evening Herald,* 10 April 1873, p. 2.). Étienne-Jules Marey made frequent use of the scientific press to communicate his progress to his peers (e.g., *La Nature* no. 608, 24 January 1885; *La Nature,* no. 278, 28 September 1878; or "Le vol des oiseaux," *La Revue Scientifique,* 19 October 1889). John Carbutt's and George Eastman's innovations were reported in the trade and mainstream press (e.g., "Dry Plates and Films: Photographic Devices in Mechanics Hall," *Boston Globe,* 7 August 1889, p. 4; or "The New Rollable Transparent Film," *Photography,* 23 January 1890).

◼ For the early history of photography and motion pictures:

Batchen, Geoffrey. *Burning with Desire: The Conception of Photography.* MIT Press, 1999.

Bitzer, G. W. *Billy Bitzer: His Story.* Farrar, Strauss and Giroux, 1973.

Boyd, Jane E. "Celluloid: The Eternal Substitute." *Science History Institute,* 11 November 2011, https://www.sciencehistory.org/distillations/celluloid-the -eternal-substitute.

Chanan, Michael. *The Dream That Kicks.* Routledge & Kegan Paul, 1980.

Charney, Leo, and Vanessa R. Schwarts, eds. *Cinema and the Invention of Modern Life.* University of California Press, 1995.

Cohen, Paula Marantz. *Silent Film and the Triumph of the American Myth*, Oxford University Press, 2001.

Daniel, Malcolm. "Daguerre (1787–1851) and the Invention of Photography." *Heilbrunn Timeline of Art History.* Metropolitan Museum of Art, 2000.

Eyman, Scott. *Lion of Hollywood: The Life and Legend of Louis B. Mayer.* Simon & Schuster, 2008.

Fielding, Raymond, ed. *A Technological History of Motion Pictures.* University of California Press, 1967.

Fornäs, Johan. "Passage across Thresholds: Into the Borderlands of Mediation." *Convergence: The Journal of Research into New Media Technologies* 8, no. 4 (2002): 89–106. 2002.

Friedel, Robert. *Pioneer Plastic: The Making & Selling of Celluloid.* University of Wisconsin Press, 1983.

Gernsheim, Helmut, and Alison Gernsheim. *The History of Photography.* McGraw-Hill, 1969.

Gordon, Colin. *By Gaslight in Winter: A Victorian Family History through the Magic Lantern.* Elm Tree Books, 1980.

Heinsohn, Bastian. "Carl Laemmle's Protégés: Everyday Life in Exile after Escaping Nazi Germany Through Help from Hollywood's Film Mogul." In *Exile and Everyday Life,* edited by Andrea Hammel and Anthony Grenville. Brill Rodopi, 2015.

Herbert, Stephen, and Luke McKernan, eds. *Who's Who of Victorian Cinema.* British Film Institute, 1996.

Lacassin, François. *Pour une Contre-Histoire du Cinéma.* Union Générale d'Éditions, 1972.

Leprohon, Pierre. *Le Cinéma, Cette Aventure.* André Bonne, 1970.

"A Mere Phantom."[pseud.] *The Magic Lantern, How to Buy, and How to Use it. Also How to Raise a Ghost.* Houlston and Wright, 1866.

Musser, Charles. *Before the Nickelodeon: Edwin S. Porter and the Edison Manufacturing Company.* University of California Press, 1991.

———. *The Emergence of Cinema: The American Screen to 1907.* University of California Press, 1994.

Norton, Charles Goodwin. *The Lantern and How to Use It.* Watson & Viney, 1895.

Pinel, Vincent. "Chronologie Commentée de l'Invention du Cinéma." Numéro hors-série, Association Française de Recherche sur l'Histoire du Cinéma, 1895, 1992.

Potonniée, Georges. *Les Origines du Cinématographe.* Publications Photographiques Paul Montel, 1928.

Ramsaye, Terry. *A Million and One Nights: A History of the Motion Picture through 1925.* Simon & Schuster, 1986.

Rossell, Deac. *Living Pictures: The Origins of the Movies.* State University of New York Press, 1998.

Sadoul, Georges. *L'Invention du Cinéma: 1832–1897.* Éditions Denoël, 1948.

Segel, Harold B. *Pinocchio's Progeny: Puppets, Marionettes, Automatons and Robots in Modernist and Avant-Garde Drama.* Johns Hopkins University Press, 1995.

Seymour, Raymond B. *Pioneers in Polymer Science.* Kluwer Academic Publishers, 1989.

Solomon, Matthew. *Disappearing Tricks: Silent Film, Houdini, and the New Magic of the Twentieth Century.* University of Illinois Press, 2010.

Sontag, Susan. *On Photography.* Penguin Books, 1979.

Soulard, Robert. "Le Cinématographe Bouly." *Revue d'Histoire des Sciences* 16, no. 4 (1963): 317–22.

Stainton, Walter. "The Prophet Louis Ducos Du Hauron and His Marvellous Moving Picture Machine." *Cinema Journal* 6 (1966–1967): 46–51.

Stanca-Mustea, Cristina. *Carl Laemmle: Der Mann der Hollywood Erfand.* Lindhardt og Ringhof, 2016.

Toulet, Emmanuelle. *Discoveries: Birth of the Motion Picture.* Abrams, 1995.

Vivié, Jean. *Prélude au Cinéma: De la Préhistoire à l'Invention.* L'Harmattan, 2006.

Warner, Marina. *Phantasmagoria.* Oxford University Press, 2008.

Watson, Roger, and Helen Rappaport. *Capturing the Light: A True Story of Genius, Rivalry and the Birth of Photography.* Pan Books, 2014.

Williams, Linda, ed. *Viewing Positions: Ways of Seeing Film.* Rutgers University Press, 1997.

Woolf, Virginia. "The Cinema." *The Nation and Athenaeum,* 3 July 1926.

Zone, Ray. *Stereoscopic Cinema and the Origins of 3-D Film, 1838–1952.* University Press of Kentucky, 2014.

PATENTS

Thomas Alva Edison

"Kinetographic Camera." US Patent 403,534. Filed August 24, 1891. Issued August 31, 1897.

"Apparatus for Exhibiting Photographs of Moving Objects." US Patent 403,536. Filed August 24, 1891. Issued March 14, 1893.

Louis Aimé Augustin Le Prince

"Method of and Apparatus for Producing Animated Pictures of Natural Scenery and Life." US Patent 376,247. Filed November 2, 1886. Issued January 10, 1888.

"Improvements in the Method of and Apparatus for Producing Animated Photographic Pictures." UK Patent 423. Filed January 10, 1888. Issued November 16, 1888.

"Méthode et appareil pour la projection des tableaux animés." French Patent 188,089. Issued January 11, 1888.

■ On the workings of the US Patent Office and motion picture patent litigation:

Dobyns, Kenneth W. *The Patent Office Pony: A History of the Early Patent Office.* Sergeant Kirkland's Press, 1997.
Post, Robert C. "Liberalizers versus Scientific Men in the Antebellum Patent Office." *Technology and Culture* 17, no. 1 (1976): 24–54.
Rogers, Walter F. "Patent Office Practice [United States of America]." In *The American Corporation Legal Manual,* edited by Charles L. Borgmeyer. Corporation Legal Manual Company, 1898. (Cites law R. S. U. S., par. 4902, rules 197–209).
Sopocy, Martin. "The Edison-Biograph Patent Litigation of 1901–1907." *Film History.* vol. 3 (1989): 11–27.
White, Leonard D. *The Republican Era, 1869–1901: A Study in Administrative History.* Macmillan, 1958.

SELECTED REFERENCE WORKS

Bazin, Jean-François. *Histoire de Dijon.* Éditions Jean-Paul Gisserot, 2001.
Caron, François. *Histoire des Chemins de Fer en France (1883–1937).* Fayard, 2005.
D'Heylli, G., and D. Jouaust. *Gazette Anecdotique, Littéraire, Artistique et Bibliographique,* 21st year, vol. 2. Rue de la Victoire, 1896.
Fenteman, Thomas. *An Historical Guide to Leeds and Its Environs, with a Plan of Leeds, View of the Town Hall, &c &c.* T. Fenteman, 1858.
Fraser, Derek, ed. *A History of Modern Leeds.* Manchester University Press, 1980.
Haigh, Thomas (compiled under the superintendence of). *A General and Commercial Directory of the Borough of Leeds, etc.* Baines & Company, 1839.
Kendall, John. *History of New Orleans.* Lewis Publishing, 1922.
Trow's New York City Directory. Trow Directory Company, for the years ending 1 May 1882 to 1885.
Webster, Noah. *A Brief History of Epidemic and Pestilential Diseases, with the Principal Phenomena of the Physical World, which Precede and Accompany Them, and Observations Deduced from the Facts Stated.* Hudson & Goodwin, 1799.
Williams' Directory of the Borough of Leeds. Edward Baines & Sons, 1845.

■ As well as past issues and records of the:

American Annals of the Deaf
Annual Report and Documents of the New York Institution for the Instruction of the Deaf and Dumb
Bulletin de l'Association Française des Ingénieurs et Techniciens du Cinéma
Bulletin de la Société Française de Photographie
Gallaudet University Deaf Biographies
Leeds Philanthropic Lodge, Register of Contributions
London *Gazette*
Scientific American

▨ Other works that inspired and broadened my understanding of these times:

Adams, Amanda. *Performing Authorship in the Nineteenth Century Transatlantic Lecture Tour.* Routledge, 2016.

Anbinder, Tyler. *City of Dreams.* Mariner Books, 2017.

Asbury, Herbert. *The Gangs of New York.* Albert Knopf, 1928.

Bertherat, Bruno. "L'Élection à la chaire de médecine légale à Paris en 1879. Acteurs, réseaux et enjeux dans le monde universitaire." *Revue Historique* 644, no. 4 (2007): 823–856.

Bill, Buffalo [William F. Cody], and William Lightfoot Visscher. *The Life and Adventures of Buffalo Bill.* Stanton and Van Vlet, 1917.

Boeglin, Noémie. "Paris, ville morte dans le roman français au XIXe siècle." *Sociétés et Représentations* 41, no. 1 (2016): 47–62.

Bonnerot, Jean C. *Saint-Saëns, sa vie et son oeuvre.* A. Durand & Fils, 1923.

Brouardel, Pierre. *Organisation du Service des Autopsies à la Morgue: Rapports Addressés à M. Le Garde des Sceaux.* Imprimerie E. Martinet, 1879.

———. *Le Secret Médical.* Librairie J.-B. Baillière et Fils, 1887.

———. *La Mort et la Mort Subite.* Librairie J.-B. Baillière et Fils, 1893.

———. *La Pendaison, La Strangulation, La Suffocation, La Submersion.* Librairie J.-B. Baillière et Fils, 1897.

Byrnes, Thomas F. *Professional Criminals of America.* Cassell, 1886.

Cherbuliez, Ernest. "La Morgue de Paris." *Revue des Deux Mondes (1829–1971)* 103, no. 2 (1891): 344–81.

Costello, Augustine E. *Our Police Protectors: History of the New York Police from the Earliest Period to the Present Time.* Published for the Benefit of the Police Pension Fund and printed by Chas. F. Roper, 1885.

Flanders, Judith. *The Invention of Murder: How the Victorians Revelled in Death and Detection and Created Modern Crime.* HarperCollins, 2011.

Gilder, Rodman. *The Battery.* Houghton Mifflin, 1936.

Gluckstein, Danny. *The Paris Commune: A Revolution in Democracy.* Haymarket Books, 2011.

Gonzalez-Quijano, Lola. "Le système réglementariste dans les communes annexées. Le cas de Grenelle (1842–1914)." *Histoire Urbaine* 49, no. 2 (2017): 54–74.

Guillot, Adolphe. *Paris Qui Souffre: La Basse Geôle du Grand Châtelet et les Morgues Modernes.* P. Rouquette, 1887.

———. *Paris Qui Souffre: Les Prisons de Paris et les Prisonniers.* E. Dentu, Éditeur. 1890.

Hazan, Eric. *A Walk Through Paris.* Verso, 2018.

Lichtenstein, Therese. *Twilight Visions: Surrealism and Paris.* University of California Press, 2011.

Osborne, Harold S. "Biographical Memoir of Alexander Graham Bell, 1847–1922." Presented to the National Academy of Sciences of the United States of America annual meeting, 1943.

Swaine, Robert T. *The Cravath Firm and its Predecessors, 1819–1947*. Lawbook Exchange, 2007.

Tainter, Charles Sumner. "The Talking Machine and Some Little Known Facts in Connection with its Early Development." Unpublished, undated manuscript. US National Museum Collection.

Weisz, George. *The Medical Mandarins: The French Academy of Medicine in the Nineteenth and Twentieth Centuries*. Oxford University Press, 1995.

INDEX

ABOUT THE AUTHOR

Paul Fischer is an author and screenwriter based in London. His first nonfiction book, *A Kim Jong-Il Production*, was translated into sixteen languages. It was nominated for the Crime Writers' Association Gold Dagger for Non-Fiction and chosen as one of the Best Books of 2015 by NPR and as a Top Ten Book of the Year by *Library Journal*. Paul's writing has appeared in the *New York Times*, the *Los Angeles Times*, the *Guardian*, the *Independent*, *Bright Wall/Dark Room*, and the *Narwhal*. His first feature screenplay, *The Body*, was produced by Blumhouse for Hulu in 2018.